DAILY LIFE IN

CHAUCER'S ENGLAND

Recent Titles in
The Greenwood Press "Daily Life Through History" Series

Post-Cold War
Stephen A. Bourque

The New Testament
James W. Ermatinger

The Hellenistic Age: From Alexander to Cleopatra
James Allan Evans

Imperial Russia
Greta Bucher

The Greenwood Encyclopedia of Daily Life in America, Four Volumes
Randall M. Miller, general editor

Civilians in Wartime Twentieth-Century Europe
Nicholas Atkin, Editor

Ancient Egyptians, Second Edition
Bob Brier and Hoyt Hobbs

Civilians in Wartime Latin America: From the Wars of
Independence to the Central American Civil Wars
Pedro Santoni, editor

Science and Technology in Modern European Life
Guillaume de Syon

Cooking in Europe, 1650–1850
Ivan P. Day

Victorian England, Second Edition
Sally Mitchell

Daily Life of the Ancient Greeks, Second Edition
Robert Garland

DAILY LIFE IN

CHAUCER'S ENGLAND

Second Edition

JEFFREY L. FORGENG
AND WILL McLEAN

The Greenwood Press "Daily Life Through History" Series

GREENWOOD PRESS
Westport, Connecticut • London

Library of Congress Cataloging-in-Publication Data

Forgeng, Jeffrey L.
   Daily life in Chaucer's England / Jeffrey L. Forgeng and Will McLean. — 2nd ed.
      p. cm. — (The Greenwood Press "daily life through history" series, ISSN 1080-4749)
   Includes bibliographical references and index.
   ISBN 978–0–313–35951–4 (alk. paper)
   1. England—Social conditions—1066-1485.   2. England—Social life and customs—
1066-1485.   3. Chaucer, Geoffrey, d. 1400—Homes and haunts—England.   I. McLean,
Will. II. Title.
   DA185.S48   2009
   942.03'7—dc22   2008037469

British Library Cataloguing in Publication Data is available.

Library of Congress Catalog Card Number: 2008037469
ISBN: 978–0–313–35951–4
ISSN: 1080–4749

First published in 2009

Greenwood Press, 88 Post Road West, Westport, CT 06881
An imprint of Greenwood Publishing Group, Inc.
www.greenwood.com

Printed in the United States of America

The paper used in this book complies with the
Permanent Paper Standard issued by the National
Information Standards Organization (Z39.48–1984).

10 9 8 7 6 5 4 3 2 1

Copyright Acknowledgments

Additional illustrations by Will McLean, John Vernier, and Kitten Reames.

The publisher has done its best to make sure the instructions and/or recipes in
this book are correct. However, users should apply judgment and experience
when preparing recipes, especially parents and teachers working with young
people. The publisher accepts no responsibility for the outcome of any recipe
included in this volume.

CONTENTS

PREFACE TO THE SECOND EDITION

When the first edition of *Daily Life in Chaucer's England* came out in 1995, we were naturally both proud of the work, a labor of love into which we have both put a great deal of effort. Yet we were probably both a bit surprised by the welcome it received: it would seem that the hands-on, experiential perspective of the work had a real appeal for readers, and it was gratifying to think that we had created something that was clearly being appreciated by such a large number of people.

A dozen years down the line, we are both very happy to have the opportunity to furnish a second edition of the work. During the intervening years, other researchers have added to the information available on the period, and the interval has also been very full for both of us in ways that will contribute substantially to this book. Will McLean has added more than a decade of research and experience as a practitioner of living history focusing on the period of Chaucer's lifetime, and has become an active participant in the fast-growing world of Web-based medieval studies. Jeffrey Forgeng (who coauthored the original version of this book under the surname Singman) has accumulated a decade of experience interpreting the Middle Ages for diverse audiences as a professor of history and as curator of the Higgins Armory Museum, and has authored a number of additional titles in Greenwood's *Daily Life* series, as well as a variety of other publications both scholarly and popular. The accumulated study and experience has allowed us to deepen and reshape this work in ways that we feel will make it an even more valuable resource than the original edition.

This second edition is over a third longer than the original. Aside from the general addition of new material throughout the work, this increased length reflects the addition of primary-source sidebars in all chapters, as well as a substantial guide to resources at the end to account for the changing landscape of information available for the study of the Middle Ages in the digital age. The illustrations have also been revised and expanded, supplementing the original line drawings with photographs. Finally, the work as a whole has been reorganized based on ideas that have proved successful in Forgeng's more recent *Daily Life* books.

In addition to the thanks offered in the first edition, the authors would like to give credit to Tobias Capwell of the Wallace Collection for his insights on the quintain; Stephen Bloch and Deborah Peters for their advice on music and for finding and transcribing "Si quis amat" and "Danger me hath"; Robert MacPherson for his updated breeches pattern, Robert and Jenna Reed for their contributions to the Digital Resources section; to Christine Drew and Tasha Kelly McGann for serving as readers for this second edition; to Sarah Kolba for her invaluable work as research assistant to the project; and to Laura Hanlan Robinson, reigning queen of Interlibrary Loan, for once again proving her ability to track down any book in the world, whether or not it has actually been written.

Once more we are pleased and proud to be able to share the fruits of our labors, and hope that our work will prove of value to many over the years to come.

ACKNOWLEDGMENTS

The authors wish to thank the following: Robert MacPherson for his breech design; Daniel Jennings for his shirt design; Karen Walter for her design for a veil and wimple and for her instructions on gussets; David Meddows-Taylor and John Vernier for their work on earlier drafts of the section on Shoes and Pattens; David Kuijt for the original draft of the section on Cards and for the rules for Karnoeffel and Glic; David Tallan for the original draft of the chapter on Food and Drink and of the recipes for Salad and Mustard; Kitten Reames for the original draft of the section on Spoons; Maren Drees for her work on the recipes; Trish Postle for her research into songs; and Karen Weatherbee for the original draft of the text on handwriting.

Illustrations by Poul Norlund of the Herjolfsnes garments appear by permission of *Meddelelser om Groenland*.

Special credit is due to Kitten Reames for her illustrations of spoons, and to John Vernier for his illustrations of shoes and pattens and of arms and armor.

The authors also wish to thank the following individuals who assisted in this book in its various incarnations: Elizabeth Bennett, Robert Charrette, David Carroll-Clark, Susan Carroll-Clark, Gerry Embleton, Jeremy Graham, Victoria Hadfield, Marianne Hansen, Tara Jenkins, Daniel Jennings, Wendy McLean, Aryeh Nusbacher, and Karen Walter. *Daily Life in Chaucer's England* is a revised and expanded version of *The Chaucerian Handbook*, itself a revision and expansion of *The Tabard Inn*, a manual for Chaucerian living history published by the University Medieval and Renaissance Society of Toronto in February 1991 for its "Tabard Inn" living history event.

INTRODUCTION

The life of medieval people has fascinated English speakers for over two hundred years, since the romantics and antiquarians of the late eighteenth century began to rediscover the medieval past. There is indeed good reason why we should be so interested in the Middle Ages. Childhood plays an enormous role in shaping adult life, and in many respects the Middle Ages were the infancy of the society we know today. Between us and the classical world there lies a real historical break, for the fall of the Roman Empire broke off the development of Greco-Roman culture. Since the Middle Ages, however, there has been more of a historical continuum. The institutions that shape our world evolved during the medieval period: cities, universities, nation-states, and the common law are all inherited from the medieval world. Today, even people from lands unknown to medieval Europe are profoundly influenced by the medieval heritage. The language of the Beatles and of Martin Luther King is the language they inherited from Chaucer—the medieval world shapes our own in ways that are more far-reaching than we can ever fully perceive.

This book focuses on the daily life of people during a particularly fascinating period of the English Middle Ages. By custom, the Middle Ages in England are reckoned to have lasted from the fall of Rome (roughly the fifth century C.E., depending on what historical event one chooses to mark Rome's fall), until the end of the Wars of the Roses with the accession of Henry VII in 1485. Sometimes the term is used in a more limited sense to indicate the period after the Norman Conquest in 1066. In either case, the Middle Ages spanned a number of centuries. In order to focus this book sufficiently to make meaningful statements about people's lives, it concentrates on the period of a single man's lifetime, from 1342 to 1400.

This man is Geoffrey Chaucer, generally considered the first great poet in English since the time of the Conquest and unsurpassed until the time of Shakespeare. This book is about ordinary people rather than about Chaucer, but he is a particularly apt choice as a figure around which to center the text. His *Canterbury Tales* are in many ways about ordinary people, whom he portrayed with a vividness that brings them alive even today; the tales are themselves a rich source of information on people's daily lives.

The latter part of the fourteenth century is also a very effective vantage point from which to observe medieval life. Many major events of the English Middle Ages happened during Chaucer's lifetime. The English archers of the Hundred Years' War won their great victories at Crécy and Poitiers, the Black Plague swept across Europe, the peasantry of England rose in revolt against their feudal overlords, the Papacy was split in two, and Henry Bolingbroke unseated Richard II as king, an act that would ultimately lead to the Wars of the Roses in the fifteenth century.

In social and cultural terms, the fourteenth century offers an opportunity to see the medieval world at its fullest. On the one hand, the traditional feudal structures were still at work, the Catholic Church held sway over the religious life of the nation, the French language enjoyed the prestige it had acquired since French-speaking Normans conquered the Anglo-Saxons in 1066, and Latin was the international language of learning. At the same time, new, market-oriented arrangements were reshaping the old feudal system, London and its merchant class were becoming a significant political force, John Wycliffe and his Lollards were challenging the teachings of the Catholic Church, and English was reasserting itself as a language of law, culture, and education.

In fact, quite a number of books have already been written about daily life in Chaucer's England. However, this book differs from any that has gone before, for it is the first such book to be written from the perspective of living history. Living history encompasses a broad range of activities. In its most general sense, it can include any attempt to recreate materially some aspect of the past. In this sense, playing medieval music or practicing medieval calligraphy are both living history activities. In its most comprehensive form, living history tries to recreate an entire historical milieu.

Living history of this last sort is relatively rare for the medieval period, partly because the lack of information makes it rather difficult. This book began as a brief manual written by members of the University Medieval and Renaissance Association of Toronto (now called the Tabard Inn Society) for a Chaucerian-period event held at the University of Toronto in 1991. It included information on clothing, games, songs, dances, and historical background, so that the participants could recreate the atmosphere of an evening at a London inn in 1391.

That original manual has undergone many substantial revisions since 1991, and very little of this book comes from that document, but the connection with living history remains. It has shaped this book in two important ways. First, living history encourages a hands-on approach to the past. Whereas other books on medieval daily life will tell you what kinds of clothes people wore, what kinds of games they played, or what kinds of songs they sang, this book includes actual patterns for medieval clothes, rules for medieval games, and music for medieval songs. History need not only live on the pages of books: there is both fun and learning to be had from trying it out first-hand.

Second, living history is a great means of focusing one's attention on the essential facts of daily life. Engaging in living history doesn't itself teach us how people lived their lives, but it does help us decide what sorts of questions we might want to ask about the past. When you spend a day trying to live as a medieval person would, you soon discover what sorts of information are really important. For this reason, you will find that this book is much more focused on the underlying fundamentals of daily life than is generally the case, and that it offers information on significant subjects that are sometimes glossed over in previous works on the subject: water sources, nutrition, waste management, and the core technologies that produced such essentials as food, clothing, and shelter.

One final important feature of this book is our belief that quality scholarship need and should not be inapproachable to the general reader. We have worked to make this text accessible and enjoyable for a wide audience, while ensuring that it is written to a high standard of fidelity to the sources. Of course, we can never fully recover the past: even if all the necessary information were available, it would be impossible for anyone to master all of it, and in the case of the Middle Ages our information is often fragmentary or inaccessible. However, we can ensure that we remain as faithful as we can to our available primary sources (i.e., original documents or artifacts from the period), so the margin of error is kept to a minimum.

This is precisely what we have striven to do in this book. Moreover, we have included samples from the sources (such as original medieval food recipes and patterns of surviving clothes) to allow the reader even closer contact with the original material. In some of the hands-on sections, we have had to use other sorts of sources (some of the rules for games, for example, are based on later texts), but in each case we felt that the degree of conjecture was justifiable and we have been careful to make it clear where the information is coming from, if not from contemporary sources. For those who want to pursue a particular topic more deeply, we have added footnotes and a bibliography to help point you in the right direction.

This book has been a labor of love in which quite a number of hands have had a part over the years. We hope it will give you as much enjoyment in reading and using it as it has given us in creating it, and that for you, as for us, it will help make history come alive.

A CHRONOLOGY OF CHAUCERIAN ENGLAND

1327   Edward III is brought to the throne in a coup d'état against his father, Edward II.

1330   Edward III assumes royal authority.

1337   Edward III lays claim to the French throne, initiating the Hundred Years' War.

1339   Edward III invades France.

1340   English naval victory at Sluys.

1342   Probable year of Chaucer's birth.

1346   English victory at Battle of Crécy, France.

Battle of Neville's Cross, England. English troops defeat Scottish invasion force.

1347   Truce between England and France.

Plague arrives in Italy.

1348   Edward III establishes the Order of the Garter.

Plague reaches England.

1351   Parliament passes the Statute of Laborers to keep down wages.

1353   Boccaccio's *Decameron*.

1356   English victory at Battle of Poitiers, France.

At about this time Chaucer is serving in the household of Elizabeth de Burgh, countess of Ulster and wife of Prince Lionel of Antwerp.

1360   Treaty of Bretigny ends the first phase of the Hundred Years' War.

Chaucer is ransomed from French captivity and serves as a courier in the peace negotiations.

1361   Outbreak of plague.

1362   First version of William Langland's *Piers Plowman*, the first major literary work to be written in English since the Norman Conquest.

1367   Edward Prince of Wales (the "Black Prince") leads an expedition to Spain in aid of Pedro the Cruel, the deposed king of Castile.

By this time Chaucer is serving in the king's household.

1369   Outbreak of plague.

Hostilities resume in the Hundred Years' War; Chaucer is paid for service in the war effort.

Chaucer composes his first major work, *The Book of the Duchess*, at about this time.

1375   Outbreak of plague.

1376   Death of the Prince of Wales. Parliament impeaches royal servants belonging to the faction of John of Gaunt, duke of Lancaster.

1377   Chaucer is sent on a delegation to arrange a peace treaty with the French.

Death of Edward III, accession of his grandson Richard II, still only 11 years of age.

Poll Tax levied.

The papacy returns to Rome from Avignon, where it had resided since 1309.

1378   Pope Gregory XI dies. The French-dominated College of Cardinals is intimidated by the Roman mob into electing an Italian as Pope, Urban VI. Urban antagonizes the cardinals, who declare him deposed, and elect a Frenchman, Clement VII. Clement moves to Avignon, but Urban remains as Pope in Rome. England, as well as the countries of Scandinavia, Germany, and northern Italy, support the Roman Pope; France, Scotland, Naples, Sicily, and the various kingdoms in Spain follow the Pope of Avignon. This schism is not healed until the fifteenth century.

Chaucer is sent on a diplomatic mission to Italy, where he meets with Bernabò Visconti, ruler of Milan, and the English mercenary leader John Hawkwood.

1381   Peasants' Revolt.

1382   Richard II marries Anne of Bohemia.

At about this time the religious reformist John Wycliffe and his Lollard followers are producing the first full English translation of the Bible.

Chaucer is composing *Troilus and Criseyde* at about this time.

1384   Death of Wycliffe.

1385   Richard II and his uncle, John of Gaunt, undertake a fruitless military campaign in Scotland.

1386   John of Gaunt leads an expensive and unsuccessful expedition to Spain in an effort to win the crown of Castile, which he claims by right of his second wife, Blanche.

Chaucer serves as knight of the shire for Kent in Parliament.

Chaucer begins to assemble the framework of the *Canterbury Tales* at about this time.

1388   Scottish victory at Otterburn.

Parliament impeaches several of the king's favorites.

1389   Richard II reaches the age of majority and assumes the functions of government in person.

Chaucer is appointed Clerk of the King's Works.

Boniface IX becomes Pope at Rome.

1390   Outbreak of plague.

Sir Gawain and the Green Knight is composed at about this time.

1394   Richard II campaigns in Ireland.

Death of Queen Anne.

1396   Truce with France; Richard II marries Isabella of France.

1399   Death of John of Gaunt.

Richard II is deposed by Henry of Bolingbroke (John of Gaunt's son), who becomes King Henry IV.

1400   Death of Richard II.

Death of Chaucer.

Outbreak of plague.

1

HISTORICAL BACKGROUND TO CHAUCER'S ENGLAND

The Middle Ages in England, in their broadest sense, are generally taken to begin around the fifth century C.E. at the time of the Roman withdrawal from Britain and the invasion of the country by Angles, Saxons, and Jutes from what is now Denmark and northern Germany. Over the following centuries, the invaders expanded their area of control at the expense of the native Celtic Britons and eventually consolidated into a single Anglo-Saxon kingdom of England. By the last years of this kingdom in the first half of the eleventh century the Anglo-Saxons had established control over all of present-day England, including western Cornwall, which still spoke Cornish, a descendant of the language of the Britons. They also had considerable authority over Wales, whose inhabitants spoke Welsh, another descendant of the British language. To the north, Scotland was an independent kingdom albeit with close ties to England.

In 1066, King Edward the Confessor died, and there was a dispute over the English crown between an English lord, Harold Godwinson, and William, duke of Normandy. William invaded England, and Harold was defeated and killed at the Battle of Hastings. William became king, and the native English aristocracy was largely supplanted by French-speaking Normans.

Under the Norman kings, England began to expand its authority. In 1166, Norman lords under Henry II invaded and conquered Ireland, although over the centuries many of the invaders assimilated to the native Irish culture and effective English control came to be limited to parts of the eastern coast. Henry also succeeded in acquiring most of northern and western France, establishing an Anglo-French empire that was to remain a persistent dream of English monarchs for the rest of the Middle Ages.

Henry II's empire disintegrated after his death, and in 1204 his youngest son, King John, lost the Duchy of Normandy, leaving only a distant holding in southwestern France under English control. However, this loss opened the way for a revival of English national identity. No longer did the English aristocracy have close connections and lands in France, and over the following century they became increasingly likely to speak English as their native tongue.

English imperial ambitions were revived during the reign of John's grandson, Edward I, in the late thirteenth century. Edward at last succeeded in subjugating Wales in 1284, and in 1301 the title of the Prince of Wales was given to his son, the future Edward II; the eldest son of the English monarch has held this title ever since. In 1296, Edward managed to subject the king of Scotland to the English crown, but this overlordship was lost in 1314 by Edward II at the battle of Bannockburn.

The young Edward III came to the throne in 1327 in a coup d'état against his father, Edward II, who had become unpopular with the English aristocracy. The coup was led by Edward II's wife, Isabella, the daughter of King Philip IV (Philip the Fair) of France, and by Roger Mortimer, the Earl of March, who was Isabella's lover. Edward was forced to abdicate, then imprisoned, and secretly murdered. Mortimer and Isabella became the effective rulers of England but soon managed to antagonize the nobles themselves. In 1330 Edward assumed the royal authority in person: Mortimer was executed, and Isabella was confined for the remainder of her life.

As Isabella's son, Edward had French royal blood as well as English. In 1328, when the French king Philip IV's sons had all died without male issue, the French crown passed to Philip VI, the son of Philip IV's younger brother, Charles of Valois. In 1337 Philip declared Edward's French holdings confiscated over a legal squabble, and later that year Edward took the offensive by claiming the French throne for himself. He invaded France from the Low Countries in 1339, starting the Hundred Years' War.

The early years of the war went well for England. In 1340, Edward won a major naval victory at Sluys (in the Low Countries), securing control over the English Channel. At Crécy in 1346 his archers and dismounted knights soundly defeated a much larger force of French knights and noblemen, whose losses were catastrophic. Edward's eldest son, Edward of Woodstock, the Prince of Wales, distinguished himself in the battle, marking the beginning of a lasting military reputation; he came to be known in later centuries as the Black Prince. In the aftermath of the battle Edward captured Calais. At Poitiers in 1356, English archers once again defeated a larger French force, and King John of France, the son and heir of Philip VI, was among those captured. By the terms of the Treaty of Bretigny signed in 1360, Edward renounced his claim to the French throne but was to hold

Calais and his lands in southwestern France independently of the king of France.

Simultaneous with the war with France was the ongoing conflict with Scotland, which increasingly allied itself with France against England. Edward III had more success against the Scots than had his father. His victory at Halidon Hill in 1333 re-established English overlordship over the king of Scotland, and at the battle of Neville's Cross in 1346 the Scottish king, David II, was captured.

In 1347, in the middle of these wars, Europe was hit by the Black Plague, which reached England in 1348. This disease had come from the east and decimated Europe, killing as many as a third to a half of the population. The sudden collapse in the population reverberated through the economy. The value of labor skyrocketed, while the value of land plummeted—much land went uncultivated for lack of people to till it. In response, the government instituted a series of measures to keep wages at their pre-plague levels. Such legislation proved impossible to enforce in the face of market pressures, and its primary effect may have been to inflame anti-government sentiment among wage-earning commoners.

In spite of the impact of the Plague, Edward III continued to enjoy considerable popularity among his subjects, largely thanks to his military successes, and this popularity was shared by the Prince of Wales. However, public opinion was less enthusiastic during the later years of Edward's reign. In 1367 the Prince of Wales led an expedition to Spain in aid of Pedro the Cruel, king of Castile, whose throne had been seized by his brother Henry with French support. The campaign was successful, but the Prince financed it by imposing heavy taxes in Gascony. The Gascon lords refused to pay and appealed to King Charles V of France, son of King John. Charles gave judgment in favor of the Gascons. The move was a direct infringement of Edward III's sovereignty in his French holdings. Edward resumed his claim to the French throne, and the war began again in 1369.

This time, things did not go nearly so well. The French had learned the lessons of Crécy and Poitiers: they avoided large pitched battles, relying instead on smaller raids to undermine Edward's control of French territory. In 1371 the Prince of Wales, debilitated with disease, returned to England. The aging Edward III was losing effective control over his government, which came to be dominated by factions led by his mistress Alice Perrers and his youngest son, John of Gaunt, duke of Lancaster. The Prince of Wales died in 1376, and Edward III a year later. By this time, all that remained of their French conquests was Calais and a thin strip of the Gascon coast.

Edward was succeeded by Richard II, son of the late Prince of Wales. Richard was still underage, and the early years of his reign were dominated by factions. The reign was also dogged by chronic revenue shortages. To redress this problem the government levied the Poll Tax in 1377; the tax was repeated in 1379 and tripled in 1380. This tax on every head fell especially hard on the poorest people, and helped ignite the Peasants' Revolt in 1381. The rebels were concentrated in the east and southeast. A force of peasant rebels from Kent actually managed to capture London and forced the King to promise the abolition of villeinage and reduction of rents. However, their leader, Wat Tyler, was killed in parlay with the King, and the rebellion collapsed. The King abandoned his promises, and harsh reprisals followed.

Richard had shown some personal courage at a very young age during the Peasants' Revolt, but the remainder of his reign proved less successful. He allowed himself to be dominated by factions and favorites, which alienated many of his subjects, and he failed to revive the military successes of his father's reign. In 1385 he and John of Gaunt conducted an expensive and unsuccessful invasion of Scotland, and in 1388 an English army was severely defeated by the Scots at the Battle of Otterburn. Anglo-French relations were largely peaceful. Indeed, in 1396 Richard married a French princess, temporarily sealing a peace between England and France.

The last decade of Richard's reign was dogged by problems in Ireland, where English control was weakening. In 1394, Richard led an expedition

---

JEAN FROISSART DESCRIBES THE PEASANTS' REVOLT (1381)

The wretched peasantry . . . began to rebel, saying that the servitude in which they were kept was excessive, and that at the beginning of the world no man was a slave . . .

A mad priest in the county of Kent, John Ball by name, had for some time been encouraging these notions, and had several times been confined in the Archbishop of Canterbury's prison for his absurd speeches. For it was his habit on Sundays after mass . . . to collect a crowd round him in the market-place and address them more or less as follows: "My friends, the state of England cannot be right until everything is held communally, and until there is no distinction between nobleman and serf, and we are all as one. Why are those whom we call lords masters over us? How have they deserved it? By what right do they keep us enslaved? We are all descended from our first parents, Adam and Eve; how then can they say that they are better lords than us, except in making us toil and earn for them to spend? They are dressed in velvet and furs, while we wear only cloth. They have wine, and spices and good bread, while we have rye, and straw that has been thrown away, and water to drink. They have fine houses and manors, and we have to brave the wind and rain as we toil in the fields. It is by the sweat of our brows that they maintain their high state. We are called serfs, and we are beaten if we do not perform our tasks. . . . Let us go to the King. He is young, and we will show him our miserable slavery, we will tell him it must be changed, or else we will provide the remedy ourselves."

From Jean Froissart, *Chronicles of England, France, Spain, and the Adjoining Countries,* transl. Thomas Johnes (London: William Smith, 1842), 652.

that succeeded in subduing the Irish lords for a time. In 1399 another rebellion erupted, and he set out to suppress it. During his absence Henry of
Bolingbroke, the eldest son of John of Gaunt, returned from exile to claim
estates belonging to his father that had been unjustly seized by Richard at
John's death that year. The invasion quickly became a rebellion. Richard
returned to England but was captured and forced to abdicate. With the
approval of Parliament, Henry assumed the crown as Henry IV, first of
the Lancastrian kings of England, and Richard died in captivity the following year.

Richard II's reign was not a political success, but it was a high point in
the history of English culture. Richard was a generous patron of the arts,
and during his reign Geoffrey Chaucer produced most of his best work.

Chaucer was probably born around 1342, the son of John and Agnes
Chaucer (the latter née Copton). His family were prosperous Londoners:
his father and grandfather were wine-merchants, although his surname
suggests that a prior ancestor had been a shoemaker. Chaucer's own career
demonstrates the possibilities that were opening up for the middle classes
in late medieval England. He received an excellent education at the school
of St. Paul's Cathedral in London, as well as some study of law at the emerging Inns of Court. During his teenage years he served in the household of
Elizabeth de Burgh, countess of Ulster. Not only was this service prestigious, but it brought the young man into the orbit of the royal court: the
countess was wife to Prince Lionel of Antwerp, the second son of Edward III
by his queen Philippa of Hainault (a region in modern-day Belgium).

As part of the extended royal household, Chaucer was involved in the
1359–1360 English military campaign in France; he was captured by the
French, and subsequently ransomed with the assistance of the king. By
1367 he was in service to the king himself, and had won a substantial
lifetime grant of 20 marks a year—about £14, a handsome annual income
that would later be supplemented by additional annuities from the royal
family.

Chaucer's connections to the royal household brought him into con-
tact with the Hainaulters who had become a significant presence at court.
Probably during the 1360s he married Philippa, daughter of the Hain-
aulter Paen de Roet and lady-in-waiting to Queen Philippa. The marriage
to Philippa sealed Chaucer's place in the highest circles of English society.
His wife's elder sister Katherine was married to Sir Hugh Swynford. After
Swynford's death in 1371, Katherine became governess to the daughters of
John of Gaunt, duke of Lancaster. Katherine would eventually become the
duke's mistress and ultimately his wife, stepmother to the future Henry
IV, and ancestor to the later Tudor monarchs of England. Chaucer's connections to the Lancastrian circle doubtless ensured his continued royal
favor after the fall of Richard II.

Throughout his adult life, Chaucer enjoyed a successful career in service
to the crown. During the late 1360s into the 1380s, as a yeoman and later

squire to the king, he served on multiple diplomatic missions to Spain, France, and Italy. From the 1370s onward he held a series of governmental positions, including Comptroller of Customs for Wools, Skins, and Hides for the Port of London, justice of the peace and member of Parliament for Kent, Clerk of the King's Works, and deputy forester for the royal forest of North Petherton in Somerset.

Chaucer's chief claim to fame is his extensive and diverse body of writings, ranging from devotional verses to a technical treatise on the use of the astrolabe. He was above all an accomplished poet, probably winning royal recognition as early as about 1370 with his *Book of the Duchess*, an elegy composed for John of Gaunt in memory of his first wife, Blanche of Castile. Not long afterwards he may have begun composing some of the material that would eventually be incorporated into *The Canterbury Tales*, his most famous work. The *Tales* are presented as the story of a company of pilgrims traveling from London to the shrine of St. Thomas à Becket in Canterbury; they are related as a series of stories told by the various pilgrims to entertain each other en route. The work had taken shape by about 1387, and Chaucer added new tales throughout the rest of his life, leaving it unfinished at the time of his death on October 25, 1400.

By the time of Chaucer's death, England had a new king and a new dynasty on the throne. The dubiousness of Henry IV's claim to the crown helped provoke the Wars of the Roses in the fifteenth century, which pitted Henry's Lancastrian heirs against the Yorkist descendants of Lionel, duke of Clarence, the second son of Edward III. These civil wars finally ended with the accession of Henry Tudor in 1485. Henry was a descendant of John of Gaunt by Katherine Swynford; his accession is customarily taken to mark the end of the Middle Ages in England.

JEAN FROISSART DESCRIBES CHAUCER'S PART IN THE PEACE NEGOTIATIONS OF 1377

Around Shrove Tuesday there was a secret treaty between the two kings . . . The English sent to Calais Guichard d'Angle, Richard Stury, and Geoffrey Chaucer, and the French sent the lords of Coucy and la Rivière, and Sir Nicholas Braque and Sir Nicholas Mercier. And they negotiated for some time over this marriage treaty, and the French offered, as I have been informed, twelve cities; but the English insisted on having something else, or nothing at all.

Translated by J. L. Forgeng from the French in Martin M. Crow and Clair C. Olson, *Chaucer Life-Records* (Austin: University of Texas Press, 1966), 50.

2

SOCIETY

At the time of Chaucer's birth in about 1342, the population of England was around 5 million, although the ravages of the plague reduced it to about 2.5 million by the end of the century. The densest concentrations of people were in the central, southern, and eastern parts of the country. The geography of these regions is mostly flat or with gently rolling hills, and the land is fertile, supporting intensive cultivation of nutrient-rich wheat. The northern and western parts of the country were generally rougher country and less fertile. At the westernmost edges were Cornwall and Wales, regions that spoke their own languages and had cultures quite different from that of England itself. Much of northern Wales had only come under the authority of the king of England in the late 1200s.

Within England itself there was considerable variety in local cultures, and an individual's experience of life depended greatly on the circumstances into which they were born. In theory, every English man and woman had a well-defined position in the social hierarchy, reflected in forms of address, in clothing, and in precedence in public places. In reality, the social hierarchy was nuanced and complex, and people's places in it were not always clear-cut. A wealthy commoner might live better than a poor aristocrat, and an individual's standing could change from year to year depending on how they were perceived by those around them. Ranks in the hierarchy of the church and in the upper aristocracy were fairly clear—knights, lords, priests, and bishops received formal titles in a well-defined hierarchy of authority and precedence. However, informal designations like squire, franklin, and husbandman could be

The hierarchy of secular society, from simple pilgrims to king and emperor. Andrea di Bonaiuto, Fresco, 1365–1368. Spanish Chapel S. Maria Novella, Florence. Photo Credit: Scala/Art Resource, NY.

somewhat fluid, and it might be hard to tell whether the local miller was a more important man than the local smith. Disputes about who had the right to go into church first on Sunday sometimes came to blows: Chaucer says of the Wife of Bath that "In all the parish, wife was there none,/That to the offering before her should go" (*The Canterbury Tales* [hereafter *CT*] A.449–50).

Social confusion was aggravated by social mobility. It was possible, although hardly easy, to rise in social rank. Sir John Hawkwood, the greatest English mercenary captain of the age, was a tanner's son who eventually married the daughter of the duke of Milan. On the other hand, people could lose social status if they failed to maintain a mode of living appropriate to their rank.

Feudal Society

Overall, English society in Chaucer's lifetime was in a period of transition that was acutely visible if not always comprehensible to contemporaries. In principle, society was organized by the structures that modern historians came to call feudalism. Feudalism had taken shape centuries earlier, around 500–1100 C.E., and it had already been strained by the growing population and burgeoning economy of the 1200s. During the 1300s, the breakup of feudalism accelerated. The early part of the century saw multiple years of livestock disease, poor harvests, and famine, bringing a sharp decline in population. Population fell even further after 1348, with the arrival of the Plague, which returned periodically for the rest of the century. Classic feudalism was not well suited to deal with rapid change, and by 1400 English society had adopted a kind of "market feudalism." Nonetheless, feudal structures continued to play a major role in shaping society, and in many ways the social realities of Chaucer's day were informed by the material realities of half a millennium earlier.

Feudal society had emerged as an organic response to the social and military vacuum left in Europe after the collapse of the Roman Empire. In the absence of Rome's military machine, the threat of violence was endemic, and those who could muster local military forces were in a position to claim political authority. The disappearance of Roman military organization also shifted the tactical balance of power. The classic Roman military system had centered on infantry, who relied on coordinated discipline and training. In the post-Roman world, the emphasis shifted toward cavalry, who could dominate the battlefield through individual physical prowess and expensive personal equipment.

Rome's fall also reduced commerce to a trickle, leaving agriculture as the only major sector of the economy. Almost everyone made their livings either by controlling the use of agricultural land or by working on land controlled by others. Agricultural production under imperial Rome had been concentrated on large estates owned by upper-class Romans. As the Roman territories were carved up by the invading Germanic tribes, many of these estates were simply taken over by the tribesmen. Coinage was also scarce, so it was impractical to make payments in cash, and since the new rulers of the Roman territories were generally illiterate, oral culture displaced written contracts as the vehicle for political and legal transactions.

In this environment, a new mode of social organization emerged that was grounded on personal relationships between individuals and relationships between people and land. These relationships provided a framework for social organization during the lifetimes of the people involved; they were also made enduring across the generations through the principle of inheritance.

Because cash was an unreliable mode of exchange in a world without trusted central authorities to issue coinage, feudalism took shape as a system for exchanging service for land. At the top of the feudal hierarchy was the king, who was the theoretical sovereign owner of all the land in the country. The king granted holdings of land to aristocratic "tenants-in-chief" in exchange for military support. The tenant-in-chief paid for his landholding by promising military service in time of war, bringing a stipulated number of armed followers to fight under the king's command for a specified number of days.

The tenants-in-chief in turn granted landholdings to lesser aristocrats under similar terms. The smallest unit of aristocratic landholding was the manor, which was a parcel of land (commonly a few hundred to a thousand acres) more or less sufficient to support a mounted knight. The manor lord granted parts of his manor to peasant farmers, who paid for their holdings with labor service. The income generated for the manor lord by his tenants supported the equipment and training for his military service. The distinction between landholding by military service and land-holding by labor service defined the line between the aristocrat and the commoner, although custom also allowed commoners to be pressed into service as footsoldiers in a feudal levy when the lord needed to assemble a military force.

At each level of tenancy, the land was held rather than owned. A land-holder inherited the right to a landholding much as he might inherit owned property. If he fulfilled the customary obligations required by his holding, he kept that right for life and passed it on to his heir on the same terms. However, landholders were not free to buy or sell their landhold-ings at will: the laws and customs governing transference of land were extremely restrictive. Even a great lord might be unable to transfer a hold-ing to someone else if the terms of the holding required that it remain in the family. Nor was a landlord entirely free to grant holdings to his tenants under terms of his own choosing. The terms of each holding were shaped by law and custom, though a determined landlord could use his power to overcome tradition. For the tenant, the holding was not necessarily a right but a responsibility, since villeins, or unfree tenants, could not give up their holding without their lord's permission.

At each level, the feudal relationship between lord and subordinate also served as a vehicle for political and legal organization. Everyone who owed service was also expected to show personal loyalty, or fealty, to that lord, and the lord in turn was expected to protect the interests of his subordinates. Legal and political authority was distributed through this feudal network, as parts of the king's authority as sovereign were delegated to his tenants-in-chief, and through them down to the level of the manor lord.

Instead of written contracts, the terms of a landholding were made binding by public oath and by custom. The commoner's main assurance that his landlord would not extort extra labor services was the fact that since time out of mind the holding had entailed certain services and no more. A lord's main security that his knight would not default on his ser-vice was the knight's public promise to serve, sworn in front of people whose respect he valued. Custom was a powerful force in a society in which other mechanisms to preserve stability were weak.

Feudalism in Decline

Feudalism had evolved in an environment where both lords and sub-ordinates had an interest in preserving the status quo. By Chaucer's day, various pressures were undermining its viability. Subsistence agriculture was no longer the rule. Even ordinary peasants were producing goods for sale rather than sustenance, and agrarian crop-raising was beginning to lose some ground in favor of the lucrative pursuit of sheep-farming for the wool trade. Coin was more plentiful, while commerce and industry were becoming significant elements in the economy. Increased literacy and a developed legal system made it more practical to use and enforce written contracts. At the same time warfare was becoming professionalized, so that the fixed, part-time service of the feudal host had been almost entirely replaced by long-term service for cash wages, often by full-time profes-sional soldiers.

In an increasingly market-oriented economy, the rigid arrangements of feudalism were unsatisfactory for everyone. Both landlords and ten-ants found it advantageous to change service-rents to more flexible cash payments. The arrival of the Black Plague in 1348 hastened the decline of feudalism. With the sudden drop in population, there was intense com-petition for labor and tenants. This made it difficult to continue exact-ing unpopular service-rents, and prompted some landowners to convert arable land into pasture, exchanging labor-intensive agriculture for labor-minimal pastoralism.

Although service-rents were disappearing, the traditional feudal link between the individual and the land persisted. Service-rents may have been commuted to money rents, but tenancy remained a legal right and responsibility, and the relationship between people and the land they held was still relatively restrictive. Some landlords were quite aggres-sive in trying to keep their villeins in their place. In 1390, six villein tenants of the Archbishop of Canterbury's manor at Wingham tried to avoid the embarrassment of bringing their required cartloads of hay and straw to the archbishop's palace by carrying it secretly and on foot. They were summoned before the manor court, and were sentenced to a ritual of humiliation in which they were obliged to carry sacks of hay and straw barelegged around Wingham church. This was precisely the kind of cultural conflict that had exploded in the Peasants' Revolt a decade earlier.[1]

Meanwhile, feudal military service was being replaced by monetary rents that supported a system of written contracts, typically called indentures. Instead of doing military service in person, aristocratic landholders were typically making cash payments to their feudal superiors. When the king needed an army, he would draw up contracts with his chosen commanders, experienced captains or great lords to whom he promised a specified payment for a specific number of men.

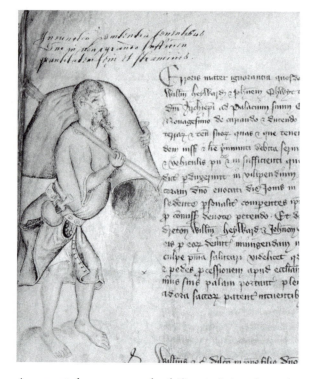

A peasant does penance for failing to bring the arch-bishop of Canterbury's straw as required by his tenure. Reg. Courtney f.337v Kentish Peasant, from the Register of the Bishop of Courtney, c. 1381–1396 (ink on vellum), English School (fourteenth century)/ © Lambeth Palace Library, London, UK/Bridgeman Art Library.

In this way the king was assured willing soldiers who would serve as long as required. The commanders would provide part of the force from their own personal followings and would subcontract the rest. The larger subcontractors might in turn subcontract a portion of their own obligation.

The usual arrangement under such subcontracts was that the lord or captain would retain men to serve under him, paying them a fixed annual fee to hold themselves ready to serve when required, plus set wages for each actual day served. The arrangement was much like the retainer paid to a modern lawyer. The advantage of the system was that the men were not expensive full-time employees, but were paid wages only when they were actually needed.

No prudent man trusts his life to total strangers if he can avoid it, and such retainers, or retinues, were recruited from a man's relatives, tenants, and neighbors whenever possible. They were given badges or distinctive clothing, called livery, to indicate their allegiance. The retainers became a sort of extension of a great man's household: not precisely part of it, but affiliated with it. The lord would typically give his patronage as well, supporting his followers in legal or political matters, and they would return the favor where they could.

Modern historians call this practice bastard feudalism, since subordinates were paid in money rather than landholdings and were bound by written contracts rather than oaths of fealty. Contemporaries called it livery or maintenance. Like the new relationship between the lord and his peasant tenants, bastard feudalism was a distinctly market-oriented arrangement,

A knight in full armor. Sir John de Argentine 1360. Ashdown.

An aristocratic household at table. The lord and lady of the house sit in the center, with their sons and daughter-in-law on the right, two Dominican friars on the left, and two servants waiting table. English, before 1340 (LP, f. 208). McLean.

since it was not bound by the traditions of inheritance or the physical tenancy of land which were a part of true feudalism.

Bastard feudalism allowed the king to put a large force into the field quickly without incurring the expense of a standing army, and the links of kinship and service that knit it together avoided the worst vices of a purely mercenary force. Yet the system also had weaknesses. The maintenance of retinues encouraged the corruption of legal and political institutions, as powerful lords would bend the rules in favor of their followers. Armies raised by indenture tended to find unpleasant alternate employment when they were put out of work, turning to brigandage and pillage to support themselves. Above all, bastard feudalism made it all too easy for turbulent subjects to raise troops on their own account. This aggravated the factional strife of Richard II's reign and helped tear the country apart when the houses of York and Lancaster struggled for supremacy in the Wars of the Roses during the following century.

THE RURAL COMMUNITY

Village, Manor, and Parish

England in Chaucer's day was still predominantly a rural country: about 80–90 percent of the population lived in the countryside. The stereotypical agricultural community was the village, consisting of a grouping of peasant households living close to each other and some miles away from the next concentrated settlement. The geographical unit of the village was roughly equivalent to the administrative unit of the manor in the hierarchy of feudalism and the parish in the hierarchy of the church, but village, manor, and parish did not always cover exactly the same people or territory.

A village might number anywhere from a few dozen to a few hundred peasant households. In the central and southern parts of England, the usual settlement pattern had the houses clustered together, surrounded by the agricultural lands. In this kind of community, known as a champion or open-field village, each peasant landholder had a certain allotment of lands in the village fields, scattered among multiple strips. In the periphery and upland regions of England—the southwest, west, and north—homes tended to be more scattered, each lying on its individual plot of land, a form of settlement known today as woodland.

Manorial Landholdings

In principal, the village lands belonged to the manor lord, who farmed them out to the peasant landholders. Every landholding included a home plot called a messuage, with a house and a small adjoining parcel of land for gardening and keeping animals. The messuage commonly came with a

THE POLL TAX RETURN FROM
THE VILLAGE OF BROCTON, STAFFORDSHIRE, 1377

Brocton

Thomas Wolseley, mason; Matilda, wife: 2s. 1d.
William Shyngeler, carpenter; Margery, wife: 2s. 0d.
Margery Bulbete, widow: 12d.
William Wayte, cultivator; Julian, wife: 2s. 4d.
John Spendour, cultivator; Margery, wife: 22d.
John Trumwyn, cultivator; Alice, wife: 2s. 1d.
John Carles, laborer; Denise, wife: 2s. 0d.
Richard Bole, cultivator; Sybil, wife: 2s. 4d.
Richard Symond, cultivator; Juliana, wife: 2s. 0d.
John Plummouth, cultivator; Matilda, wife: 2s. 1d.
William Cok, cultivator; Margery, wife: 2s. 0d.
John Forde, cultivator; Isolde, wife: 2s. 0d.
Adam Baker, tailor; Elena, wife: 2s. 1d.
Richard Tayllour; Agnes, wife: 12d.
Hugh Bromburgh, cultivator; Alice, wife: 2s. 4d.
Richard del Forde, carpenter; Margery, wife: 2s. 2d.
Margery his servant: 12d.
John Harr, cultivator; Alice, wife: 2s. 0d.
William Bate, cultivator; Joan, wife: 2s. 2d.
William Cartwright; Amice, wife: 2s. 0d.
Henry They, carpenter; Felice, wife: 2s. 0d.
Robert servant of William Wayte: 12d.
Juliana Laurence, laborer: 8d.
Petronilla Sharp, laborer: 10d.
Margaret Kyry, laborer: 8d.
Sum: 44s. from 44 people

Translated by J. L. Forgeng from the Latin in Carolyn C. Fenwick, ed., *The Poll Taxes of 1377, 1379, and 1381: Part 2 Lincolnshire-Westmorland* (Oxford: Oxford University Press, 2001), 475.

certain acreage in the agricultural fields of the village, along with rights to keep animals in the village pastures and other incidental rights in village resources. When the landholder died, the holding normally passed to the heir. Most manors had been in existence for centuries, and their landholdings had well established customs that dictated the terms under which they were held.

The most advantageous form of landholding was the freehold, to which the holder and their heirs had a clear right in perpetuity. The freeholder might owe some kind of rent to the manor lord, but this was generally a nominal amount, often paid in produce at a few major holy days in the year, serving as little more than a nod to the lord's nominal authority over the holding.

Other village tenants held their land as unfree or villeinage holdings. Villeinage land was also passed from one generation to the next, although villeins were required to pay an entry fee upon taking up their holding. Opinion varied as to the heritability of villeinage holdings. Manor lords liked to think that they let it out by choice, even if they almost always granted the holding to the landholder's heirs. Villeins naturally felt that their right to their holdings was absolute. When push came to shove, the law tended to side with the landlord.

Villein landholders were typically required to pay some rent, sometimes in the form of produce, as well as special fees and fines on particular occasions. Among other impositions, the landlord could generally claim their best farm animal when they died (a custom known as heriot); they owed a payment of recognition when a new lord inherited the manor; and they might be required to pay when the landlord married off a daughter. But the main portion of a villein's rent was labor-service, which the manor lord could generally command for two to three days a week for those who held larger holdings, a single day for those whose holdings were not large enough to support their households. Extra service would be due during harvest time. Villein landholders were also obliged to attend the lord's manor court, and both villeins and free tenants might also be called on to perform boon work, working on special tasks such as bridge and road repair.

Typical of a villeinage holding was the custom at the Somerset manor of Orchard, owned by the Bishop of Winchester. Here holders of a quarter-virgate (about 10 acres of agricultural land, plus the messuage) typically owed cash payments of from 2 shillings (s.) 10 pence (d.) to 3s. 10d. a year, one day of labor service a week (sometimes commuted for a 1/2d. cash equivalent), plus additional service for mowing in June and July, reaping in August and September, a day of plowing in winter, and a day of sowing in Lent. They were also required to attend the manor court, and to use the manorial mill to grind their grain.[2]

Manor lords also kept a part of their land in their own hands. Parts of this demesne land could be let out to tenants under terms negotiated by the landlord and tenant. A common option was the leasehold, in which the tenant was granted use of the land for a term of years or even for several lifetimes, for example passing from the holder to his widow and child before reverting to the manor lord. Leaseholds were becoming increasingly popular during Chaucer's lifetime, providing a measure of stability for both lord and tenant, while also allowing some flexibility in a changing economic environment. Other parcels might go to "tenants at will," who rented their land merely at the pleasure of the manor lord.

In a world where custom was paramount, the status of a landholding was not always clear or immutable. A villein who could avoid doing labor service might be able to convince a manor court that his holding was a freehold; conversely, a freeholder who ended up doing labor service could

A husbandman reaping grain. Italian, c. 1400 (TS Casanatense, f. lxxvi). McLean.

be judged to hold his land in villeinage. A single landholder might have both free and unfree holdings.

Villeins and Freemen

A villager's landholding was a major determining factor in their social status in the village community; however, the equation was complex, reflecting the size of the holding, the nature of the holding, and the personal status of the peasant. There was a fundamental distinction between free peasants and unfree ones. In principle, free peasants were those who held free holdings or who were born to free parents, while unfree peasants, known as villeins or bondmen, held unfree holdings or were born to unfree parents. The villein was the closest English equivalent of the Continental serf. Estimates vary, but it is believed that in the early 1300s villeins accounted for about half the peasant population or a bit more.

Free peasants had access to the king's courts and were free to leave the manor if they chose. Villeins were entirely under the jurisdiction of the lord's manorial court, except in severe criminal cases. They needed their lord's permission to leave the manor, to marry, or to enter the priesthood—although this permission could usually be secured for a fee.

In practice, free or unfree status was not always easy to determine. A single individual might inherit or otherwise acquire both free and unfree holdings; a person born to free parents might acquire an unfree holding, or vice versa; and mixed marriages of free and unfree peasants were common (in such cases, the children would normally inherit their status from the father).

A characteristic example of the complexities of personal status is the case of Alice Comyn, a tenant of the Countess of Norfolk at the manor of Earl's Soham in Suffolk. In 1373, Alice was challenged in the manor court for having married without a license. She produced a charter from the countess's father, by which she was made free. However, the manor was held under terms that did not permit the manor lord to give away property except during his lifetime, so the countess argued that the charter became void at the earl's death. The court accepted this argument and Alice was fined 13s. 4d.[3]

Although custom dictated that both lord and peasant had rights and responsibilities in the manorial relationship, the playing field was far from even, and manor lords had the power to twist the system in their favor. In 1356 the manorial court of Elmley summoned Adam le Bedel for having left the manor without permission of the lord, Thomas Beauchamp, earl of Warwick. Adam testified that he was a freeman, although he held a villeinage holding. When the jury of manorial tenants agreed with him, the earl's officials convened a special jury who decreed that Adam was a villein, and ordered the previous jury to pay a severely punitive fine of £20. Warwick had a history of high-handed behavior towards his villeins: in 1346 he had decided to rebuild his castle at Elmley, and compelled his villeins to provide free boon-work for the massive project.[4]

This degree of arbitrary treatment of villeins was exceptional, but in the late 1300s the English peasantry were increasingly resentful of the burdens and stigma of villeinage. The persistence of villeinage helped fuel the Peasants' Revolt in 1381. Among the main demands of the rebels were the abolition of villeinage, commutation of labor service, and the curtailing of landlords' judicial powers in manorial courts.

The peasants who risked their lives in their unsuccessful attempt to abolish villeinage in 1381 probably did not realize that the institution was already dying a natural death. Labor services were rigidly fixed by custom, and villeinage was poorly suited to the needs of a changing economy: many landlords were willing to forego labor service in favor of cash rents. With the drop in population after the Black Plague, landlords found themselves competing for tenants and it became even harder to continue exacting the services associated with villeinage. The proportion of villeins to freemen declined rapidly during the second half of the 1300s, and in another two centuries villeinage would disappear entirely.

Although villeins resented the social stigma and practical burdens placed upon them by their status, a peasant's quality of life and status in the community was probably less determined by free or unfree status than by the size of their landholding. It was easier and more pleasant to be a freeholder with 30 acres than a bondman with the same lands, but a villein with 30 acres was better off than a free man with 10 and probably

---

FROM THE CUSTOMS OF LACKFORD MANOR, SUFFOLK, 1399

William Douwe, for one cottage with three acres of land lately of William Poke, 18d. per annum. And owes suit of court, and shall reap one acre of oats, give one hen, and mow the lord's meadow, namely *le merchmede*. And he shall find one man for one boonwork to reap the lord's corn in the harvest.

From Mark Bailey, *The English Manor, c. 1200–1500* (Manchester: Manchester University Press, 2002), 83.

---

carried more weight in local affairs. It was by no means unusual for a villein to be a man of considerable wealth and standing in the community. The Reeve in *The Canterbury Tales* is roughly equated in status with the Miller, who would have been a leading freeman in the village community. Yet the reeve was by definition a villein: he was a manorial official recruited from among the villeins to help administer the estate.

Franklins or Yeomen

In terms of the size of landholdings, the most privileged peasants were those known as franklins or yeomen, freemen with holdings of 50 acres or more, enough to offer a reasonable standard of living and the prospect of economic advancement. Such men lived comfortably by the standards of the age, and many were wealthier than some squires. Yeoman was traditionally the term for the servant that ranked below a squire, and in Chaucer's day the word was coming to be applied to the class of people from which such servants were drawn. This class also provided the archers who distinguished themselves in the wars against France. Perhaps one-fifth of the peasantry were yeomen in the early fourteenth century, and the number appears to have grown during the century. Villeins with exceptionally large landholdings might enjoy a standard of living equivalent to a franklin, even if they did not enjoy the same prestige.

Husbandmen

Below the franklins were the husbandmen, who were freemen or villeins with holdings typically ranging from about 15 to 40 acres, a size sufficient to maintain a peasant family. Such men may have constituted a third of the peasant population in the early fourteenth century. Many villein landholdings fell in this range.

Cottars

The smallest landholders were commonly known as cottars or cottagers. They held little more than their home messuages—generally five acres or less. This was too little land to support a family, so they needed to supplement their land-based income by selling their labor. Probably about half the peasantry were cottars in the early fourteenth century, many of them villeins, although the lot of such people likely improved in the latter half of the century.

Laborers and the Rural Poor

At the bottom of rural society were those who held no land at all and were entirely dependent on their earnings as laborers: carters, plowmen, herdsmen, threshers, and other hired hands. Younger sons of landholders, and girls who were unable to marry landholders, were likely to end up in this class. The most fortunate might find long-term employment in the household of a landholder; others traveled from village to village in search of seasonal work. Those who could find no work in the country ended up migrating to the towns in search of a living.

The Manor Lord

The manor lord was sometimes but not always a resident of the manor itself. Many of them owned multiple residences, moving from one site to another during the course of a year and leaving the manor in the hands of a hired steward while they were away. The manor lord was not necessarily an individual person. Many churches, monasteries, bishoprics, and schools had received manors as donations from wealthy benefactors at some point in their history, and used the income from these manors to support their operations.

The manor lord enjoyed some income from rents and fees, but equally important was the demesne, a portion of the manor's agricultural lands kept in the lord's hands rather than farmed out. The demesne was traditionally worked through the labor services of the lord's unfree tenants, though as labor services were commuted for cash rents, landlords shifted toward hired help, or even leased out their demesne lands.

In addition to receiving the largest share in the income generated by the manorial lands, the landlord also enjoyed legal jurisdiction over the manor. A manor court was summoned several times a year, often meeting in the manor lord's hall, or else in the church or outdoors. The court administered all manner of petty complaints and administrative needs of the manor residents. The villeins of the manor were entirely subject to the court's authority, except in major criminal cases, where the royal courts might become involved. Decisions of the court were in the hands of a jury of villeins impaneled by the authority of the manor lord. To some degree, the manor court served as a mechanism for local self-government by the manorial tenants, though the manor lord was generally capable of determining the outcome of a case if he deemed it important.

THE ARISTOCRACY

The manor was the point of contact between the village community and the aristocratic hierarchy. In all, the aristocracy probably accounted for about one percent of the total population, spanning a vast economic range, with annual incomes varying from around £20 a year for a poor manor lord to £3,000 or even £12,000 for the upper nobility. The aristocracy included both the titled nobility and those who were simply "of gentle birth," meaning that their forebears had belonged to the landed warrior class.

In the early part of the Middle Ages, clerical political theorists had begun to explain society in terms of three estates: aristocrats, clergy (accounting for another 1% of the population), and commoners (the remaining 98%). The clergy were responsible for society's spiritual well-being; commoners were responsible for physical work. The purpose of the aristocracy was to fight on behalf of the rest: war was its profession and justification. In reality, the fourteenth-century aristocracy was beginning to lose its pre-eminence on the battlefield. Yet if the aristocratic man-at-arms was no longer the only kind of soldier that mattered, he was still a force to be reckoned with; and in the cultural sphere the aristocrat enjoyed a kind of prestige that even the richest commoner lacked.

Although diverse in power and wealth, the aristocracy were unified by a set of shared ideals. These included the martial virtues of prowess and courage, but also the outward signs that a person came of a certain station in life and could comfortably maintain it: social graces and a certain generosity of spirit. Not all aristocrats lived up to these ideals, but they remained a unifying principle that helped define the aristocracy as a class: in many ways, the English aristocrat had more in common with his counterparts in Scotland or France than with the English peasants who worked his estates.

The King

At the top of the feudal hierarchy was the monarch. Although he was lord of all England and hedged about with the glory of kingship, the king's power was far from absolute. The great lords of England were not afraid to rebel against a truly unpopular king. Edward III had come to the throne in one such rebellion, and his successor, Richard II, lost the throne in another. The king also needed to worry about his relations with the petty aristocracy and the more powerful commoners. His normal revenue, derived principally from crown lands and various tolls and customs, was greater than any subject's, but it was not enough to run a country, especially in time of war. He had to rely on the consent of Parliament to levy taxes to make up the difference, and the lower house of Parliament consisted of the lowest echelons of the aristocracy and the upper ranks of the commons. Even with tax revenues, medieval monarchs were chronically short of money.

The Nobility

Below the king were the titled nobility, beginning with a handful of dukes who were only slightly less wealthy and powerful than the king himself. They could be numbered on the fingers of one hand, had incomes of thousands of pounds, and were almost always close relatives of the king. The dozen or so earls were only slightly less wealthy and powerful. They were the equivalent of the continental count, and their wives were called countesses. A few dozen barons, with incomes of several hundred pounds a year, rounded out the lay peerage—that is, the major feudal lords who received summons to Parliament. The entire lay peerage amounted to only some 50 lords.

Knights

Below the nobility were the aristocracy without hereditary titles. Knights ranked highest in this group. A knight received his title during his lifetime and did not pass it on to his heirs. In earlier centuries, the knights of England had been more or less all those men whose lands yielded enough income that they could afford a horse and armor. By the fourteenth century this was no longer the case. Any man who had lands worth £40 a year could become a knight. In fact, the king would fine him if he didn't. Yet many who could be knighted declined the honor. The rank was both prestigious and burdensome. The ceremony was expensive; knighthood entailed a number of local administrative and legal duties, mostly unpaid; and land held by knight-tenure exposed the owner to various feudal expenses that the ordinary landholder could avoid.

There were something fewer than 1,000 knights in Chaucer's England. The most important, able to afford to raise substantial retinues to fight under their banner, were called knights banneret, the remainder knights bachelor. The distinguishing symbol of knighthood was a pair of golden spurs, buckled on as part of the knighting ceremony. Also during the ceremony the new knight would be belted with a sword belt, often white in token of purity. The spurs were sometimes worn afterwards on ceremonial occasions, although this does not appear to have been the case with the belt.

Squires

As the chivalry decreased in numbers, untitled gentlemen, sometimes known as squires, rose in status to fill the gap they had left. Originally, a squire had been a gentle-born assistant to a knight—the word meant shield-carrier. The term was still used in this way, as in the case of the Squire in *The Canterbury Tales,* who is the son and attendant of the Knight.

But squire could also be a general designation for men of gentle birth who were not knights. Many were wealthy enough to become knights. The great majority of fully armored horsemen, or men-at-arms, were squires. In most fourteenth-century armies they outnumbered the knights by three to one or more. Along with the knights they formed the backbone of the English and French armies, took part in tournaments, and shared a chivalric set of values. While some squires eventually became knights, most did not.

Most squires were drawn from the ranks of the moderate landowners. Some had incomes of £40 a year or more from land, enough to become knights if they wished. In 1436, fully 1,200 reported landed incomes of £15 or more. But many were younger sons, or those had not yet inherited, or had lands that would not support them as they wished to live. These took service with richer men. They might serve as men-at-arms or high-ranking domestic servants. They might also be bureaucrats or diplomats or independent military commanders, or they might be several of these in turn.

THE URBAN COMMUNITY

Townsmen

Towns in Chaucer's England accounted for a minority of the population, probably between 10 and 20 percent, with 1.5 percent in London, and another 1 percent in Bristol, York, and Norwich combined. London's population was around 80,000 in the early part of the century, although the ravages of the plague brought it down to around 50,000 in the latter part. At the other end of the urban scale, there were around 700 smaller market towns, with populations of only a few thousand.

An olive oil vendor. Italian, c. 1390 (TS Paris, f. 15). McLean.

Most urban populations were small, but as economic and social hubs, towns exercised an influence beyond their actual populations. Country-dwellers sold their surplus produce and purchased necessary supplies at the local market town, which was usually less than 10 miles from home. Towns also served as markets for surplus labor as well as surplus produce. Those who could not make a living in their village would move to the nearest town, and from there perhaps to a regional center, and eventually to London. These immigrants were the lifeblood of the towns. Urban health conditions were poor, and death rates in the towns exceeded birth rates. Towns would have been depopulated were it not for a constant stream of immigration from the countryside.

For some, towns offered not only a living, but a prospect of advancement. Richard Whittington, as the third son of a Gloucestershire knight born around the middle of the century, had a limited future, since he was unlikely to inherit his father's landholding. Instead of choosing the obvious backup options of service in the military or the church, Whittington relocated to London to learn to be a cloth merchant. He grew rich on trade in the 1380s and 1390s, eventually becoming a major money-lender whose clients included Richard II and Henry IV. Known in legend as Dick Whittington, he became famous as a medieval emblem of social advancement, serving multiple terms as Mayor of London, an office that made him among the most important individuals in the kingdom.

Whittington rose from a moderately privileged youth to a position of great wealth and power. Parallel stories occurred further down the social scale for those who combined talent with a healthy measure of good luck. As a young man in 1351, John Brampton was serving on a team of glaziers in Westminster, breaking glass and laying it out for stained glass windows at wages of 6d. a day. Not long after he did similar work for the royal residence at Windsor Castle. He rose to become Warden of the London guild of Glaziers, saving enough money to buy a house of his own, and eventually landing a position as the king's principal glazier, for which he was paid a shilling a day—as much money as a man-at-arms.[5]

The opportunities afforded by the towns were in large measure due to their less rigid systems of landholding and personal status. Since feudal structures were poorly adapted to the needs of commerce, feudal lords in the early Middle Ages who wished to foster urban commercial centers established towns as zones free from the usual strictures of feudalism. These towns enjoyed a greater or lesser degree of self-government, and owed minimal feudal responsibilities to their overlord, who was usually the king himself. Land was held in burgage tenure, a mode of tenancy that was based on fixed cash rents, and allowed the tenant to sell, bequeath, divide, or sublet a holding. Burgage tenants also had the free right to trade in the town without paying the market fees required of outsiders.

Nonetheless, towns had a hierarchy of their own. Only a portion of the population of a town were citizens or burgesses with full rights and a say in the town's governance. In London less than half were citizens. The bulk of the urban population were laborers, servants, apprentices, and aliens from outside the town.

Citizenship could be purchased, or it could be acquired by rising through the hierarchy of a trade. Each trade in a city had its own guild, which regulated the practice of the trade within that city. People entered the trade as apprentices and, if they were fortunate, might rise to the position of master (for more on social hierarchy, see Table 2.1).

Table 2.1:
The Social Hierarchy

First Estate	Second Estate	Third Estate	
Clergy	Aristocracy and their servants	Rural Commons	Urban Commons
	King, Queen		
Archbishop	Duke, Duchess		
Bishop, Major Abbot	Earl, Countess		
Abbot, Abbess	Baron, Lady		Mayor of London
	Knight Banneret, Lady		Alderman of London, Mayor of great town, major legal officer
Prior, Prioress, Archdeacon, Dean, Rector	Knight Bachelor		Other mayor or civic or legal officer, great merchant
Vicar, Master of Arts	Squire		Lesser merchant
Monk, Friar, Nun	Yeoman	Franklin	Craftsman
Clerk	Groom	Husbandman	Journeyman
	Page	Cottar	Apprentice
		Laborer	Laborer
		Pauper, Vagrant	Pauper, Vagrant

A schematized table of the social hierarchy. Ranks at the same horizontal level could be considered roughly equivalent to each other.

Laborers and Paupers

The opportunities offered by the cities were not equally accessible to all. To secure a place as an apprentice required connections, and only those who had access to the necessary capital and other resources could ever hope to become masters. For most, survival in the city was a matter of finding employment in someone else's household or business. The most fortunate laborers might build connections that allowed them to be confident of long-term work. For others, employment was a hand-to-mouth affair. The laboring poor whether in town or country inevitably went through periods of unemployment. Living at the margin of subsistence, they were always at risk of slipping into destitution, although this risk was lower in the latter half of the century, once the plague had substantially reduced the supply of labor.

The elderly and disabled were highly vulnerable to poverty if they had no independent source of support. Prisoners were also vulnerable, especially since they had to pay for their own provisions. Widows and orphans were at risk when the man of the family died without leaving them a secure source of income. Such people depended on the charity of others. A few were taken in by charitable institutions, called hospitals, that offered long-term lodging for the destitute, particularly the elderly, infirm, and orphans. Most had to resort to begging, and many turned to crime or prostitution.

The hierarchy of the church, from ordinary monks and friars to bishop, cardinal and the pope. Andrea di Bonaiuto, Fresco, 1365–1368. Spanish Chapel S. Maria Novella, Florence. Photo Credit: Erich Lessing/Art Resource, NY.

THE CHURCH

The Clergy

The concept of the three estates divided society into clergy, nobles, and commons. Since it was a clerical invention, it is no wonder that the clergy constituted the first estate, but this also reflected the privileged position of religion in medieval society. The idea of a separation between church and state was unthinkable, and the Church was firmly embedded in the structures of society and government.

There were two sorts of clergy in the fourteenth century. The secular clergy, such as the parish priest, lived *in seculo*, "in the world." Their primary responsibility was to attend to the spiritual needs of the laity, the nonclerical people of the other two estates. The regular clergy consisted of monks and friars, who were regulated by rules that dictated lives of asceticism and discipline.

In all, the clergy may have accounted for something over one percent of the population. They were instantly recognizable by their tonsure, or clerical haircut. Their heads were shaven on top, with the rest of the hair worn short, and their facial hair was shaven too. In addition, members of the regular clergy wore habits, or special clothing indicating the order to which they belonged. Secular clergy did not necessarily wear distinctive dress except during religious rituals—moralists railed against clergymen who insisted on wearing the latest immodest fashions. Aside from nuns, the clergy were all male; and aside from the minor orders, they were sworn to a life of celibacy.

Unlike the other two estates, nobody was born into the clergy. Every clergyman had been raised either as an aristocrat or as a commoner, and this distinction often played a role in their clerical life. Aristocratic clergymen had the connections that gave them better chances of reaching the upper levels of the clergy and the more coveted positions in the Church. Commoners sometimes reached these positions, but the climb was more arduous and less often achieved, although a clerical career was the best chance many commoners had for social advancement.

At the top of the secular clergy in England were the prelates, two archbishops and a bit more than a dozen bishops under them. On a par with the prelates were the abbots of great monastic abbeys and priors of the larger priories. Such clerics had incomes and status comparable to that of an earl, and they sat in Parliament in the House of Lords.

Below them were the lesser officers of the church hierarchy, such as the dean who supervised a bishop's or archbishop's cathedral, or the archdeacon who helped administer the bishopric. Likewise, an abbot would have a prior and a few other major officers to help administer the monastery. The bishops oversaw a hierarchy of archdeaconries and deaneries that administered the local parishes.

Clergymen at the upper levels might have incomes and lifestyles that ranged from gentle to lordly, and they often had more in common with the aristocracy than with the lesser clergy. Such was the priest William of North Berwick, who, according to the chronicler Jean Froissart, distinguished himself fighting beside the Earl of Douglas at the battle of Otterburn in 1388, and "thereby the same year he was made archdeacon of Aberdeen."

The Parish Priest

Towards the bottom end of the church hierarchy was the parish priest. There were probably upwards of 9000 parishes in England in Chaucer's day. The parish was the smallest unit of church organization, typically corresponding to a village in the countryside or to a neighborhood in the towns; it had its own church and, theoretically, its own priest. Simple parish priests of rural parishes often came from peasant families and lived a life not much different from their peasant neighbors.

Some parishes produced revenues of hundreds of pounds, but most were worth less than £10 a year. Often much of the revenue was siphoned off to an absentee rector. The rector might be a clergyman working at the royal court, a clerk pursuing higher learning on a scholarship endowed by the parish revenue, or even a monastery or cathedral which used the funds to support its expenses. The actual care of the souls in the parish would then be in the hands of a vicar, whose income might be as little as £4 a year. The poorest must have been particularly dependent on the harvest from the parson's share of the village fields (called a glebe). Many had to work those fields themselves, and some kept beasts or threshed corn in the churchyard or stored malt in the church.

On such low wages it was hard to attract good help. One chronicler complained that many of the men who became priests after the plague "knew nothing except how to read to some extent." Medieval clerics were expected not simply to be able to read and write but to be able to do so in Latin—a fourteenth-century clerical illiterate might not have been so by twentieth-century standards. Still, the poorer parishes can hardly have attracted well-educated parsons.

It is difficult to judge the moral quality of the fourteenth-century priesthood at a distance of six centuries. Certainly contemporaries thought there was a problem. In 1373, 10 priests were accused of unchastity in Norwich alone, one of them with two women. In some ways the character of priestly offenses is more informative than their number: charges included haunting taverns, dicing, theft, assault, and poaching. Yet there must also have been many priests like the early fourteenth-century vicar of Staverton in Devon, who, according to his parishioners, "behaves himself well and honestly, and informs them excellently in spiritual matters, nor, as they say, is he at fault in that. They know nothing of any hidden mortal sin."

Minor Orders

At the very base of the secular clergy were the clerics in minor orders. They were ordained but not sworn to celibacy, so they could marry. They bore only a small tonsure at the crown of their head instead of the full tonsure of the priest. Many were acolytes and readers, assisting in church services. Physicians, university students, and parish clerks were likely to be in minor orders as well. The clerk Absolon in Chaucer's *Miller's Tale* is in this category—a young man who assists the local priest in his duties, but who has not yet fully committed to the priesthood, and takes advantage of his situation by flirting with the women of the parish.

Monks and Friars

The oldest form of the regular clergy were the monks, who had been present since the early Middle Ages. The original intent of monasticism had been to foster spirituality by placing the monks in a monastery, secluded from the world outside, where they would lead austere lives devoted to prayer and holy contemplation. Every monastery and every monk belonged to a particular order, which had its own administration and its own rules governing the monks' way of life. The oldest order was the Benedictines; more recent orders included the Carthusians and Cistercians. The principal responsibility of monks was originally a daily cycle of prayers called the canonical hours, but over the centuries they had assumed important roles as scribes, teachers, and healers, and it was by no means unusual for them to be seen outside their monasteries, like the Monk who is among the pilgrims in *The Canterbury Tales.*

The thirteenth century had witnessed the emergence of a new kind of regular clergy, known as the mendicant orders or friars. Friars, like monks, lived under the authority of the rule of their order; in particular, they were not allowed to own private property—all their possessions belonged to their order. However, rather than retiring from the world, their mission was to minister to the spiritual needs of the lay public, particularly through preaching, teaching, and hearing confession. There were two principal mendicant orders: the Dominicans, also known as the black friars or friars-preachers, and the Franciscans, also called gray friars or friars-minor. In all, there may have been some 12,000 monks and friars in England toward the end of the Middle Ages.

The ideals of the regular clergy were difficult to sustain, especially when pious bequests had enriched the landed income of the orders, making it easy to enjoy a comfortable life in the cloister. Few abbeys were as lax as Flaxley in 1397, where nine monks were unchaste and where the abbot was found to have slept with three different women. Gross immorality was a less common problem than creeping worldliness, a falling away from the austere ideals that had defined the monks and friars in the

first place. Chaucer's portraits of the Monk and the Friar are in keeping
with contemporary satirical attitudes to the orders: the Monk delights in
horses, hounds, and hunting; the Friar flirts with the women to whom he
is administering Confession, and can wheedle a widow out of a donation
even if she has "not a shoe." By contrast, Chaucer's secular clergy are presented more positively: the Clerk of Oxford is poor but eager both to learn
and teach; the Parson is teaches "Christ's lore and his apostles twelve . . .
but first he followed it himself."

On the whole, monks and friars were probably no more worldly than other
men—most were probably less so—but their failings were considered much
more grievous because of their religious profession. However, the worldliness of the regular clergy had its benefits too, since friars and monks contributed significantly to society as teachers, physicians, and administrators.

Nuns

In addition to the male clergy there was a smaller number of nuns. Nuns
effectively belonged to the first estate, but they did not enjoy the same
privileges as their male counterparts. They could not become priests, their
abbesses did not have a place in the House of Lords, and in general they were
appended to the male clerical hierarchy rather than integrated into it. Nonetheless, some nunneries were quite wealthy; the abbess of such an establishment could be an important woman in her own right, enjoying a degree
of independence and authority rare for a medieval woman. The activities
of a nun's life were in many ways similar to those of monks, and, like
monks, they were not always confined to their nunneries—there are several of them among Chaucer's pilgrims. Nuns also belonged to orders and
wore distinctive habits, and their hair was cropped close under their veils.

LAW AND GOVERNMENT

The political and legal system in Chaucer's England had evolved organ-
ically over the centuries in tandem with feudalism, and mirrored many
of the complexities of the feudal hierarchy. Governmental authority was
further complicated by the sometimes overlapping jurisdictions of church
and secular authorities, and by emerging systems of national governance
that were in the process of displacing feudal jurisdictions.

The first major component in this system was the dispersed network of
authority represented by feudalism and by burghal self-governance. This
dispersed authority was manifested primarily at the local level, through
manorial courts in the country, or borough courts in the towns. Such courts
were generally administered by local officers known as stewards or bailiffs, and met several times a year. These courts served both legislative and
judicial functions, regulating matters pertaining to the common interest of
the community, and judging local civil disputes and petty criminal cases.

PROCEEDINGS AT THE MANOR COURT OF BILLINGHAM, DURHAM, 1378

All the tenants of the village . . . were ordered to seek to the repair of the sheep-cot before the next court, under penalty of 40s. William del Toune came into court and took possession of two cottages previously held by John Waux, to have for the term of his life, giving and doing for it the same as John had done before, because neither John's wife nor any of his blood wished to take the cottages. And William shall return the cottage at the end of his term in a satisfactory state. . . . It was ordered that every one of them shall be responsible for the pigs, and that every one of them shall look after them when his turn comes, until they have a common piggery, under penalty of 12d. It was ordered that none of them should dig in the high street in the village of Billingham, under pain of 40d.

Translated by J. L. Forgeng from *Halmota Prioratus Dunelmensis,* ed. William Hylton Dyer Longstaffe and John Booth (Durham: Surtees Society, 1889), 148–49.

Royal Governance

The second major player was the crown itself. Royal authority was exercised through some three dozen shires or counties, each under a sheriff appointed by the king (though the northern counties of Durham, Chester, and Lancaster were semi-independent feudal jurisdictions where this system did not apply). The shires were further subdivided into local administrative units called hundreds or wapentakes, depending on local customs. Both the shires and hundreds had courts of their own, administered under the supervision of the sheriff. The local representative of this system was the constable of the hundred, who was the chief law enforcement officer at the local level.

By Chaucer's day, the sheriff was no longer as important a figure as he had been a century earlier, and the authority of the county and hundred courts was being displaced by local justices of the peace on the one hand, and by a system of national circuit courts on the other. The justice of the peace was emerging during Chaucer's lifetime as an important agent of royal law at the local level, capable of independently adjudging minor cases, and by the second half of the century meeting with other justices of the peace from the county in quarterly sessions to handle more serious matters. The justices were drawn from local landlords, and although they were nominally appointed by the crown through a system administered by the sheriff, the selection process seems to have been effectively in the hands the local elites.

Complementing the growing power of these local elites was the increasingly regular system of traveling circuit courts emanating from the central royal courts of King's Bench and Common Pleas in Westminster, the seat of royal government just west of the City of London. Justices of the central courts would spend part of the year traveling regular circuits of the counties to preside over courts known as the assizes. The assizes handled major cases that might otherwise have to be brought to London for adjudication.

Among the London courts, the proceedings of King's Bench, Common Pleas, and the Exchequer were all based on common law, the legal system founded on custom and precedent that remains at the heart of legal systems in the English-speaking world today. In principle, King's Bench heard cases in which the Crown had a direct interest, Common Pleas was for cases between the king's subjects, and the Exchequer handled cases that touched on royal finances. In practice, plaintiffs could often find ways to bring their cases to the court of their own choosing— someone who happened to owe money to the king might bring choose to bring an unrelated case to the Exchequer if he thought it would be to his advantage.

The customs and precedents of common law did not govern the court of Chancery. Petitions might be brought before Chancery in difficult or sensitive cases that could not readily be handled by common law, for example cases involving foreign nationals or relating to actions on the seas. Such matters could also be handled by the king's council, an advisory body of a few dozen leading nobles and legal experts. The members of the council might be chosen by the king, or forced upon him by political necessity.

The highest legal and legislative authority was that of the king and Parliament. Parliament was summoned at the will of the king, and was divided into the House of Lords, made up of the country's leading noblemen and clergy, and the House of Commons, consisting of two representatives from each shire and borough (chartered town). Parliament had traditionally been a consultative body used above all to facilitate the royal will, and particularly to levy taxes for the crown. By the late 1300s it was increasingly being manipulated by aristocratic political factions that were sometimes hostile to the king or his relatives, paving the way for a growing level of independence in the centuries to come.

Church Courts

The final major player in governance was the church. The country was divided into about 9000 parishes, grouped in a hierarchical network of deaneries, bishoprics, and archbishoprics. The church had jurisdiction over many aspects of daily life. All laypeople were required to pay tithes to the church, consisting of one-tenth of their income in money or produce. Church courts had jurisdiction in matters of marriage and sexuality, wills, heresy, and a host of other areas relating to the precepts and practices of medieval Christianity. In the *Friar's Tale* Chaucer describes the business of the archdeacon's court:

> In punishing of fornication,
> In witchcraft, and also of bawdry,
> Of defamation, and adultery,
> Of church reeves, and of testaments,
> Of contracts, and lack of sacraments,
> Of usury, and of simony also.
> But certainly, lechers he did the greatest woe. (*CT* D.1304–10)

Chaucer's Summoner is an agent of such a court. The poet's unflattering portrayal of this character reflects something of the popular hostility toward these courts, especially in an age when many people in England felt that the Church was in dire need of reform.

Procedure and Punishment

Legal procedure varied within the various legal hierarchies. Manorial courts and many of the royal courts reached their verdicts by impaneled juries, although these juries were often subject to political manipulation. Local courts relied on juries who already knew the parties involved, and typically decided cases based on prior knowledge of the circumstances and the local reputations of the parties in the case. The courts in London had a more developed system for presenting and evaluating evidence. Church courts had inherited their structure from Roman law, and were conducted as investigations on behalf of the presiding authority, typically the archdeacon or his representative, who gave judgment based on the testimony he heard.

Minor infractions were known as trespasses, and included assault, wounding, and damage to property; such infringements did not require the involvement of royal courts, and could be handled by a local court. Typical punishments for trespasses included fines and ritual humiliations such as confinement to a pillory. Church courts might impose a light penance in comparable cases. More serious matters were punished by heavier fines, or by corporal punishment such as beating or whipping, though church courts could not impose penalties that involved shedding blood. Crimes such as homicide, arson, rape, robbery, and grand larceny (defined as theft of more than 12d. worth of goods) were classed as felonies, and subject to the death penalty, normally by hanging. Long-term imprisonment was not a major part of the penal system, and since death was the only penalty available for felony, many juries were reluctant to convict in such cases.

NOTES

1. F.R.H. DuBoulay, *The Lordship of Canterbury: An Essay on Medieval Society* (New York: Barnes and Noble, 1966), 189.

2. Phillipp R. Schofield, *Peasant and Community in Medieval England, 1200–1500* (New York: Palgrave-Macmillan, 2003), 26–27.

3. E. B. Fryde, *Peasants and Landlords in Later Medieval England* (Stroud: Sutton, 1996), 26.

4. Fryde, *Peasants and Landlords,* 26, 16.

5. E. M. Veale, "Craftsmen and the Economy of London in the Fourteenth Century," in *The Medieval Town: A Reader in English Urban History 1200–1540,* ed. Richard Holt and Gervase Rosser (London and New York: Longman, 1990), 136–37.

3

HOUSEHOLDS AND THE COURSE OF LIFE

The Household

The fundamental building block of medieval society was the family. A person's place in society was determined by the family into which they were born, and they were integrated into the social hierarchy through the household in which they lived.

The medieval family was not necessarily a nuclear family but a household. At the upper end of the social spectrum it might include relatives beyond the core married couple and their children. Such extended-family households were not common among ordinary people, and it was generally rare for more than one married couple to live in the same house—the younger generation would get married once they were ready to live on their own. However, it was common for servants or apprentices to live with the family. Even a family of modest means might have a servant or two; a lesser gentleman might have seven or eight people in his household, a wealthy knight from 12 to 30, a baron 20 or more, a major aristocrat from 40 to 150, and the king around four hundred.

The larger aristocratic households were divided into administrative departments. These might include a pantry for dealing with bread; a buttery responsible for drinks; a kitchen for other foods, and perhaps even a separate saucery, cellar, larder, and poultry; a marshalsea for looking after horses; hall staff responsible for the public spaces; chamber staff for the private areas; a chapel; and an almonry charged with distributing the household alms to the poor.

An evening at home. Italian, c. 1395 (TS
Vienna, f. 100v). McLean.

Among commoners, the family was the typical unit of economic production: the family business was the rule rather than the exception. A well-run
aristocratic household was also a unit of production. One contemporary,
Christine de Pisan, described how a lady living on a manor should not
only carefully oversee the agricultural production, but in winter "she will
reflect that labor is cheap" and put her men to work cutting firewood and
making vine props for later sale, or threshing in the barn if the weather is
bad. She will put her women to work in the herb garden, and work with
them spinning and weaving, and making clothing for the household, "or
to sell if she needs to do so." Christine noted with approval the Countess
of Eu, who ran her household so well that she received more income from
it than from her lands

The Householder

An individual's role in the household was shaped by gender norms.
The head of the household was expected to be an adult man. Becoming a
householder was essentially an economic transition. A man would marry
when he acquired the ability to support a family. For countrydwellers,
this meant acquiring some sort of landholding, at least in the form of a
home messuage where the family might live. For citydwellers, it meant
acquiring the skills, connections, and other resources that were necessary
to make a living in the town. The householder had legal responsibility for
the members of his household: the legal status of a wife or servant was

A woman being distracted from her spinning. Her simple wheel is not equipped with a treadle. c. 1340. From decretals of Pope Gregory IX. BL Roy 10 E IV. Folio No: 139 London. Photo Credit: HIP/Art Resource, NY.

roughly equivalent to that of the children, and a husband was expected to discipline his wife and servants if they misbehaved much as he would discipline his children. Inevitably these kinds of expectations could lead to domestic abuse, but society also condemned excessive violence on the man's part: abused wives or servants could seek legal redress through church or secular courts, although the legal system's ability to intervene effectively in domestic affairs was predictably uneven.

Women

In theory, females were expected to be subordinate to a male householder. A girl was subject to her father until she married, at which time she would become subject to her husband. She did not normally inherit land unless her father died without leaving any sons. Women did not officially participate in governmental activities, were rarely allowed to become citizens of a town, and had only limited independent standing under the law.

The reality for women was a bit more complex than the legal theory. A householder's wife was expected to be responsible for the management of the household. This included domestic activities such as cooking, cleaning, and childrearing, but it also included a significant economic component. Both urban and rural households kept gardens and livestock that

**CHAUCER'S REEVE DESCRIBES SIMKIN
THE MILLER AND HIS WIFE, c. 1390**

The parson of the town her father was;
With her he gave full many a pan of brass [i.e., as dowry]
So that Simkin should in his bloodline ally.
She was fostered in a nunnery—
For Simkin would have no wife, as he said,
Unless she were well bred, and a maid,
To preserve his estate of yeomanry.
And she was proud, and pert as a magpie.
A full fair sight it was upon the two;
On holy days before her he would go
With his tippet bound about his head;
And she came after in a gown of red;
And Simkin had hose of the same.
There dared no man address her but as "dame."
There was none so hardy that went by the way
That with her dared to sport or ever play,
Unless he wished to be slain by Simkin
With a dagger, knife, or bodkin.

Translated by J. L. Forgeng from the Middle English in *CT* A.3942–60.

fell within the woman's domain. Vegetables from the garden and meat, dairy, and eggs from the livestock were important parts of the diet, and the surplus could be sold to supplement the household income—bringing produce to market was normally the job of the woman of the house. Women could also add to the family coffers by spinning, weaving, brewing, and laundering—the modern surnames Brewster, Baxter, and Webster derive from the medieval names for female brewers, bakers, and weavers. Many women worked outside of the home, taking on part-time employment as servants or day-laborers. The income generated by these activities was typically less than that earned by men, but for many families it was an important part of the household equation.

For women as for men, towns could offer a degree of social mobility that was harder to achieve in the country. An urban woman of some means might engage in trade, property speculation, retailing, or brewing, and a poorer woman might find work as a laborer, vendor, or servant. In some cases a townswoman might take part in her husband's trade. The York metalfounders' guild in 1390 decreed that masters were allowed to instruct their wives in the craft; in 1404, York armorer Adam Heche bequeathed his tools for plate armoring to his son, but his mailmaking tools to his daughter.[1]

Other women achieved independence in widowhood, a state that was all too common in this age of high mortality. A widow was guaranteed a share of her husband's property for support during her lifetime; if her husband had practiced a craft or trade, she might take over the business after his death and might even be admitted into the guild.

Servants

An important social class in fourteenth-century England that has largely disappeared today was the servants, who were a common feature of the medieval household: some 20–30 percent of the urban population may have been servants. Like women and children, they were legally subject to the householder's authority, but there was nothing demeaning about domestic service. Indeed, service to a prestigious employer could raise one's status: Chaucer's outstandingly successful career was launched by his service to the Countess of Ulster in the 1350s, which led to service in the royal household by the 1360s.

Many servants were adolescents or young adults at a stage in their life where they needed to learn their way in the world, but not yet ready to strike out on their own; for such people, service was often a stepping stone on the way to social and economic advancement. Even a young aristocrat might spend time in service in some noble household, a boy as a page and later as a squire, a girl as a lady-in-waiting, acquiring social polish and learning the skills appropriate to their class. For commoners, service could be a means of saving up money and making useful social contacts.

In ordinary households, servants did much the same sorts of tasks that the children of the family might otherwise perform: male servants helped the man of the house in his work, female servants helped the woman in hers. In large aristocratic households, servants would be assigned to one of the household departments to perform much more specialized functions. Servants were normally hired for a year at a time, living with the family and receiving quarterly wages as well as food and perhaps additional perquisites such as a suit of clothing—since servants reflected on the householders' social status, it was in their interest to ensure that they had decent clothes to wear.

THE LIFE CYCLE

Birth

The final component of the household was the children. The basic biological facts of birth in the fourteenth century were of course much the same then as now, but the human context was rather different. The scene is described in John Trevisa's late fourteenth-century translation of the thirteenth-century encyclopedia *De Proprietatibus Rerum* by Bartholomeus Anglicus:

A midwife is a woman that has the craft to help a woman that labors with child, so that she may bear and bring forth her child with less woe and sorrow. And so that the child should be born with the less labor and woe, she anoints and balms the mother's womb, and helps and comforts her in that manner. Also she takes the child out of the womb, and knots his navel four inches long. With water she washes away the blood of the child, and balms him with salt and honey to dry up the humors and to comfort his limbs and members, and swathes him in cloths.[2]

As Trevisa suggests, birth was in the hands not of a physician but of a midwife. A physician would not normally be involved unless there was a pathological complication. The setting was also different, since childbirth almost invariably took place at home. Hospitals in this period were principally a place for long-term care of the infirm poor, rather than for short-term intervention in acute medical circumstances. The birth was often attended by other women as well—friends, neighbors, and relatives of the mother. In places where a midwife was not available, these women would take the lead in facilitating the birth.

Another difference between medieval and modern childbirth was the degree of risk to the mother. We have no accurate figures for childbirth deaths in England during this period, but they were certainly higher than they are now. Some historians have suggested as high as 20 percent, but this is a gross overestimation—England would soon have been empty at so catastrophic a rate of maternal death, and the evidence of wills suggests that a majority of women survived their husbands rather than vice versa. In fifteenth-century Florence the rate of maternal mortality was 14.4 per 1,000

Childbirth—a representation of the birth of the Virgin Mary in a fourteenth-century home. North Italian, c. 1385 (Bibliothèque Nationale MS Lat. 757, f. 351v). McLean.

births, which is probably nearer the mark. This would still be very high by modern standards: the equivalent estimated figure for sub-Saharan Africa in 2005 was 9 per 1,000 births, and if a woman had a 1.4 percent chance of dying every time she gave birth, this would make death in childbirth a very real possibility over the course of her childbearing years.[3]

The Newborn

Although a number of people might be involved in the birth, the birth-day itself was not seen as an important date. Most people would be unable to name the day on which they were born, and in many cases even the year: in legal proceedings where ages had to be established, witnesses were usually able to recall no more than the holy day nearest the birth.

The first formal event in the newborn's life was the ceremony of baptism, or christening. This was the most important of the rituals administered by the Church, for without it one could never enter heaven. Baptism was so important that everyone was encouraged to learn the basic words of the ritual, even if only in English, so as to be able to pronounce them at need. In a doubtful birth, midwives were urged to baptize the infant as soon as its head appeared. The formula was quite simple: *Ego baptizo te in nomine Patris et Filii et Spiritus Sancti. Amen;* or in Middle English, *I crystene the [thee] in the nome of the Fader, and the Son and the Holy Gost. Amen.*

If the infant survived the birth, the christening could take place within the week. There might be more haste if the child's survival seemed uncertain, although important families preferred more preparation time in order to make a major occasion of the event. When the time came, the godparents were summoned and the family proceeded to the church, where the ceremony was celebrated by the parish priest. Ironically, the mother would not normally be present, since it was the custom for her not to enter the church prior to her own ceremony of purification or churching, which was supposed to cleanse her from the spiritual stain of childbirth—although some people felt this restriction was not a proper part of Christian observance.

Baptism marked the child as a part of the Christian church; because church and society were considered equivalent, this also meant bringing the child into society. The child would have two godparents of the same sex and one of the opposite. The bond between the infant and the godparents was a significant one that was akin to that between blood relatives: people who were related by godparentage were forbidden to marry each other. The word gossip, or god-sib, originally meant someone related by godparentage—a god-sibling. It later came to mean "an intimate friend," and is now applied to the kinds of discussions people have with close friends. As part of the baptismal ceremony, the godparents were charged with providing the infant with basic religious instruction: they were expected to teach it the Paternoster, Ave Maria, and the Apostles' Creed, and how to sign itself with a cross; they were also called on to bring the child to the local

A baptismal procession. French, late fourteenth century (TBH, p. 262). McLean.

bishop for the ceremony of Confirmation when it came of age. They were even expected to play a part in child care: the priest admonished them to protect the child "from fire and water" until the age of seven.

The core baptismal ritual involved smearing oil on the infant's chest and back, then totally immersing it three times in the font, once to the right side, once to the left, and once face-down. After the immersion, the infant was lifted from the font from the senior godparent of the same sex, who had the responsibility of naming the newborn.

Names

As a rule, the child was supposed to be baptized with the name of the senior godparent, although some children were named for a relative or saint. For boys, most names were either a saint's name or a name of French origin. The single most common masculine name fell into the first category: perhaps a third to a half of the male population of England was named John. Other common saints' names included Matthew, Thomas, Andrew, James, Simon, Peter or Pierce, Stephen, Nicholas, Bartholomew, Edward, and Edmund. Names from the Old Testament were less common: Adam, Joseph, David, and Daniel were the only ones widely used. French names had become fashionable since the Norman Conquest in 1066, the most common being Robert and William; other popular names in this class included Roger, Richard, Walter, Henry, Hugh, and Philip. In the north of England there was a slightly greater diversity, including the occasional Alexander (perhaps from Scottish influence), Alan, Brian, and Conan (names imported by Breton participants in the Norman Conquest), and even Tristan (a name from Arthurian legend).

The trends in girls' names were quite different. A few saints' names were common, notably Katherine, Julian, Cecily, Lucy, Christine, Elizabeth, Annice or Agnes, and Margaret (with its variant, Margery), although none dominated in the way John did among men. Of Old Testament names, only Sarah was common. Joan was also common, as were Isabel, Alice (and its diminuative Alison), Lettice, Emma, Maud (Matilda), Rose, and Beatrice. Some women even bore names from legend, such as Isold or Sybil. A distinctive feature of English names in this period is the extreme rarity of Mary or Martha.

Among the lower classes, these names might be reduced to an abbreviated or diminutive form. Richard might be called "Dick" or "Hick"; Roger "Dodge" or "Hodge"; Robert "Dob," "Hob," or "Robin"; John "Jack"; Nicholas "Coll"; Gilbert "Gib"; Thomas "Tom"; David "Daw"; William "Will"; Walter "Wat"; Catherine "Kit"; Cecily "Cis." Diminutive versions of a name were often formed with the suffix "-kin," such as "Jankin" for John, "Perkin" for Pierce, "Simkin" for Simon, "Malkin" for Maud, or "Watkin" and "Wilkin" for Wat and Will.

With a relatively small pool of available names and strong pressures to choose certain ones, it was not uncommon for more than one sibling to have the same name: the children of the Carew family in 1414 were called Guy, John, John, John, John, William, William, Eleanor, Agnes, Agnes, Margaret, and Anne.[4]

In previous centuries, individuals of a given name had been distinguished from each other by second names. These were usually one of three types: patronymics designating the person's father (such as Robertson, Roberts, Robinson, Robins, Dobson, Hobson, and Hobbes, all of which originally meant "the son of Robert"), place names designating the individual's place of origin (such as "of Lincoln," later "Lincoln"), or professional names indicating the person's trade ("the Smith," later "Smith"). In London it had become customary for children of well-established families to inherit their father's second name as a surname by the mid-fourteenth century—Chaucer's surname had been in his family for at least three generations. By the end of the century surnames were almost universal, although names continued to fluctuate as late as the sixteenth century. The shift toward surnames was slower in the countryside than in the towns, and slower among the lower classes than among the well-to-do.[5]

Infants and Toddlers

From the outset, the shape of the infant's life depended on its social background. All medieval babies were breast-fed for the first two years or so, but while most women nursed their own children, the babies of privileged families were often given to a wet-nurse. The nurse was by definition a woman of lower social standing who had recently given birth, and was therefore lactating. With the high rate of infant mortality, many of these women had lost their own child, and the milk represented an economic opportunity that could bring some extra money into their household. Nursing a child from a wealthier family could also prove a useful

A woman carries a swaddled child in a cradle on her shoulders. MS G. 24 f. 10r The Pierpont Morgan Library. McLean.

social asset in the long term. If the nurse still had her own child, the bond of fosterage between the two children could likewise be valuable to the lower-born child.

Trevisa's description of the infant's world seems familiar in most respects:

Nurses rock children in cradles to promote natural heat with gentle and moderate moving. . . . Also they sing lullabies and other cradle songs to please the wits of the child.

A nurse . . . takes him up if he falls, and gives him suck if he weeps, and kisses him if he is still . . . and cleans and washes him if he fouls himself, and feeds him with her fingers against his own will. And because he cannot speak, the nurse pronounces the words childishly, the more easily to teach the child that cannot speak. And she uses medicines to bring the child to suitable state if he is sick. And she heaves him up, now on her shoulders, now in her hands, now on her knees and lap; and so she heaves him up and down if he squeals and weeps. And she puts food in her own mouth and makes it ready for the toothless child, that he may the more easily swallow that food.

The child would be weaned somewhere between one and three years of age. The typical starter food was a mixture of milk with grain or flour as a kind of pap. As the child grew and developed more teeth, it would shift from pap to solid foods.

One major difference between medieval and modern methods of infant care was the practice of "swaddling," also described by Trevisa:

Because of tenderness of the limbs, the child may easily and quickly twist and bend and take diverse shapes, and therefore children's limbs are bound with strips of cloth and other suitable bonds so that they will not be crooked or ill shaped.[6]

In addition to its supposed benefit of making the infant's limbs grow straight, swaddling kept it warm and out of trouble. For added warmth, the baby would have a bonnet to cover its head. As the baby grew, it would be unwrapped at times so that it might crawl about, and older babies might be swaddled with their arms and shoulders free to allow some freedom of movement.

During the first years of life, there was little differentiation between boys and girls. During the toddler years, the child would be dressed in a loose gown, perhaps with a padded roll around the head to prevent injury while it was learning to walk. Whether male or female, the child was almost exclusively in female care, either of its mother or a nurse. However, girls seem to have had a higher mortality rate, which may indicate that more attention was lavished on a son's well-being.

Childhood in the Middle Ages was a time of enormous danger, due primarily to the ever-present risk of illness and disease for an immature immune system. Accidental death was also a problem, especially in poorer families where the requirements of household labor meant that the child was not always closely attended. The risk was highest just after birth. In the latter half of the fourteenth century, nearly 300 of 1,000 children died in their first year (by comparison, even among the poorest Third World nations today an infant mortality rate of 125 in 1,000 is exceptionally high). After 10 years, only 500 of the 1,000 would still be living, and only 300 would survive to age 20.[7] Of course, these figures were extreme even by medieval standards, as Chaucer's lifetime corresponds to the worst ravages of the Black Death.

The early life of children was mostly a combination of learning and play. For most children, the only formal education was their religious instruction. This was seen primarily as a familial responsibility, especially that of the godparents, who were expected to ensure that by the age of five or seven the child knew the basic elements of Christian belief and observance. This included knowing the proper way to cross oneself and learning how to recite (in Latin) the Pater Noster, the Ave Maria, and the Credo (all of which are reproduced here in Latin and in Middle English). It was also considered important to know the meaning of the Latin, especially in the case of the Credo, which was regarded the definitive summary of the Christian faith.[8]

THE APOSTLES' CREED (CREDO)

Credo in Deum Patrem omnipotentem	I beleve in God, Fader almyghty,
Creatorem coeli et terrae	Makere of heven and erthe,
Et in Jesum Christum Filium eius unicum	And in Jhesu Crist, his onely sone
Dominum nostrum	oure Lorde
Qui conceptus est de	that is conceyved
Spiritu Sancto	by the Holy Gost,
Natus ex Maria Virgine	born of the Mayden Marye
Passus sub Pontio Pilato,	suffred under Pounce Pylate,
crucifixus	crucyfied,
Mortuus, et sepultus	ded, and beryed;
Descendit ad inferna	descendid to helle;
Tertia die resurrexit a mortuis	the thridde day he aros fro dethes

Ascendit ad coelos	styed [rose] up to hevene
Sedet ad dexteram Dei Patris omnipotentis	sitte on his Fader half [side];
Inde venturus judicare	schal come to deme [judge]
vivos et mortuos	the quick and dede.
Credo in Spiritum Sanctum,	I beleve in the Holy Gost,
Sanctam Ecclesiam Catholicam,	holy Chirche, that is alle that schulle be saved,
Sanctorum communionem	and in communion of hem,
Remissionem peccatorum	remissioun of synnes,
Carnis ressurectionem	risyng of flesch,
Et vitam aeternam. Amen.	and everlastynge lyf. Amen.

Translation of the Credo from the *Book to a Mother*, ed. Adrian James McCarthy, *Elizabethan and Renaissance Studies* 92 (Salzburg: Institut für Anglistik und Amerikanistik, 1981), 1.

Children's religious education was expected to extend further to encompass the fundamentals of Christian belief and conduct. These had been identified by the Lambeth Council in 1281 as

the Fourteen Articles of the Faith (which are the statements in the Apostles' Creed)

the Ten Commandments

the Two Laws of the Gospel ("Love God" and "Love Thy Neighbor")

the Seven Virtues (Faith, Hope, Charity, Justice, Temperance, Prudence, Fortitude)

the Seven Deadly Sins (Pride, Sloth, Envy, Avarice, Lust, Wrath, and Covetousness)

the Seven Sacraments (Baptism, Confirmation, Confession, Communion, Ordination, Matrimony, and Extreme Unction)

the Seven Works of Bodily Mercy (feeding the hungry, giving drink to the thirsty, clothing the naked, sheltering the stranger, nursing the sick, visiting the prisoner, and burying the dead).

In these early years, children would also learn good manners. They were taught not to pick their nose, or scratch or rub themselves, or swear, and were expected to learn to keep their hands and faces clean and to pare and clean their nails.[9] Some children may even have been taught letters as early as age three, four, or five, at least in aristocratic families

In laboring-class families, a child of age four or five might be set to do small tasks about the house, such as fetching water or minding a younger sibling. However, the bulk of a child's time in these early years was given to play and to exploration of the world around them. Much of what we know about the early life of children comes from the records of coroners'

THE PATER NOSTER AND AVE MARIA

THE LORD'S PRAYER (PATER NOSTER)

Pater noster qui es in coelis	Fader oure that art in heven,
Sanctificetur nomen tuum	halwed be thi name;
Adveniat regnum tuum	come thi kyngdom,
Fiat voluntas tua	fulfild by thi wil
et in terra sicut in coelo	in hevene as in erthe;
Panem nostrum quotidianum	oure ech-day bred
da nobis hodie	yef us to day,
Et dimitte nobis debita nostra	and foryeve us oure dettes
sicut et dimittemus debitoribus nostris	as we foryeveth to oure detoures;
Et ne nos inducas in tentationem,	and ne led us nought in temptacion,
sed libera nos a malo. Amen.	bote delivere us of evel. So be it.

HAIL MARY (AVE MARIA)

Ave Maria, gratia plena	Heil Marye, ful of grace
Dominus tecum	God is with the [thee]
Benedicta tu in mulieribus	of alle wymmen thou art most blessid
Et benedictus fructus ventris tui.	and blessid be the fruyt of thi wombe, Ihesus.
Amen.	So mote it be.

Translation of the Pater Noster from a fourteenth-century version in William Maskell, Monumenta Ritualia Ecclesiae Anglicanae (Oxford: Clarendon Press, 1882), III.249; translation of the Ave Maria from the *Book to a Mother,* ed. Adrian James McCarthy, *Elizabethan and Renaissance Studies* 92 (Salzburg: Institut für Anglistik und Amerikanistik, 1981), 1.

investigations into accidental deaths, so we tend to see rather a grim side of children's play: a child tries to fetch a white feather out of a brook and falls in, a two-year-old girl tries to follow older children across a stream and drowns, a three-year-old girl wanders out into a London street and is run down by a rider who has lost control of his horse.[10]

As toddlers grew into childhood, they began to engage in the more complex and structured play of older children. The allegorical figure of Youth in John Lydgate's translation of Guillaume de Deguileville's fourteenth-century *Pilgrimage of the Life of Man* describes something of the pastimes of a fourteenth-century child:

> Play at the closh [croquet] at times I shall,
> And sometimes run at the ball

Boys playing at the quintain. Flemish, 1338–1344 (RA, f. 82v). McLean.

> With a staff made like a hook,
> And I will have a camp-ball crook . . .
> Sometimes fish, and catch fowls,
> And sometimes play at the bowls,
>
> At times shoot at bersels [targets],
> And after play at merels,
> Now at the dice in my young age,
> Both at the hazard and passage;
> Now at the chess, now at the tables,
> Read no stories except for fables.[11]

Parents and Children

It is a popular myth that medieval parents responded to the high rate of child mortality by investing little emotion in their children, but contemporary evidence suggests otherwise. Trevisa's description of a mother's devotion to her child is amply supported by other contemporary sources:

The mother conceives with pleasure, and labors and brings forth her child with sorrow and with woe, and she loves the child tenderly, and hugs and kisses him and feeds him and nurtures attentively.

Medieval theory expected the father to be less emotional, but not less loving:

A man loves his child, and feeds and nurtures him, and sets him at his own table when he is weaned, and teaches him in his youth with speech and with words,

---

CHAUCER'S DEDICATION TO HIS SON LEWIS OF
THE *TREATISE ON THE ASTROLABE*, 1391

Little Lewis, my son, I perceive well by certain evidences your ability to learn sciences touching numbers and proportions, and as well I consider your diligent request in special to learn the use of the astrolabe. . . . Therefore I have given you a sufficient astrolabe for the sky we see, based on the latitude of Oxford, upon which by means of this little treatise, I intent to teach you a certain number of conclusions pertaining to the same instrument . . . This treatise . . . I will show you under very easy rules and plain words in English, for of Latin you still have very little, my little son. But nonetheless these true conclusions in English are as good for you as are these same conclusions in Greek to the noble Greek clerks, and to Arabians in Arabic, and to Jews in Hebrew, and to Latin folk in Latin . . . And God knows that in all these languages and in many more these conclusions are adequately learned and taught, and yet by diverse rules; right as diverse paths lead diverse folk the right way to Rome.

Translated by J. L. Forgeng from the Middle English in Geoffrey Chaucer, *Treatise on the Astrolabe,* in *The Works of Geoffrey Chaucer,* ed. F. N. Robinson (Oxford: Oxford University Press, 1974), 546–47.

---

and chastises him with beating, and sets him to learning under ward and keeping of wardens and tutors. And the father shows him no glad cheer lest he become proud. And he . . . gives to his children clothing and food as their age requires, and acquires land and heritage for his children constantly and makes it greater and greater, and improves his acquisition, and leaves it to his heirs.[12]

As Trevisa suggests, corporal punishment was seen as a normal component in childrearing, though many people, including Chaucer himself, were already thinking seriously about the limitations of physical punishment:

A philosopher, who meant to beat his student for his great trespass, which had greatly angered him, brought a stick to beat the child. And when this child saw the stick, he said to his master "What think you to do?" "I will beat thee," quoth the master, "to correct thee." "Forsooth," quoth the child, "you ought first correct yourself, since you have lost all your patience for the guilt of a child." (*CT* I.670–73)

Language

One of the first and most important things a child learned was its mother tongue. In previous centuries, this would have been French for an aristocrat and English for a commoner. The Norman Conquest of 1066 had placed French-speaking Normans in charge of England, and for several centuries French remained the language of government and aristocratic life. In the 1300s this situation had changed substantially. By the early part of the century, aristocrats no longer necessarily spoke French as their native tongue, and by the end of the century John Trevisa could remark that the English aristocracy knew "no more French than their left heel." A few years later two English ambassadors to France—a knight and a lawyer—had to confess that they were as ignorant of French as of Hebrew. French continued to enjoy considerable prestige, being extensively used among the most cultured Englishmen as well as in the legal system, but its use was now purely artificial.

English gained ground as French lost it. In 1353 the law courts of London abandoned the requirement that proceedings be conducted in French, and the rest of the courts in the country followed soon after. In 1363 the Chancellor opened Parliament in English. The latter half of the fourteenth century witnessed the re-emergence of English as a fully developed language of literature and learning. In the 1360s a London clerk of northwestern origin named William Langland produced *Piers Plowman*, the first

A man and boy, after a contemporary Italian painting—the boy is dressed in a smaller version of an adult's gown. Italian, c. 1385 (Altichiero, "The Beheading of St. George"). McLean.

major work in the new literary tradition. Around this time Geoffrey Chaucer was beginning his own poetic career, which was to culminate in *The Canterbury Tales,* composed between about 1380 and 1400. It was also during these years that the school of religious reformers known as Lollards wrote the first complete translation of the Bible in English; John Trevisa's late fourteenth-century translations of the encyclopedia *De Proprietatibus Rerum* (*On the Properties of Things*) and the massive history *Polychronicon* marked the entry of English into the world of learning. For the first time in three centuries, it was no longer necessary to know Latin or French in order to participate in the learned or literary culture of the day.

To a modern English speaker, fourteenth-century spoken English would be extremely difficult to understand. For a start, the long vowels sounded more like their equivalents in Spanish or German, and final *-e* was pronounced: *have* would sound (roughly) as if it rhymed with lava, *be* with say; *liking* would sound like leaking, *moon* like moan, and *town* like toon. Some consonants that are silent today were pronounced, such as the *k* in *knight,* the *g* in *gnat,* and the *gh* in *light* (which resembled a rough *h* sound). The grammar was different too. For example, thou was used as a familiar form of you—people might call their close friends or family thou (thee was used for thou in exactly the same ways we use him for he).

Childhood

According to medieval ideas of child development, infancy, as the first stage of life, ended by age seven or so. At this point the child began to be integrated more directly into society. Trevisa again offers a recognizable description of these years:

A child that is between seven years and fourteen . . . is able to receive chastising and learning, and then he is put and set to learn under tutors and compelled to receive learning and chastising. . . . Such children . . . are able and light to move, clever to learn ditties, and without industriousness, and they lead their lives without care and industriousness and are interested only in mirth and pleasure, and dread no peril more than beating with a stick; and they love an apple more than gold. . . . When they are praised or blamed they set little thereby. . . . For tenderness of body they are easily hurt and injured, and they cannot well endure hard work. . . . Since small children often have evil manners and faults, and think only about things that are and care not for things that will be, they love playings and games and vanities. . . . When they are washed of filth and dirt they soon dirty themselves again. When the mother washes and combs them they kick and prance and push with feet and hands, and resist with all their might and strength. They think only of the pleasure of the stomach, and know not the measure of their own stomach. They covet and desire to eat and drink all the time. With difficulty they rise out of their bed, and they ask for food at once.[13]

Medieval understanding of childhood development is reflected in legal practices. Below age seven, children could not be punished as felons.

Between 7 and 12 or 14 was seen as a transitional age, where the punishment depended on the degree to which the child was seen as guileful. Also around age seven the process of sexual differentiation began in earnest, and religious counselors recommended separating the sleeping arrangements for boys and girls at this age.[14]

As Trevisa suggests, play continued to be an important part of children's lives at this stage, but adults expected them to begin learning the industriousness that they would need in the future. Girls continued to operate in the female sphere of the home, where they learned domestic skills appropriate to their station in life. For commoners, this meant tasks such as cooking, brewing, spinning, sewing, laundry, and basic medicine. Boys meanwhile began to play a part in the world of men. The sons of commoners were set to lighter forms of work, helping out the adult men with their work: in the country, this might mean helping with harvesting or thatching, or going out on their own to run errands, gather fuel, or look after livestock.

For children of the privileged classes, the settings and skills were rather different. Boys could be given to the care of male tutors or teachers, often known as masters: John of Gaunt's son Henry Bolingbroke during the 1370s was entrusted to the tutelage of a French knight named Guillaume de Mountendre. Many were eventually sent away to another aristocratic household, usually one of higher standing than their own family, where they would act as pages and squires while acquiring the skills they would need as adults. At this stage, these would include genteel etiquette, the aristocratic arts of riding and hunting, music and singing, probably some book-learning, and the rudiments of combat. Such are the skills attributed to the Squire in *The Canterbury Tales:*

> He could make songs and well compose,
> Joust and also dance, and well draw and write. . .
> Courteous he was, humble, and serviceable,
> And carved before his father at the table. (*CT* A.95–100)

Aristocratic girls learned the skills necessary for household management, as well as embroidery, music, and other adorning accomplishments. Like boys, they were often sent away to other households at some point, or they might be entrusted to mistresses who were charged with caring for them: Katherine Swynford, the wife of one of John of Gaunt's knightly retainers, served in this capacity for the duke's daughters during the 1370s, eventually becoming the duke's own mistress in a different sense—she would ultimately become his third wife in 1396.

Both boys and girls of aristocratic families were often sent to monasteries or nunneries at this stage of life, where they could be taught and looked after until they reached puberty. This was a particularly common choice for aristocratic girls: in the early 1400s, Philippa de la Pole, a daughter of the early of Suffolk, was in the keeping of the nuns of Bungay Priory, although she was allowed two weeks to come home each year at Christmas.

A GUARDIAN ANSWERS CHARGES
OF BEATING HIS WARD, 1381

The aforesaid John by Henry Gatington his attorney came in and denied the force and wrongdoing . . . And as to coming by force and arms, he said that he is not at all guilty. . . . And as for the beating he said that the Isold is his kins- woman, and at the time when the supposed transgression was said to have been done, Isold was of tender age living in John's company, and because Isold was inclined to pass her time among boys and in company inappropri- ate for her estate, and not to behave herself as she should, John reproved Isold for the sake of punishment and correction and to get her to abstain from this kind of company, and he chastised her with small rods on various occasions, but in no way did he beat Isold with force and arms or out of malice.

Translated by J. L. Forgeng from the Latin in Morris S. Arnold, *Select Cases of Trespass from the King's Courts 1307–1399* (London: Selden Society, 1985), 26.

Education

While Philippa de la Pole was being looked after by the nuns, her brother Thomas was at Oxford studying for a career in the church, and another brother, Alexander, was boarding with the town schoolmaster in Ipswich. As the children of an earl, all were in an unusual and highly privileged position. Formal education was much rarer in the Middle Ages than it is today: in general, it was the preserve of a privileged fraction of society, consisting mostly of the aristocracy, the clergy, and the more prosperous townsfolk. Children who were destined for a full education would begin studying by age seven, or even younger in some cases. Those who were to be taught only basic literacy might begin later.

There were several ways a child might receive an elementary educa- tion. The most privileged children had private tutors. A less expensive option was to send the child to a commercial school in a town, or to a school attached to a religious institution such as a church, cathedral, or monastery. The poorest children were unlikely to receive any education at all, except for boys who were marked for a career in the church: such boys might receive basic education from their parish priest, and eventu- ally be sent to a religious school, with the costs paid for by some form of scholarship.

The first stage in a formal education was learning how to read. Lit- eracy was a relatively rare skill in the fourteenth century, although it was becoming more widespread. Just how rare it was depends on how one defines it. There is a broad gray zone between total literacy and total illit- eracy, and many medieval people lived within it.

Some could read but not write. Ordinarily, the medieval student would be taught reading first; only when he had mastered that would he be taught how to write. Some never got beyond the ability to read, and some learned only the bare rudiments of writing.

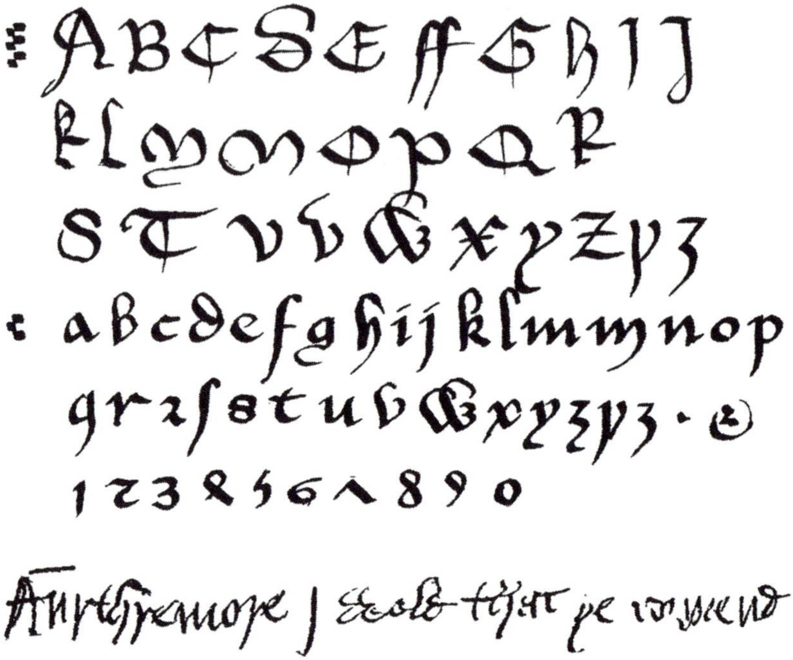

An exemplar for a Cursive Batarde script from the late fourteenth century based primarily on Chaucer's hand (Public Record Office c 81/1660 BP/126). Missing letters are drawn from similar contemporary English hands. This is the rapid cursive script of a professional clerk. The minims, lower case letters without ascenders or descenders, are about three pen nibs in height, and baselines are about ten pen nib widths apart. Hairline strokes can be drawn with the corner of the nib. Two versions of m, r, and s are shown in lower case. The second form of m and s is used to end words, and the second form of r can be used after o and similar rounded letters. Fourteenth-century writers did not systematically distinguish between i and j or between u and v as separate sounds. V tends to be used initially and for the Roman numeral five. J is often used as the first letter in a word and as a final Roman numeral one. The letters after z are thorn and yogh. In Middle English, thorn could be used for th, and yogh for sounds like the y in York and the ch in loch. The lower-case letters are followed by a period, typically at mid-minim height rather than on the baseline, and an ampersand. Arabic numerals from ca. 1360 are shown, although Roman numerals were much more typical. The exemplar is oversized for clarity: surviving document hands could be a third the size shown here. Below is a related but less practiced hand: Henry V writing home in 1419. (Brit. Mus. Cotton Ms. Vesp. F. III. F5.). McLean.

STUDENTS AND THEIR BOOKS, 1345

You may happen to see some headstrong youth lazily lounging over his studies, and when the winter's frost is sharp, his nose running from the nipping cold drips down, nor does he think of wiping it with his pocket-handkerchief until he has bedewed the book before him with the ugly moisture. Would that he had before him no book, but a cobbler's apron! His nails are stuffed with fetid filth as black as jet, with which he marks any passage that pleases him. He distributes a multitude of straws, which he inserts to stick out in different places, so that the halm may remind him of what his memory cannot retain . . . He does not fear to eat fruit or cheese over an open book, or carelessly to carry a cup to and from his mouth . . . Continually chattering he is never weary of disputing with his companions, and while he alleges a crowd of senseless arguments, he wets the book lying half open on his lap with sputtering showers. Yes and then hastily folding his arms he leans on the book, and by a brief spell of study invites a long nap. . . . Again it is part of the decency of scholars that whenever they return from meals to their study, washing should invariably precede reading . . . Nor let a crying child admire the pictures in the capital letters, lest he soil the parchment with wet fingers . . . Moreover the laity, who look at a book turned upside-down just as if it were open in the right way, are utterly unworthy of any communion with books.

From Richard de Bury, *Philobiblion*, ed. E. C. Thomas (London: Moring, 1903), 155.

Some could read but not understand what they read. Most of the business of the church and royal administration was still conducted in Latin or French. The priest of a remote parish might be able to read familiar phrases of ritual but not be able to understand the Latin very well. Some could read and write but chose not to. Many people of gentle birth preferred to employ scribes to read and write for them, even though some were perfectly capable of writing for themselves when necessary—much as a modern executive dictates letters to a secretary.

Overall, male literacy at the end of the 1400s may have been around 10 percent. It was certainly lower in Chaucer's day, although there is little information on which to base a precise figure. The most literate men were scholars and the professional clerks who carried out the business of administration for secular and clerical authorities. They needed to be able to read, write, and express themselves in Latin, French, or English. Many, but not all, were clerics, and not all clerics were men of letters in this sense.

Among aristocratic men, most could read and write, at least in English. Yet there were exceptions. The squire who commanded the La Rochelle garrison in 1372 was easily tricked by the pro-French mayor of the town because he could not read. When the mayor showed him a letter from the king of England, the squire recognized the king's seal but was entirely unable to read the letter. This allowed the mayor to pretend to have the letter read aloud, but he actually gave a fabricated message that led to the

Jean de Meun composing the *Romance of the Rose*. With his left hand he uses his penknife to steady the parchment without soiling it with his fingers. His book table is adjustable like a piano stool. c. 1380. Roman de la Rose BL Yates Thompson 21, f.69v, London. Photo Credit: HIP/Art Resource, NY.

capture and betrayal of the entire garrison. Even in the seventeenth century there were still illiterate men among the aristocracy.

Literacy was higher in the city than in the country. The richer merchants could read and write as a matter of course. Many of the poorer merchants and shopkeepers could read and write as well. Among craftsmen, practitioners of well-paid sedentary crafts like limners (manuscript painters) or goldsmiths might well be literate, while tanners and smiths were probably not. By the late fifteenth century, many urban guilds expected their members to be able to read and write.

At all levels of society, women were less literate than men. As of the late 1400s, female literacy appears to have been about one-tenth that of men. As among men, female literacy was most common among the aristocracy and the richer merchant families. A wealthy citizen such as the one who wrote the *Goodman of Paris* (*Le Ménagier de Paris*), a collection of instructions for running an urban household, expected that a prosperous townsman's wife would be able to read letters from her husband and perhaps "answer them in your own hand, if you know how." The Knight of la Tour-Landry, another French contemporary, had a somewhat different opinion: "As for writing, it is no matter if a woman knows nought of it, but as for reading, I say that it is good and profitable to all women."

Few husbandmen were literate, and even fewer poor laborers. Most rural folk had little opportunity or incentive to learn to read and write. Not all were completely illiterate, however. Two of the seven husbandmen called in to witness John Fastolf's will in 1466 signed their names, and as early as the thirteenth-century manuals were being written on the office of the reeve. The reeve was almost always a villein, although usually a substantial one. He had an important role in the running of the manor and was often responsible for keeping manorial accounts. Such a man would find literacy valuable, as would any husbandman who did not want to be utterly at the mercy of others in dealing with a lease or a will or financial accounts. Apparently literacy was common enough among the lower orders that the revolutionary priest John Ball could circulate subversive letters during the Peasants' Revolt of 1381 and expect them to find readers.

The first stage of literacy was to learn to read from a "tablet-book," a piece of paper or parchment nailed to a board, small enough to be easily handled by a child. To judge from later hornbooks, this probably had the alphabet written out on it, and very likely a basic text such as the Lord's Prayer. As the child began to learn to write, he would probably begin with a wax tablet and stylus, practicing the letters in wax, and rubbing them out afterwards with the blunt end of the stylus, or leaving the tablet in the sun to erase it entirely.

Eventually the child would need to learn the art of handling pen and ink. The writing-quill was made from a goose feather with the vane cut off, and the tip had to be carefully trimmed with a pen-knife to the shape necessary for holding the ink and allowing it to flow properly onto the writing surface. Increasing literacy was doubtless encouraged by the growing availability of paper. In previous centuries, the main permanent media were parchment, derived from sheepskin or goatskin, and vellum, from calfskin. Each sheet had to be laboriously cleaned, scraped, and smoothed, making it comparatively expensive. Paper was made from old linen rags, which could be efficiently pulped in water-powered paper mills, making it a much more economical option, although less durable—legal documents would continue to be written on skins for centuries after paper had become common.

Children at the first stage of education might acquire numeracy as well as literacy, particularly if they were headed for a career in which they would need to keep accounts. Prior to Chaucer's lifetime, numbers had been reckoned in Roman numerals, but by the 1300s ciphers, the early version of Arabic numerals, were becoming more common. The child might also learn to use a counting board, an apparatus similar to a set of checkers, used like an abacus in keeping accounts. Even unlettered people learned to count, of course, and might also use visual aids like notched tally-sticks in helping to keep track of numbers.

Advanced Education

After learning the fundamentals of reading and writing, a child might go on to other studies. By about age 10 or so, a boy might be sent to a grammar school to learn Latin, especially if he was destined for a career in the church. Once he had learnt the rudiments of Latin grammar, he progressed by reading a variety of works in the language. Because Latin was the international language of learning, the grammar-school curriculum could include works on topics including literature, history and science, providing students with the medieval equivalent of a general education.

At this stage a child of a privileged family might also be learning French, which was the international language of upper-class culture in western Europe. Chaucer's Prioress Eglentyne, undoubtedly born into a privileged family, takes pride in her French, which she speaks "full fair and prettily, after the school of Stratford-at-Bow—for French of Paris was to her unknown." Since Stratford-at-Bow was an abbey outside of London, we may presume that she learned the language as a girl under the instruction of nuns.

A boy headed for a career in the church or as a physician might continue on to university—Oxford, Cambridge, or a university on the Continent. University teaching was conducted in Latin. The course of study for the baccalaureate degree concentrated on Grammar, Logic, Rhetoric, Geometry, Arithmetic, Astronomy, and Music. Advanced degrees were available in Canon Law (that is, church law), Philosophy, and Medicine.

Prospective students applied to study with specific masters, although by this time the system was increasingly managed through the students' residential halls, which survive today as the colleges of modern Oxford and Cambridge. The curriculum consisted chiefly of attending lectures and observing and taking part in disputations. In lectures, the master would read and comment on an important text, while disputations involved debating selected topics. Completion of a degree was by no means a required outcome of the university experience. Some students remained for only a year or two, enough time to acquire a smattering of advanced learning in preparation for their careers, but not enough for the baccalaureate. Others might remain for years without finishing: one student, Robert Lincoln, resided at college from 1382 until his death in 1440 without attaining a degree.

Alternative forms of advanced education with a secular focus were available in London. Young men who wanted to learn the workings of English law would attend sessions of the law courts. By Chaucer's day, there were permanent residences, or inns, at the western end of the city, catering to the needs of these students. These inns provided both lodgings and a curriculum of study, and by the time Chaucer died, they were coalescing into what would be known the Inns of Court, the chief institutions for legal education in England.

The presence of young men looking for an education in Oxford, Cambridge, and London also gave rise to specialized schools in these towns, usually consisting of a single tutor offering subjects not available at university: Thomas Sampson of Oxford in the late 1300s ran a school where he taught the skills needed for commerce and management, such as keeping accounts, writing formal letters, and conveying property.

Confirmation

At some point before or at puberty, the child marked their next religious rite of passage with the sacrament of Confirmation, administered by the bishop to signify the child's full entry into the Christian community. Opinions varied as to when Confirmation should take place. Some authors thought it should happen as early as age five, others felt it should wait as late as age 12 or 14. Because Confirmation had to be administered by the bishop, the actual age often depended on when the bishop was coming through the area.

Adolescence

By age 14, children were becoming integrated as subordinate participants in the world of adults and specializing for their role in society and the economy. They also began to acquire legal responsibility as adults: at age 14 a child was treated as an adult in the legal system, and was subject to the national poll tax that was levied in 1377; at age 15 a boy could be called into military service; full legal majority came at age 21. In the opinion of the thirteenth-century legal scholar Henry of Bracton, a girl of the commons reached majority "whenever she can and knows how to order her house and do the things that belong to the arrangement and management of a house," which he put at no earlier than 14 or 15 years of age.

Aristocratic teenagers generally continued on the path established in their younger years. A girl might continue residing in a nunnery until she was ready for marriage, although by age 14 she might relocate to an aristocratic household to begin her integration into adult secular society. Aristocratic boys at this age were unlikely to remain in monastic hands unless they were destined for a career in the church. At this age they were ready to begin learning the arts of war in earnest: Edward the Black Prince was only 16 when he "earned his spurs" at Crécy. Contemporary writers recommended 14 to 16 as an appropriate age to begin military training.

A peasant girl by this age would be engaged in exactly the same sorts of work as her mother, such as spinning wool into thread, cooking, cleaning, tending to the garden and dairy, and looking after the younger children. Peasant boys took a bit longer to assume the full work of farming. At age 14 they had not yet achieved the physical development they needed to handle the heaviest agricultural tasks, but as they matured through their teenage years their work patterns assimilated to those of their elders. By the time they were 21, they were performing the same work as the rest of the men, although it might be years before they actually inherited their own landholding.

Urban adolescents, or those whose families had urban connections, might be apprenticed to a craft or trade. Apprenticeship was a privileged position, since completion of apprenticeship was a stage on the way to membership in the guild and citizenship in the town. For this reason there seem to have been two tracks, one for those with the connections that would lead to guild membership, and another for those who were destined to spend their lives working for other craftsmen.

The apprentice lived with his master, perhaps along with one or more other apprentices. Apprenticeship traditionally lasted seven years, although it could be longer or shorter depending on the craft and its specific regulations in the town where the apprenticeship was served. Girls as well as boys might be apprenticed, though this was rare; their choices were more limited, principally such crafts as silkworking, embroidery, and dressmaking. Girls' apprenticeships were not expected to last as long, and were often regarded as an interim measure prior to marriage.[15]

Young people in both town and country who had no expectations of advancement through inheritance or family connections were more or less already in their lifetime economic roles by the age of 14 or so. For people in this position the usual route was selling one's labor, whether in domestic service, in agriculture, or in a craft or trade as an unskilled worker.[16]

Entering the Clergy

The teenage years were also the stage at which a child might begin a clerical career. Earlier in the Middle Ages it had been accepted practice for noble families to commit children to a life in the church from a very early age, but this practice had been forbidden by the Fourth Lateran Council in 1216. It was still possible for a boy as young as seven to be ordained as a doorkeeper, reader, or exorcist; at 13 or 14 he could become an acolyte. Ordination in these minor orders involved a partial tonsure, but not a binding commitment to a clerical career, and clerks in minor orders were free to continue a secular life of employment and marriage. Only at age 17 could a boy be ordained as a subdeacon: this involved a binding vow that committed the individual to a clerical and celibate life. At 19 he could become a deacon or monk, but he could only become a priest at 24. Similar age restrictions applied to girls, though their only clerical options were in regular orders as a nun.

Coming of Age

For the duration of his teens, a boy remained a subordinate participant in the society and economy of adults. The transition from subordination to independence varied from class to class. In theory, people came fully of age at 21, the official age of inheritance, but this age was not necessarily significant in practice. The age of 21 was most likely to be significant for a male aristocrat, since his family might have the means to set him up in some sort of independent position. A youth who had been apprenticed as a part of the guild system remained under tutelage until the end of his apprenticeship, at which point he became a journeyman, allowed to sell his skills to others for a daily wage. If he had the means and connections, he might eventually acquire permission from the guild to set up independently as a master; otherwise he would remain a journeyman for the rest of his working life.

A peasant remained in a semi-dependent position until he inherited a landholding; those who did not stand to inherit would spend their lives working for others. For laborers or servants, coming of age would not be a very meaningful event: they would have been fully participating members of the workforce since their early teens and they too would probably remain dependent on others for employment for the remainder of their working lives.

For women these professional considerations were of less importance. Women were essentially treated as adolescents until they were married (unless they entered religious life), at which point they exchanged subordination to their family or employer for subordination to a husband. Girls might inherit property at age 16 if they were married and their husbands were age 21 or older.

Marriage

For both men and women, marriage was probably the most important step in the transition to independence. Marriage was a religious rather than a civil procedure, and it fell under the jurisdiction of the Church. Canon law prohibited marriage before the age of 12 for girls, or 14 for boys. In reality, such young marriages were practically unknown. As it was unusual for two couples to live in a single house, marriage was delayed until the prospective couple had some sort of household to occupy, whether by inheritance or by economic or professional advancement. This meant that most commoners married rather late: statistically reliable data is lacking, but most men seem to have married in their late 20s, women in their mid-20s. Aristocrats, whose economic opportunities were less restricted, usually married younger: the men in their mid-20s, the women in their late teens. The urban elite tended to marry at ages similar to that of the aristocracy.[17]

There were occasionally very young marriages among the upper aristocracy, such as Mary de Bohun, who married Henry Bolingbroke in 1380 when she was only 12. Such marriages were driven by the political needs of leading families in the country, rather than by any sense that marriage was truly appropriate for such young girls. Mary would give birth to seven children before dying around age 25, something of a martyr to her family's need for heirs.

A more common aristocratic practice was child betrothal, which could technically take place as early as age seven. Such a betrothal could protect the family property from falling under royal custody if the parents died while the child was under 21, but they could not be consummated before the children reached the minimum canonical age, and they could be dissolved prior to consummation.

The Wedding

Marriage in the Middle Ages was an involved process, beginning with the eternal dance of scouting prospective spouses. The interest of young people in meeting others of the opposite sex was counterbalanced by a social imperative that girls avoid even the rumor of sexual activity outside of marriage. This imperative was largely driven by concern among men and their families that their heirs should be genuinely their own. It was most pronounced among the aristocracy, for whom inheritance involved very high stakes. Equally important for aristocratic families were the political and economic dimensions of marriage: it was considered essential that any marriage should advance the interests of the family as a whole.

The danger posed by youthful sexuality to the ambitions of an aristocratic family was highlighted by the story of Elizabeth, daughter of John of Gaunt. At age 16 she had been betrothed to the seven-year-old Earl of Pembroke. The engagement appears to have been broken off by the time she was 23, when she was sent to the court "to study the behavior and customs of courtly society." Here she met Sir John Holland, the king's constable, who "fell violently in love with her at first sight," and pursued her, eventually getting Elizabeth pregnant. Happily for the couple, Holland was deemed a suitable match, and the two were subsequently married, but the scandal must have been seen as an object lesson for many English aristocrats—hence the aristocratic practice of secluding girls in nunneries until they were ready to marry.

For most people from privileged families, the normal course was for potential matches to be explored through the social network, and for the young people to be introduced to each other by arrangement. The church required consent as a prerequisite for marriage, so in principle either of the prospective couple might refuse to take things any further. How much freedom the couple had in accepting or refusing a match probably depended heavily on the political and economic stakes. In very high-status families, there was considerably more pressure for the young people to conform to the family's will.

Further down the social scale the stakes were lower, and families exerted less control over their children's choice of spouse. Among ordinary commoners, there were plenty of opportunities for young people to meet each other at public occasions: feasts, festivals, fairs, and markets were all settings in which men and women had ample opportunity to meet the opposite sex. For such people, sexual attraction doubtless played a larger role in choosing a spouse than it did for the aristocracy, though practical considerations were not negligible: choosing the right partner could mean moving up in the world, while the wrong partner could bring a lifetime of poverty and hardship. Young people growing up in a society where poverty was always visible had ample reminders of the economic implications of their choices.

The initial meeting would be followed by a period of courtship in which the couple and their families could size each other up before committing to a marriage. Giftgiving was an important activity at this point, especially for the man: gifts served not only as a token of affection, but as evidence of financial resources and generosity of character.

Once marriage had been decided on, the next stage was an arrangement between the two families, so that each would know what property was being settled on the prospective spouses. Then a betrothal took place in which the couple promised to marry each other. The Church regarded the betrothal as a binding legal contract, and it was difficult to break except by mutual consent or by one of the parties actually becoming married to someone else. Prior to the actual ceremony, the banns, or marriage announcement, had to be proclaimed publicly in the parish churches of both partners on three successive Sundays. The theoretical purpose of the banns was to allow anyone who knew of any impediment to the marriage to come forward. Possible impediments included prior contracts to marry, familial relationships (which included relatives by marriage, godparentage, or even by promises to marry), impotence or infertility, error (such as misrepresented identities or personal status), or coercion of either party.

In canon law, what normally made a marriage was a present-tense statement before witnesses in which the partners took each other as husband and wife. The vows were normally exchanged at the door of the church, but might be followed by a nuptial Mass within.[18] The bride might wear a garland on her head, and the man gave his bride a ring as part of the ceremony. The religious ceremony would be followed by a wedding feast.

This sequence of events was mandated by the Church, but it was not the only route to marriage. According to canon law, a promise of marriage followed by sexual consummation was also considered a legally valid marriage. Such clandestine marriages were illegal and punishable under canon law, yet they remained binding. This could make for substantial problems: in the event of sexual consummation one partner might claim marriage on the grounds of a promise to marry, and the other might deny that such a promise had been made. Nor did everyone who made formal marriage vows do it at a church: in 1372, a couple in York exchanged their vows sitting on a bench in a tannery, sealing the ceremony by kissing between a garland of flowers.

Once the marriage was made, it was considered permanently binding. Divorce existed only in a form that would today be called legal separation. Since married couples were legally required to cohabit, it required a church decree of divorce to allow a married couple to live apart from each other. Such decrees could be issued in cases of cruelty or adultery, and they might include maintenance agreements akin to modern alimony payments.

Alternatively, a marriage might be annulled if it were found to have been invalid in the first place. An annulment might be procured if a prior family relationship existed between the couple (whether by blood or marriage), if either partner had been coerced into the marriage, or if the man was found to be sexually impotent, to name just a few possible reasons.

Family Sizes

Because different social classes tended to marry at different ages, family sizes varied with social status. An aristocratic woman, married in her teens, might produce many children over the course of her childbearing years. A commoner, marrying in her twenties, would have five or ten fewer years to produce children. Differences in levels of nutrition and health increased the disparity by producing a higher level of child mortality among commoners. As a result, a rich peasant family might have only three children surviving to adulthood, an ordinary peasant family two, and even fewer in a poor household.

Other factors could also influence family size. Since lactation inhibits pregnancy, upper-class women who give their children to wet-nurses could sooner return to a fertile state. Deliberate family planning could also be practiced—doubtless with limited success—through herbal medicines and other means. For many working people, the physical demands of daily labor doubtless inhibited reproduction in a way not necessarily true for the leisured aristocracy.

Not all sexual activity took place within the accepted confines of the marriage bed. Cases of premarital and extramarital sex were common in the church courts, and prostitution was well recognized as a feature of urban life. The legal system regularly handled the cases of children born out of wedlock. If the parents subsequently married, the child became legitimate in canon law, though not in common law. This meant that the child could enter the clergy without a dispensation, though it would still be restricted from inheriting property. Church courts sometimes imposed child support payments for illegitimate children.

Aging and Life Expectancy

Although child mortality was high, once a person reached adulthood, their prospects of living a full life increased dramatically. The fourteenth-century figure for life expectancy at birth—17 years—is distorted by the extremely high rate of child mortality. Even in this century of plague, a 20-year-old had a total life expectancy of 45 years, a 30-year-old of 50, and a 40-year-old of 60.[19]

Old Age

There is a popular notion that medieval people were considered aged at 40. In fact, old age was most often reckoned to begin at 60—this was the age at which a man was no longer subject to military service. A fair number of people reached this age—it has been estimated that at any given time some 10 percent of the population were over 60. In Verona in 1425 some 15 percent of the population were over age 60, and 6 percent over 70.

Retirement did not exist as an official institution, but when people became too old to work, they often made an arrangement to transfer their property to a younger person (usually their own children, if possible) in exchange for a perpetual allowance of food and lodging for the remainder of their lives. Such an agreement of support, known as a corrody, might also come from other sources, for example a long-term employer. In 1399, William Wyneford, master mason of Winchester Cathedral, was granted a corrody by the cathedral priory: the terms included lodging at the priory; permission to eat at the prior's table unless he had to be crowded out by high-ranking visitors, as well as a place for his servant to eat with the servants of the priory; a gown trimmed with lamb's fleece each year for himself and his servant; two candles a day and fuel for a fire in the winter; and use of the priory's horses for himself and his servant.[20]

Many wives, perhaps most, outlived their husbands; indeed, a woman was not infrequently widowed at a relatively young age. Widowhood could be a uniquely independent state for a woman. If her husband left her with sufficient property or a viable business, she could continue to hold it in her own right and even take over the business in person. By this means some women managed to enter professions otherwise barred to them. Under these circumstances a woman enjoyed considerable freedom and might remarry or not as she pleased.

For most people, old age or widowhood was a time of economic vulnerability. Only a minority enjoyed the material assets or long-term professional relationships that might support them in their old age. Others had to turn to the charity of relatives, friends, or strangers. A fortunate few might find a place in a charitable home founded for the support of the elderly poor—known as hospitals, such institutions could be found in large towns, but there were never enough places for all the people who needed them. The rest had to make shift as best they might, and many ultimately had to resort to begging.

Death

Rich or poor, all lives eventually come to an end, a fact that was more immediate for people in a world where the elderly, infirm, and dying were more visible than is typical today. When death was imminent, a priest was summoned to administer the last rites, known as Extreme Unction (Final Anointing). This involved hearing a last confession, administering Communion, and anointing the feet with holy oil. Those who had not provided for the disposal of their property were encouraged to make a will; even illiterate paupers sometimes had written wills.

After death, the body was laid out, washed, and clothed, and the friends and relatives of the deceased might gather for a wake—to the disapproval of moralists, who saw wakes as an occasion for drunkenness and riotous behavior. Prior to burial, the naked corpse was wrapped in a cloth shroud. The body was carried to the churchyard to the sound of the churchbell. Most people were buried outside the church in unmarked graves without any kind of casket. Only the wealthy few were buried under the church floor with a grave marker, and to be buried with an elaborate tomb with a brass or stone effigy was a mark of enormous wealth and privilege.

Funerals were occasions for the distribution of alms for the benefit of the deceased's soul, and there was often a funeral banquet for the guests. Friends and relatives grieved, yet death was a familiar occurrence. Corpses were by no means a rare sight, and, barring unforeseen accident, death, like birth, probably happened at home: this too was a part of ordinary life.

The sacrament of Extreme Unction. French, late fourteenth century (TBH, p. 178). McLean.

NOTES

1. P.J.P. Goldberg, *Women, Work, and Life Cycle in a Medieval Economy: Women in York and Yorkshire c. 1300–1520* (Oxford: Clarendon Press, 1992), 128.

2. John Trevisa, *On the Properties of Things. John Trevisa's translation of Bartholomeus Anglicus' De Proprietatibus Rerum,* gen. ed. M. C. Seymour (Oxford: Clarendon Press, 1975), 305.

3. Robert S. Gottfried, *Doctors and Medicine in Medieval England 1340–1530* (Princeton: Princeton University Press, 1986), 87.

4. Nicholas Orme, *Medieval Children* (New Haven: Yale University Press, 2001), 37–38.

5. On names, see P. H. Reaney, *A Dictionary of British Surnames* (London: Routledge and Kegan Paul, 1977).

6. Trevisa, *On the Properties of Things,* 299, 304.

7. Josiah Cox Russell, *British Medieval Population* (Albuquerque: University of New Mexico Press, 1948), 183.

8. On religious education, see *Dives and Pauper,* ed. Priscilla Heath Barnum, Early English Texts Society 275, 280 (London: Oxford University Press, 1976, 1980), I.329; John Mirk, *Instructions for Parish Priests,* ed. E. Peacock. Early English Texts Society 31 (London: Kegan Paul, Trench and Trübner, 1868), 151 ff.

9. See John Lydgate, "Stans Puer ad Mensam," in *The Minor Poems of John Lydgate,* ed. H. N. MacCracken (London: Trübner, 1934), 2.739–44.

10. Barbara Hanawalt, *The Ties That Bound: Peasant Families in Medieval England* (New York: Oxford University Press, 1986), 180–81; Barbara Hanawalt, *Growing Up in Medieval London: The Experience of Childhood in History* (New York: Oxford University Press, 1993), 65.

11. John Lydgate, *The Pilgrimage of the Life of Man,* ed. F. J. Furnivall (London: Early English Texts Society, 1899), ll. 11,181–96.

12. Trevisa, *On the Properties of Things,* 303, 310–11.

13. Trevisa, *On the Properties of Things,* 300–1, 302.

14. Mirk, *Instructions,* 216.

15. Hanawalt, *Growing Up,* ch. 8.

16. Hanawalt, *Growing Up,* ch. 11.

17. Hanawalt, *Growing Up,* 205–6.

18. Mirk, *Instructions,* 190 ff.; *Dives and Pauper,* 2.61; Robert Mannyng, *Handlyng Synne,* ed. F. J. Furnivall (London: Kegan Paul, Trench and Trübner, 1901, 1903), ll. 203 ff.

19. Russell, *British Medieval Population,* 183.

20. Joan Greatrex, ed., *Register of the Common Seal of the Priory of St Swithun, Winchester 1345–1497* (Winchester, UK: Hampshire County Council, 1978), 8–9.

4

CYCLES OF TIME

Time

The passage of time for people in the fourteenth century was not nearly as finely marked as it is in the modern world. The rural majority most often reckoned time by the daily cycle of natural events: the time of day was perceived in relationship to cockcrow, dawn, sunrise, midday, sunset, dusk or twilight, and midnight. For such people, the closest thing to a clock would be the bells of the village church, so if some precision was needed, time would be reckoned according to the canonical hours, the traditional schedule of the monastic cycle of daily prayer: Prime, Terce, Sexte, None, Vespers, and Compline. Each of these hours referred both to the time at which that period of prayer began, and to the space of time from that hour to the next; thus, "Prime" could mean either 6 A.M., or the period from 6 A.M. to 9 A.M. The canonical hour could also be subdivided: half Prime was halfway though Prime (roughly 7:30 A.M.), whole or high Prime the latter end of Prime. The system was complicated by the fact that Sexte had largely fallen into disuse, so None moved forward to cover midday as well as mid-afternoon, whence our modern word noon. The canonical hours divided the daylight period into equal parts, so the hours varied from 30 minutes in midwinter to 90 minutes in midsummer.

Town-dwellers were likely to reckon time by the equal hours used today. Urban churches might ring bells according to equal hours, and clock towers were coming into use as well: Windsor had one by the 1350s, Westminster acquired one by the 1360s. Other devices for the

THE CANONICAL HOURS

Matins (Midnight)
Lauds (around 3 A.M.)
Prime: 6–9 A.M. (sunrise and early morning)
Underne (Terce): 9–12 A.M. (morning)
Sexte: 12–3 P.M. (afternoon)
None: 3–6 P.M. (late afternoon) or noon
Vespers (Evensong): 6–9 P.M. (evening)
Compline: 9 P.M. (roughly the time of curfew)

precise reckoning of time included hourglasses and sundials, some of which were made portable for personal use. In principle, time could also be divided into minutes and seconds, but these were little used—clocks did not normally have a minute hand, let alone a second hand. In practice, the half or quarter hour was the minimum duration of reckoned time—shorter durations might be reckoned as "the time it takes to recite three Pater Nosters."

The Day

For those who had to earn a living, the working day began a bit before dawn—artificial light was expensive and relatively weak, so it was important to make the most of the sun. It was common to begin the morning with a prayer and by washing one's face and hands. Another important activity in the early morning was stoking the fire from the previous night's coals, so there would be warmth and a source of hot water for the rest of the day. In privileged households, it was the job of the servants to rise first to make the fires ready so that their employers would find it less chilly when they rose from bed. Servants might even warm their masters' clothes for a bit of extra comfort.

Some people ate breakfast upon rising, although others waited until a few hours into their workday. Morning labor began promptly: city folk often did their marketing when markets opened at sunrise, and farmers were already in the fields at this time.[1]

Work lasted all day, with breaks for meals and refreshments. The midday meal was usually called dinner, and the evening meal supper. Those who could not take a break for a full meal might have a lighter repast at noon or afterwards called a noon-shench (noon-drink), later nuncheon, the ultimate source of our word lunch.

One guild in the fifteenth century specified the working hours as from 4 A.M. to 8 P.M. in the summer, and from 6 A.M. to 6 P.M. in the winter; total time off during this workday was probably two hours or less. Rural hours of work likewise depended on the season, since they ran from dawn to dusk. As is often the case when people are subjected to lengthy hours of

Laborers pause for a meal. Italian, c. 1395 (TS Vienna, f. 64). McLean.

ENFORCEMENT OF CURFEW, 1370

Proclamation [was] made the 4th December 4, 44 Edward III . . . that no-one wander in the City after curfew is sounded at the churches of St. Mary-le-Bow, Barking Church in Tower Ward, St. Bride, and St. Giles without Cripplegate, unless he is of good repute and carries a light, on pain of imprisonment; [and] that no taverner or brewer keep open house after curfew is sounded at the above churches, and that curfew should not be sounded at any other church later than at the above churches.

Reginald R. Sharpe, *Calendar of Letter Books . . . of the City of London: Letter Book G* (London: John Edward Francis, 1904), 270–71.

---

work, the actual intensity of labor was not necessarily very high, especially among wage laborers, although independent landholders and shopkeepers obviously had incentive to work harder.[2]

At the end of the day, lights were extinguished and hearth fires were banked as a precaution against the hazard of fire. The term curfew comes from the French *couvre-feu* (cover-fire), since this was the time at which the household fires were covered so that the coals would smolder slowly through the night, to be rekindled in the morning.

One might recite a prayer in the evening before retiring. People slept in nightgowns, shirts, or nothing at all—although those who slept naked might opt for some sort of head covering, as nights became chilly once the fires were out. In towns, there was generally a curfew around 9 P.M., and the taverns and town gates closed at about that time. Great houses and castles also closed overnight, setting a porter on watch at the gate in case there were any important arrivals during the night. After curfew, only the town watch and reputable people carrying lights and going about legitimate business were supposed to be on the streets, although in reality revelers were often known to cause disturbances late at night.[3]

Buying wine from a vendor. Italian, c. 1385 (TS Liège, f. 57). McLean.

The Week

Then as now, the work week began on Monday. Villeins who owed labor services might have to spend one or more days working on the lord's land—sometimes as many as five in harvest season. Friday was set aside as a day of religious penance, observed especially by fasting: no one was supposed to eat meat other than fish. Wednesdays and Saturdays might also be observed in the same fashion. Saturday was often a half-holiday, theoretically in preparation for the Sabbath—workers might be let off in the afternoon, sometimes as early as midday. Markets took place on regular days of the week, so shopping also followed a weekly schedule.[4]

Sunday

For people who worked from dawn to dusk for five and a half to six days a week, the break in labor on Sunday was especially important. This was a day of enforced leisure when no one was supposed to work. Shopkeepers in London were permitted to sell on Sundays, since laboring people found it difficult to shop on working days, but no wares were to be placed out in the streets.[5]

Sunday morning was reserved for religious observances. The especially devout might attend Matins at dawn. Mass took place from early morning until midday, and was supposed to be attended by all parishioners. Once Mass was over, the rest of Sunday was free for a variety of secular entertainments. Strict moralists believed that games and carousal were inappropriate activities for the Sabbath, but time-honored custom entitled people to spend Sunday afternoon feasting, drinking, playing, or otherwise making merry.[6]

Religious Services

The focal point of religious observance was the ceremony of the Mass, celebrated every Sunday in every parish church. At the heart of the Mass was the sacrament of Communion, the ceremony by which the sacred wafer and wine were turned into the body and blood of Christ and received by the communicants. The bread and wine were usually received only by the priest himself: it was considered sufficient for the parishioners to participate vicariously. Mass was not always accompanied by a sermon: sermons were required only four times a year, when the priest was expected to preach on the fundamental points of the faith. The frequency of preaching probably varied with the locality. More heavily populated and prosperous areas had better trained priests and were more likely to receive sermons. During the service the parishioners were supposed to sit or kneel on the floor, although they stood during the reading of the Gospel—the pew was a later development.[7]

Most people received Communion only once a year, at Easter. The laity generally received Communion only in the form of the wafer, except on very special occasions such as a coronation. Current doctrine held that the body and blood of Christ were present in both the bread and the wine. Prior to Communion, the communicant was expected to confess his or her sins to the priest, who would assign some form of penance. This process was known as the sacrament of Confession and was intended to ensure that the communicant would receive Christ's body in a state of spiritual cleanliness. Confession was supposed to take place with the confessant kneeling at the altar. There was no confessional booth: the priest merely pulled his hood down over his eyes. He was especially enjoined to avert his glance if the confessant was a woman. Many believed that Confession and Absolution should be in the hands of the parish priest—parish priests most especially were of this persuasion—but since the previous century the mendicant orders of Franciscan and Dominican friars had also enjoyed this privilege, and many worshippers resorted to them instead.

As part of the ritual of Confession, the priest would examine the penitent on the Credo, Ave Maria, and Pater Noster; additional penance was assigned to those who failed this annual test. Penance for ordinary sins might be an imposed almsgiving, prayers, additional attendance at church, a pilgrimage, or abstinence from food or sex. From the time of the Fourth Lateran Council in 1215 all Christians were required to confess annually, although this rule was not always observed.[8]

The Year

The life of the country dweller was dominated by the cycle of the seasons. Even in towns, where the natural cycle was less important, the shape of the year played a crucial role in the ceremonial life of the community. The cycle of the rural year is evoked in this late medieval poem:

January	By this fire I warm my hands;
February	And with my spade I delve my lands.
March	Here I set my things to spring;
April	And here I hear the fowls sing.
May	I am as light as bird in bough;

June	And I weed my grain well enow.
July	With my scythe my mead I mow;
August	And here I shear my grain full low.
September	With my flail I earn my bread;
October	And here I sow my wheat so red.
November	At Martinmas I kill my swine;
December	And at Christmas I drink red wine.[9]

There were two distinct systems for dividing the year into seasons, one astronomical, the other agricultural. The astronomical year was essentially the system of solstices and equinoxes known to us today. Following the system that Europe had inherited from the Romans, January 1 was called New Year's Day, but in reckoning years, the English actually changed the number on March 25, the Feast of the Annunciation.

All of Europe was still on the Julian calendar, originally established by Julius Caesar. Because the solar year is slightly over 365 days, the Julian calendar reckoned leap years to make up the difference. This actually made the average Julian year slightly longer than the solar year, so that the seasons were inching their way earlier on the calendar. England would accumulate an 11-day discrepancy by the time it adopted the modern Gregorian calendar in 1752 (on the Gregorian calendar, three out of four years ending in -00 are not leap years, which reduces the difference between the calendar year and the solar year to a negligible amount).

The agricultural year was quite different. For the medieval peasant, Winter was the first season. It ran from Michaelmas (September 29) to Christmas. Christmas was reckoned to last the full twelve days from Christmas Day until Epiphany (January 6), and working people commonly had this period off from work. The next season, from Epiphany to Easter, was called Lent. Lent derived from the Anglo-Saxon word for Spring, so named from the lengthening of the days. The term was later adopted by the Church to designate the season of religious penance from Ash Wednesday until Easter. The term Spring did not come into common use until the Protestant Reformation of the sixteenth century did away with the Catholic observance of Lent. Easter lasted from Easter Sunday until Hocktide, which fell on the Monday and Tuesday a week after Easter. As with Christmas, working people commonly had this period free. Afterwards came Summer, which lasted from Hocktide until Lammas (August 1). The final season of the year was called Harvest; it ran from Lammas until Michaelmas. The terms Autumn and Fall began coming into use in the sixteenth century, probably owing to the waning influence of agricultural life. Sometimes the year was simply thought of as consisting of two seasons: Winter, from September to February, and Summer, from March to August.

In addition to the seasons, the year was shaped by the cycle of holidays and festival seasons. In the Middle Ages every official holiday was theoretically religious—literally a holy day—although even religious

THE KING GRANTS AN ANNUITY TO CHAUCER, 1367

From the king to all to whom [these letters shall come], greetings. Know that by our special grace and for the good service which our beloved yeoman Geoffrey Chaucer has rendered and will render in the future, we grant him twenty marks every year, to be received from our Exchequer in equal portions on the days of Saint Michael and Easter for his entire life. . . . Witnessed by the king at the castle of Queensborough on the 20th day of June.

Translated by J. L. Forgeng from the French in Martin M. Crow and Clair C. Olson, *Chaucer Life-Records* (Austin: University of Texas Press, 1966), 123.

festivals had secular aspects. In addition to the holidays familiar to us today, like Christmas and Easter, there were many commemorative days that are less well known. In particular, there was a multitude of saint's days in honor of the various saints and other holy figures; these were sometimes called feasts or feast days—the term feast was originally another word for festival. Feast days were occasions for conviviality and plentiful food and drink, which is how the word acquired its modern sense. A few particularly important saints had two or more feast days, commemorating different events in their lives. These commemorative days were extremely numerous, and only the most important were actually observed as official holidays. These days were observed in a similar manner to Sundays, with church services in the morning and leisure in the afternoon. The afternoon before a holy day might be a half-holiday and was supposed to be observed by abstaining from meat.

Reckoning Dates

Individual days could be reckoned much as they are today, for example, "xi November" or "xi of November." Similarly, one might identify a day as "the last day in July." A more learned way was to use the Roman system. This method reckoned days in relation to the Kalends ("kl.": the first of every month), the Nones ("N.": the 5th, but the 7th in March, May, July, and October), and the Ides ("Id.": the 13th, but the 15th in March, May, July, and October). The date was determined by counting forward to the next of these three days, including the day being reckoned. Thus, "xi November" could also be "iii Id. Nov."; "xv November" could be "xvii kl. Dec."; "i December" would simply be "kl. Dec."

A more common means of reckoning was according to feast days. The Feast of St. Martin was November 11. The Vigil or Eve of the Feast of St. Martin was November 10. The Morrow or Second Day of the Feast of St. Martin was November 12. The Third of St. Martin was November 13, and so on. Alternatively, a day might be identified as "Monday next after Martinmas," "the Tuesday before the Feast of St. Martin," and so on.

The reckoning of years may have been important in urban and aristo-cratic circles, but it was less important for the lower reaches of society—the poorer commons probably had only a rough idea of their own age at any given time. There were two principal means of reckoning years. One was by Anno Domini, which differed from the modern system only in that it considered the new year to begin on March 25. The other common means of reckoning, particularly in legal contexts, was by regnal year: Edward III came to the throne in 1327, so that 1350 was called "the 24th year of the reign of Edward III."

A MEDIEVAL CALENDAR

On the following calendar, major feasts are listed in **boldface**: these are the days that people would most likely have as holidays, although customs and terms of employment varied from place to place.[10] In addition to the fixed feasts listed here there were two important holidays that varied from community to community. The first was the Dedication Day of the parish church (that is, the day of the saint to whom the church was dedicated), the other was Fair Day, since many towns had a certain day or days in the year when they were permitted to hold a fair. Fairs were most often held during the summer, but some took place during the winter months. Not every saint's day is listed in this calendar, and some that are listed were not necessarily very familiar outside of ecclesiastical circles.

January

January was a month of relative leisure: the winter planting was over, and the spring planting had not yet begun. Such tasks as were done in January were not time sensitive, and fell into the category of maintenance: repair of home buildings, mending tools, hedging and ditching around fields to keep animals out, and so on.

  1 **The Circumcision of Christ** (*New Year*). This, rather than Christmas Day, was the primary occasion during the year for giftgiving.

  5 *Edward the Confessor.*

  6 **Epiphany** (*Twelfth Day*). This was the Twelfth Day after Christmas, and the end of the Christmas season. It commemorated the occasion on which the Three Kings brought their gifts to the infant Jesus. The evening before Twelfth Day was called Twelfth Night, and was an occasion for riotous merrymaking.

13 *St. Hilary the Bishop.*

15 *St. Maure the Abbot.*

16 *St. Marcel Pope and Martyr.*

17 *St. Supplis the Bishop and St. Anthony.*

18 *St. Prisce the Virgin.*

19 *St. Wolston the Bishop.*

20 *Sts. Fabian and Sebastian.* St. Sebastian had been put to death by archers and was therefore the patron saint of archers.

21 *St. Annice (Agnes) the Virgin.*

22 *St. Vincent the Martyr.*

24 *St. Timothy.*

25 *The Conversion of St. Paul.* This feast commemorated the occasion on which Paul, originally a persecutor of Christians, was converted to Christianity.

27 *St. Julian the Bishop.*

30 *St. Batilde the Queen.*

31 *St. Ignace the Bishop and Martyr.*

February

At this time the ground was soft enough to allow plowing to resume in preparation for the Spring, or Lenten, crop of oats, barley, peas, and beans, which had to be sown by about the end of March. For this purpose, cattle were driven out of the previous year's fallow fields; they were also put out of the meadows to make way for the new year's hay.

To prepare the fields, the land was first plowed. This involved hitching a plow to one or more horses or oxen to pull it up and down the fields. The plow had a knife-like coulter projecting downwards that cut through the ground, creating a trench called a furrow. The plow also had an angled mouldboard that cast dirt up sideways out of the furrow. Afterwards, the husbandman would sow the crops, walking through the fields with a box of seeds and casting them into the furrows. Finally, the ground was harrowed: a large wooden frame was hitched to a horse and dragged over the fields; this pulled the loose dirt into the furrows to cover up the seeds.

1 *St. Bride (Bridget) the Virgin.*

2 **The Purification of Mary** (*Candlemas*). This feast commemorated the churching of Mary after the birth of Christ. Churching was a ritual observed by women after childbirth in which they bore a candle to church. This day was therefore observed by the bearing of candles, and was also known as Candlemas.

3 *St. Blase Bishop and Martyr.*

4 *St. Agatha the Virgin.*

5 *Sts. Vedast and Amande the Bishops.*

10 *St. Scholaste the Virgin.*

14   *St. Valentine.* In Chaucer's day as today, this day was associated with love and romance. One of Chaucer's poems hints that there may have been a custom of "choosing one's Valentine" as was done in later centuries.

16   *St. Julian the Virgin.*

22   *The Cathedration of St. Peter.* This holy day commemorated St. Peter's establishment as the Bishop of Antioch.

24   **St. Matthias the Apostle.**

29   *St. Oswald the Bishop and Confessor.*

• *Shrove Tuesday:* This day was one of the movable feasts, being dependent on the date of Easter. It fell six weeks and five days before Easter, between February 3 and March 9. Shrove Tuesday was the last day before Lent.

• *Ash Wednesday:* This was the day after Shrove Tuesday and the first day of Lent, which lasted until Easter. Lent was a season of religious penance: all Christians were supposed to abstain from eating meat and having sexual contact for the duration of Lent. The day was named from the custom of placing ashes on one's head as a sign of penance. The following Wednesday, Friday, and Saturday were Ember Days, days of particular fasting and penance.

March

The work of planting the Lenten crops continued in this month; they were to be sown by Annunciation or Easter. Military campaigns tended to begin in March or April after the harsh winter weather had subsided. At about Easter time, the sheep were put out to their pastures once again.

1   *St. David.*

7   *Sts. Perpetua and Felice the Virgins.*

12   *St. Gregory.*

17   *St. Patrick.*

18   **St. Edward the King and Confessor.**

20   *St. Cuthbert the Bishop and Confessor.*

21   *St. Benet (Benedict) the Abbot and Confessor.*

25   **The Annunciation** (*Feast of Our Lady in Lent*). In England the number of the year changed on this day.

• **Palm Sunday:** This day was one week before Easter. It commemorated the arrival of Christ into Jerusalem just before the Crucifixion: the parishioners would bear rushes or willow wands into church (palm leaves being hard to come by in medieval England).

• *Shere Thursday:* The Thursday before Easter. This was traditionally a day for almsgiving.

- *Good Friday:* The Friday before Easter.
- *Holy Saturday:* The day before Easter.
- **Easter:** The date of Easter is variable because it is based on the Jewish calendar. This calendar follows the cycles of the moon rather than the solar year of the calendar we inherited from the Romans. Easter falls on the first Sunday after the first full moon on or after 21 March; if the full moon is on a Sunday, Easter is the next Sunday. This means that Easter comes between March 22 and April 25. Easter marks the end of Lent. It was commonly a quarter-day, on which one-quarter of the annual rent for a landholding was due.
- *Hocktide:* Hocktide consisted of Hock Monday (also called Rope Monday), Hock Tuesday (also called Hockday), and Hock Wednesday, the three days a week after Easter. Hocktide was apparently celebrated, as in later centuries, by the young men and maidens of the village catching people in the street with a rope and forcing them to pay a small ransom.

April

By about this time the spring planting was complete, allowing the farmer to turn to the task of preparing the fallow fields for the next year's crop; the fields were plowed two or three times before harvest time. At about this time the woman of the house began her dairy work, as the cows had calved by now and were producing milk.

2   *St. Mary the Egyptian.*

3   *St. Richard the Bishop and Confessor.*

4   *St. Ambrose the Bishop and Confessor.*

6   *St. Sixtus.*

13   *St. Eufemie.*

14   *Sts. Tiburce and Valerian.*

19   *St. Alphege Bishop and Martyr.*

23   **St. George the Martyr.** St. George, famous for having slain a dragon, was also the patron saint of soldiers and of England.

25   **St. Mark the Evangelist.**

26   *St. Clete the Pope and Martyr.*

28   *St. Vital the Martyr.*

May

This was regarded as the first month of summer. In this season, the time pressures of agricultural work were somewhat diminished until the hay harvest began. At some point in this season, typically May Day, Ascension, or Whitsun, there would be a festival to welcome the arrival of summer. The festival often involved gathering branches and flowers to decorate the village, and choosing a Summer Lord and Lady to preside over the festivities.

  1 **Sts. Philip and Jacob the Apostles** (*May Day*).

  3 **The Discovery of the Cross** (*Holy Rood Day in May, Crouchmass*).

  6 *St. John at Port Latin.* This commemorated the occasion when the Emperor Domitian attempted unsuccessfully to have John the Evangelist boiled in oil at the Porta Latina in Rome.

10 *Sts. Gordian and Epimache.*

12 *Sts. Nere Achille and Pancras.*

19 *St. Dunstan the Bishop and Confessor.*

25 *Sts. Urban and Aldhelm the Bishops.*

26 **St. Austin** (Augustine) **the Bishop and Confessor.**

28 *St. Germain the Bishop and Confessor.*

31 *St. Purnel the Virgin.*

- *Rogation Sunday:* This day fell five weeks after Easter, between April 26 and May 30.
- *Rogation Days* (*Gang Days*): This was the Monday to Wednesday between Rogation Sunday and Ascension Day. The Rogation Days were an occasion for asking divine forgiveness of sins. On these days the parishioners would process around the boundaries of the parish, bearing a cross and banners to the sound of the church bells; the ceremony helped preserve the knowledge of the extent of the parish.
- **Ascension Day** (*Holy Thursday*): This was the Thursday after Rogation Sunday, between April 30 and June 3.
- **Whitsunday** (*Pentecost*): This fell on the Sunday ten days after Ascension, between May 10 and June 13. The Monday, Tuesday, and Wednesday following could also be holidays. The Wednesday, Friday, and Saturday following were all Ember Days, to be observed with fasting and penance.

June

This was a month for weeding the fields and for sheepshearing. After a year of poor harvests, hard times would tend to set in around June and last until the grain harvest came in during August and September. Traditionally, the hay harvest began after Midsummer Day.

1 *St. Nichomede the Martyr.*

2 *Sts. Marcelin and Peter.*

5 *St. Boniface the Bishop.*

8 *Sts. Medard and Gildard.*

11   *St. Barnabas the Apostle.*

14   *St. Basil the Bishop and Confessor.*

15   *St. Vitus.*

16   *St. Cyriac.*

17   *St. Botulf.*

18   *Sts. Mark and Marcellian.*

19   *St. Gervase.*

22   *St. Alban the Martyr.*

23   *St. Etheldred the Virgin and Martyr.*

24   **The Nativity of St. John the Baptist** (*Midsummer*). The holiday would be celebrated with gathering of greenery and with dancing, perhaps also with bonfires. This festival was often an important civic occasion marked by a variety of festivities and displays of communal identity. It was commonly a quarter-day on which quarterly rents came due.

26   *Sts. John and Paul.*

28   *St. Leo the Pope and Confessor.*

29   **Sts. Peter and Paul the Apostles.**

30   *Commemoration of St. Paul the Apostle.*

- **Trinity Sunday:** This fell one week after Whitsun, between May 17 and June 20.

- **Corpus Christi Day:** This was the Thursday after Trinity Sunday, between May 21 and June 24. It was instituted in honor of the sacrament of Communion. In towns this day was often celebrated with major civic festivities, including elaborate religious plays.

July

This month was dominated by the hay harvest. The grass in the meadows had been allowed to grow long; then the men would go out and cut it down with scythes, lay it out in the sun to dry, stack it, and cart it indoors for storage. Hay was of great economic importance, as it would provide the fodder on which animals were kept during the following winter.

2   *St. Swithun.*

7   **The Translation of St. Thomas the Martyr.** This day commemorated the occasion when Thomas à Becket's bones were removed from their burial place to a holy shrine. Thomas, the Archbishop of Canterbury, had been assassinated in 1170 and was England's most venerated saint—a pilgrimage to his shrine is the narrative context of Chaucer's *Canterbury Tales*.

14   *St. Metheldred the Virgin and Martyr.*

17   *St. Kenelm the King.*

18 *St. Arnulf the King.*

20 *St. Margaret the Virgin and Martyr.*

22 **St. Mary Magdalene.**

23 *St. Appolinar the Martyr.*

24 *St. Christine the Virgin and Martyr.*

25 **St. James the Apostle**; *St. Christopher.*

26 *St. Ann.*

27 *Feast of the Seven Sleepers.* The sleepers were seven young Christian men who, according to legend, were walled up alive in a cave and found alive when the wall was opened 112 years later.

28 *St. Sampson.*

29 *Sts. Felix, Simplis, and Faustin.*

31 *St. Neot.*

August

The arrival of August marked the end of the hay harvest and the beginning of the harvest of grain. The grain was cut, bound into sheaves, stacked, and carted indoors for storage. It was harvested with a sickle rather than a scythe and was cut relatively high, leaving a long stem of straw. The straw was later cut with scythes to provide material for thatching, making hats and baskets, strewing on floors, stuffing beds, and other uses. This was the most demanding season of the year for the farmer. Temporary workers were often hired, and women and children commonly helped with binding and stacking, in order to finish harvesting by Michaelmas. August and September were the worst months for the plague.

1 **St. Peter ad Vincula** (*Lammas*). This holy day was named in commemoration of miracles performed by the chains (*vincula* in Latin) in which Peter had been bound while imprisoned in Rome.

2 *St. Stephen the Pope.*

4 *St. Dominic.*

5 *St. Oswald the King and Martyr.*

7 *St. Donate.*

8 *St. Cyriac.*

9 *St. Roman the Martyr.*

10 **St. Lawrence the Martyr.**

11 *St. Tyburce the Martyr.*

13 *St. Hypolite.*

15 **The Assumption of Our Lady.**

20 *St. Oswin the King.*

23 *St. Timothy.*

24 **St. Bartholomew.**

25 *St. Louis.*

28 *St. Austin the Bishop (Augustine of Hippo).*

29 *Beheading of St. John the Baptist.*

31 *St. Cuthburg the Virgin.*

September

In this month the harvest would be finished. When the weather began to get wetter, more days might be spent indoors threshing the grain—beating it with flails to crack open the husks. The husks, or chaff, were then separated from the grain by winnowing, either fanning the grain to blow away the chaff or tossing it up in a basket. The grain was stored and could later be boiled in a broth, ground in a mill to make flour, or brewed up as ale. September and October were also the time for gathering fruit. Warfare tended to diminish in September or October, as the armies sought their winter quarters.

1 *St. Giles.*

5 *St. Bertin.*

8 **Nativity of Our Lady** (*Our Lady Day in Harvest*).

14 **Exaltation of the Cross** (*Holy Rood Day in Harvest*). The following Wednesday, Friday, and Saturday were Ember Days, observed with fasting and penance.

16 *St. Edith the Virgin.*

17 *St. Lambert.*

20 *St. Eustace.*

21 **St. Matthew the Apostle.**

22 *St. Maurice.*

26 *Sts. Justin and Cyprian.*

Threshing grain. Italian, c. 1400 (TS Casanatense, f. lxxxvii). McLean.

29 **St. Michael the Archangel** (*Michaelmas*). This day marked the end of the agricultural year, at which time the annual accounts were cast up; it was also a quarter-day on which the last installment of rent came due.

30 *St. Jerome.*

October

During this month husbandmen began to plow in preparation for the winter planting of wheat and rye.

1 *St. Remigius.*

2 *St. Leodegar the Bishop and Confessor.*

4 *St. Francis the Confessor.*

6 *St. Faith the Virgin and Martyr.*

9 *St. Dennis.*

15 *St. Wolfran the Bishop and Confessor.*

18 **St. Luke the Evangelist.**

21 *Feast of the 11,000 Virgins.* According to legend, these pious Christian virgins had been martyred in Cologne.

25 *Sts. Crispin and Crispianus.*

28 **Sts. Simon and Jude the Apostles.**

31 *St. Quentin the Martyr.*

November

The winter seed was supposed to be planted by All Hallows, or by Martinmas at the latest. Martinmas traditionally marked the beginning of the slaughter and preserving of extra livestock for the winter; the remaining livestock were housed for the winter.

1 **All Hallows (Hallowmas).** This holy day was dedicated to all the holy people of the Christian religion—hallow was another word for a saint.

2 **All Souls.** On this day people were supposed to pray for the souls of the dead, to help speed their way through their time of penance in Purgatory.

6 *St. Leonard the Abbot and Confessor.*

11 *St. Martin the Bishop and Confessor (Martinmas).*

13 *St. Brice the Bishop.*

16 *St. Edmund the Archbishop.*

17 *St. Hugh the Bishop.*

20 **St. Edmund the King and Martyr.**

22 *St. Cecily the Virgin and Martyr.*

23 *St. Clement the Pope.*

25 **St. Katherine the Virgin and Martyr.**

30 **St. Andrew.**

- *Advent:* This began on the fourth Sunday before Christmas and lasted until Christmas Eve. The truly pious might observe a fast from meat during this season.

December

This was one of the more leisurely months in the agricultural year: the livestock had been housed, all planting was over, and people could look forward to the celebrations of Christmas.

4 *St. Barbara.*

6 **St. Nicholas the Bishop and Confessor.** This day was sometimes celebrated by the choosing of a "boy bishop" as a mock ruler to preside over topsy-turvy merrymaking.

7 *St. Ambrose.*

8 **Feast of the Conception of Our Lady.**

13 *St. Lucy the Virgin and Martyr.* The following Wednesday, Friday, and Saturday were "Ember Days," observed with particular fasting and penance.

21 **St. Thomas the Apostle.**

25 **Christmas.** The Christmas season, lasting until Twelfth Day, was a time for celebrations, including games, music, dancing, plays, and colorful decorations. It was also a quarter-day when quarterly rents came due.

26 *St. Stephen the Martyr.*

27 *St. John the Apostle and Evangelist.*

28 *Feast of the Holy Innocents* (*Childermas*). This feast commemorated the children slaughtered by King Herod in his attempt to slay the infant Jesus. Sometimes this was celebrated by choosing a boy bishop as on St. Nicholas Day (December 6).

29 **St. Thomas the Archbishop and Marty.**

31 *St. Silvester the Pope and Confessor.*

NOTES

1. On mornings, see G. G. Coulton, *Medieval Panorama* (New York: Macmillan, 1938), 302; G. T. Salusbury-Jones, *Street Life in Medieval England* (Oxford: Pen in Hand, 1938), 171.

2. On daily labor, see Barbara Hanawalt, *Growing Up in Medieval London: The Experience of Childhood in History* (New York: Oxford University Press, 1993), 177; Christopher Dyer, *Standards of Living in the Later Middle Ages* (Cambridge: Cambridge University Press, 1989), 224.

3. On evenings, see Robert Mannyng, *Handlyng Synne*, ed. F. J. Furnivall (London: Kegan Paul, Trench and Trübner, 1901, 1903), l. 4712; C. Pendrill, *London Life in the 14th Century* (London: Allen and Unwin, 1925), 40; Hanawalt, *Growing Up*, 30.

4. On the weekly schedule, see Pendrill, *London Life*, 171; Mannyng, *Handlyng Synne*, ll. 845 ff.; *Dives and Pauper*, ed. Priscilla Heath Barnum, Early English Texts Society 275, 280 (London: Oxford University Press, 1976, 1980), 1.287.

5. On Sundays, see Pendrill, *London Life*, 171.

6. On Sunday afternoons, see G. R. Owst, *Preaching in Medieval England* (Cambridge: Cambridge University Press, 1926), 179; *Dives and Pauper* 1.293–94; Mannyng, *Handlyng Synne*, ll. 985 ff.

7. On religious services, see Mannyng, *Handlyng Synne*, ll. 4260, 1045; John Mirk, *Instructions for Parish Priests*, ed. E. Peacock. Early English Texts Society 31 (London: Kegan Paul, Trench and Trübner, 1868), ll. 404 ff.; Owst, *Preaching in Medieval England*, 144–45.

8. On confession, see Mirk, *Instructions*, ll. 236 ff., 771 ff., 805, 1590 ff.; Mannyng, *Handlyng Synne*, ll. 4783 ff., 10297 ff., 10300, 11607. See also W. A. Pantin, *The English Church in the Fourteenth Century* (Cambridge: Cambridge University Press, 1955).

9. R. H. Robbins, *Secular Lyrics of the XIVth and XVth Centuries* (Oxford: Clarendon Press, 1952), 62.

10. These are based on the holidays listed in a Masons' Ordinance of 1474 (L. F. Salzman, *Building in England Down to 1540* [Oxford: Clarendon Press, 1952], 64–65) and on those mentioned in the journals of John Dernell and John Boys, two Norfolk carters of the early fifteenth century (*Norfolk Archaeology* 14 [1904], 125–57).

5

MATERIAL CULTURE

WORK, TECHNOLOGY, AND THE ECONOMY

Agriculture

Most people in medieval England derived their living from the land. Local practices varied, but the central part of the country was cultivated under was what is now called the three-field system of crop rotation. The village agricultural land would be divided into three large fields (each typically over a hundred acres), with every landholder having his holdings scattered among the three. The agricultural year began in October: in October–November one field would be planted with "winter crops" of wheat and rye; the following February–March the second field would be planted with "spring crops" of oats, barley, peas, and beans; the third field would lie fallow, serving as pasturage for livestock, who enriched the soil with their manure. The crops were harvested in August–September. When the cycle began again in October, the formerly fallow field would be planted with the winter crop; in the spring, the former winter field would be planted with the spring crop; and the former spring field would lie fallow. This system allowed the soil to renew its nutrients to maximize productivity, as well as balancing out the diet by supplementing carbohydrate-rich grains with protein-rich legumes (peas and beans) and animal foods (meat and dairy).

The staple grain was wheat, which has a high gluten content that made for appealingly light bread; it also has the highest caloric content by volume. However, it does poorly in marginal soils or poor weather. Rye and oats are hardier crops, and better suited to the less fertile regions of England, although they produced a coarser and heavier bread, and are less nutritive as bread grains. Barley was grown chiefly for brewing ale. Sometimes farmers would hedge their bets by sowing mixed seed: masclin, for example, was a mixture of wheat with rye, and the resulting mix of grains was used for making a cheaper form of bread.

The most important livestock in this system were the cattle. Female calves were raised to become cows, providing offspring and milk. Male calves could be used in one of three ways. A very few were allowed to grow up as breeding bulls. A larger number were gelded to become working oxen, useful for pulling plows and other heavy vehicles. The majority were destined to become beef: they were gelded while young, and slaughtered once they were fully grown.

Other important livestock included horses, pigs, sheep, and goats. Depending on local conditions, horses could be more efficient draft animals than oxen, and of course they were also valued as riding animals. Pigs were prized as a source of meat, and they could be pastured in wooded areas or fed with household scraps, allowing the farming family to maximize its use of resources. Sheep and goats were raised for meat and milk, and sheep also provided wool; they were easier to graze than cattle in the highland zones around England's periphery. The last major component in the agricultural equation was poultry, especially chickens, geese, and ducks, providing meat, eggs, and feathers.

Clothmaking

Although traditional feudalism had been geared toward grain agriculture, sheep were playing a growing part in England's economy. Wool could be a better cash crop than grain: it required comparatively little labor to produce, it traveled well, and there was a constant demand for this staple fabric of medieval clothing, especially since English sheep yielded particularly fine wool. Sheep-raising provided relatively little employment on the land itself: a single shepherd could look after the sheep on an acreage which would require many people for tending crops. However, the wool trade stimulated secondary economic activity, as the raw material required multiple stages of processing to make it ready for wearing. The various stages of clothmaking constituted one of the major engines of economic activity after agriculture itself.

The first stage was to convert raw wool into thread, a cottage industry that provided many women with extra income. The fleece first had to be washed, and then brushed out with "cards" to untangle the fibers. Once this was done, the fibers were wound around a distaff, and teased out and twisted into thread using a weighted spindle, rotated by hand. Peasant women often carried a distaff and spindle as they did their work around the house, to devote idle moments to this simple but time-consuming task.

Wool could also be spun more efficiently on a hand-powered spinning wheel.

The thread was sold to the growing cloth industry, which was one of the most mechanized parts of the English economy. Cloth was woven on sophisticated horizontal hand-looms and fulled (cleansed and thickened) in water-powered fulling mills. Clothmaking was not yet an export industry in England, so English-made cloth was only for the home market. Wool was exported raw, bound for foreign looms, especially those of Flanders; but English weavers were gaining in skill, and over the next few centuries they would come to dominate the trade in woolen cloth.

Ironworking

After clothmaking, the most important industry in medieval England was probably metalworking, particularly with iron. Although iron employed considerably fewer people than cloth, it had broad ramifications as a generator of economic activity and as an essential component in the tools that made other technologies possible.

Iron was mined domestically, although the quality of the English metal was not as high as that which came from some other parts of Europe. Iron came in the form of an ore in which the iron was chemically combined with oxygen, and physically mixed up with other matter, particularly silicon-based compounds. The process of purifying this ore was one of the most subtle technologies in use in Chaucer's England. Iron purification, or smelting, achieved complex chemical effects even though there was no understanding of the underlying chemistry—the modern concept of elements would not be discovered for almost another half-millennium.

First, the ore was subjected to intense heat in the presence of carbon. This separated the iron from the oxygen as the oxygen bonded with the carbon to make carbon dioxide. The process required a very hot fire, fueled by charcoal; since charcoal consists of almost pure carbon, it also provided the carbon for the carbon dioxide. This left pure iron mixed up with silicon impurities. Once the temperature reached 1100–1200°C, the impurities would melt and start to flow out of the metal. However, some of the impurities, known as slag, would remain trapped in the metal. The smelted metal had to be hammered repeatedly to drive out as much of the slag as possible.

The product of this process was wrought iron, which was sold to smiths and other metalworkers. Smiths were among the most common craftsmen, as their work was essential for making and repairing the tools on which everyone else relied. Every village would have at least one blacksmith, who ranked among the more important peasants in the community.

Iron was still somewhat expensive, and used sparingly if widely: an agricultural spade would have an iron tip to facilitate digging, but the rest of the blade and handle were made of wood. By Chaucer's day, early versions of the blast furnace were in use in parts of Europe. This technology would increase the efficiency of iron production by raising the ore to a temperature where the iron itself would melt, but it would not become common in England until the 1500s.

Other Crafts and Trades

Agriculture generated substantial secondary employment for people involved in transforming agricultural produce into food, especially in the towns, where households lacked the means to provide their own food. Grinding grains to make flour was a significant sector in the economy, performed in mills powered by water or wind. Millers were to be found in every village, where they ranked with the blacksmith as one of the most important community figures. They could also be found in and around the towns. Other tradesmen involved in food processing and retail included bakers, cooks, fishmongers, poulterers, butchers, and brewers.

Another major clustering of trades involved the making of apparel, including weavers, dyers, tailors, skinners, tanners, leatherworkers, glovers, furriers, and shoemakers. House construction supported specialized carpenters, masons, brickmakers and bricklayers, plasterers, slaters, and tilers.

Many crafts were organized around particular materials or technologies. Horners used the horns of cattle to make a variety of products. The material was the closest medieval equivalent to plastic: it is translucent, watertight, smooth, resistant to breakage, and it can be partially molded when subjected to heat. It was used for lantern-panes, cups, inkhorns, spoons, and combs. Metalworkers specialized in particular metals: iron, copper alloys, tin, lead, or precious metals. Woodworkers included carpenters, joiners (specializing in jointed furniture), turners (making furniture, tableware, and other household items on lathes), and coopers (barrelmakers).

Tradesmen furnished a variety of services: ostlers (innkeepers) provided food, drink, and lodging for travelers; carters and porters transported goods; water-carriers brought vessels of water door-to-door in the towns to supply the household; tinkers and grinders repaired and maintained household items. At the margin of English society was the semi-independent world of the maritime economy: boatmen providing local transport on rivers; sailors, fishermen, and merchants traveling around the coast and overseas.

Craftsmen generally sold their own wares from their shops, which doubled as both workshop and store, but many goods were sold through various layers of retailers and middlemen. At the uppermost level were the international merchants who imported goods for which the domestic supply was nonexistent, insufficient to meet demand, or of lower quality than the imports. They dealt in such luxury items as wines, spices, fine cloths, and furs, as well as bulk goods such as grains, fish, salt, and metals.

Buying turnips from an itinerant vendor. Italian,
c. 1390 (TS Paris, f. 43). McLean.

Goods acquired in bulk might be retailed or brokered through a variety
of lesser merchants: grocers purchased bulk quantities of various goods,
especially foodstuffs and spices, for retail to the public; mercers traded in
a variety of household wares, especially textiles. At the lowest level, goods
were sold on the streets and door-to-door by itinerant vendors: peddlers
and hucksters (often women) sold items such as fruits and vegetables in
the streets of the towns, while chapmen traveled from village to village
carrying wares such as linen cloth, laces, pins, and other small domestic
wares to sell to rural households. Agricultural goods were also bought
and sold at weekly town markets, and a wide variety of products were
sold at annual fairs at major towns around the country.

Crafts and trades in the towns were regulated by guilds. Each craft or
trade had its own local guild; guild responsibilities included monitoring
product quality, certifying the practitioners, overseeing wages, prices,
and working conditions, and controlling the supply of labor. The guild
was run by the masters of that trade, and the government of many towns,
including London, was through the leaders of the most important guilds.

Standards of Living

Overall, the economy and standard of living in fourteenth-century
England had more in common with the modern Third World than with

modern Europe. Discrepancies in income were comparable to those in industrialized countries today, but a much higher portion of the population was poor. Although an industrial base was growing during this period, industry in the sense of mass mechanized production was practically nonexistent. Water-powered mills had long been used for grinding grain, and were increasingly being used for fulling cloth, grinding metal ores, powering bellows, and a few other applications, but the overwhelming bulk of manufacturing processes were still done by human hands.

As a result, anything that is now mass-produced by machine was much more expensive in Chaucer's world than it is today. Plain woolen cloth, suitable for the clothes of a respectable peasant, at a shilling per yard would cost a laborer three days' wages for a single yard. On the other hand, because wages were low, anything requiring more labor than materials today was relatively inexpensive—domestic service is a prime example.

Money, Income, and Prices

Currency was issued exclusively in the form of coins, and coinage was all of silver or gold. For this reason even the smallest coin was relatively valuable. However, not all transactions were dependent on cash. Merchants with widespread international connections were able to transfer funds through personal letters of credit. Such a letter would allow the holder to draw cash from someone who trusted the author of the letter. At the local level, neighbors in both villages and towns commonly engaged in credit transactions with each other.

The design of silver coins was generally the same regardless of date or denomination: on the front was a stylized face of the king, and the reverse bore the image of a cross; the only variations were the name of the king (whoever was reigning when it was minted) and the size of the coin. Gold coins were more diverse and quite valuable: the smallest was equivalent to a laborer's wages for an entire week.

The value of a coin varied according to the actual amount of silver or gold it contained: each coin was made to a specific standard of weight and purity that guaranteed the quantity of precious metal. All coinage was alloyed to a greater or lesser extent, but English coins were generally of consistently high quality during this period. By contrast, the French kings had fallen into the bad habit of mixing more base metal into the coinage whenever they needed to make their income stretch further. Each time this was done, it produced a dramatic surge in the apparent wealth of the French crown, but it also guaranteed instant inflation. At the other end, unscrupulous individuals tried to make a profit by clipping or shaving tiny fragments from coins to capture some of the precious metal: the images on both sides of the coin helped to reveal whether a coin had been compromised in this way.

To complicate matters further, prices, particularly of staples, fluctuated greatly from year to year. Limited technologies and infrastructure for preserving, storing, and transporting foodstuffs meant that local weather conditions in a particular year had an enormous impact on food prices. After a good harvest, the price of grain could come down, while poor harvests sent it skyrocketing. The cost might double or halve from one year to the next, and these fluctuations in the price of grain rippled through the rest of the economy.

Such fluctuations meant that the cost of staples changed with each harvest, and as supplies increased or dwindled over the course of the year. Because bread and ale were the chief nutritional staples, government took an active role in overseeing their prices and quality. Regulations originating in the 1200s pegged the weight of a loaf of bread to the current cost of grain—the price of the loaf was fixed, so changing costs were reflected in a change in weight. Similarly the price of various grades of ale was stipulated in relation to the current price of barley.

English money was most often reckoned in pounds, shillings, and pence. Some denominations, such as the pound and the mark, existed only as moneys of account, used in reckoning but never existing as actual coins. Table 5.1 offers an idea of the relative value of the various denominations, but the modern equivalents should be taken as magnitudes rather than values: the differences between modern and fourteenth-century price structures make it impossible to derive a universally valid equivalence.

A clearer idea of the value of money can be had by comparing wages and prices. In Table 5.2, the column on the left represents pay in military service to the king, that on the right the income of civilian craftsmen and laborers.[1]

Laborers' wages were also subject to seasonal variation: they were paid more in the summer, when demand for labor was high and the extra daylight permitted longer hours of work. Wages were not always based entirely on money: sometimes the employer would provide food, lodging, or supplies (such as fuel or clothing) as part of the payment. Of course, many people were not paid wages at all: landowners, landholders, and independent tradesmen made whatever money their lands or professions yielded. Table 5.3 shows sample annual incomes for such people.[2]

Wages rose dramatically during Chaucer's lifetime. The Black Death drastically cut the supply of labor, and surviving wage-earners were in an advantageous market where labor had become more scarce and valuable, allowing them to negotiate better terms. In the 1340s, a skilled worker might earn 3d. a day; by the 1350s the figure was between 3 and 4d.; by the 1370s it was 4d., and by 1390 it had reached 5d. Scarcity of labor also encouraged employers to offer better benefits in the form of food allowances and other perquisites, and overall the standard of living for wage-earners in 1400 appears to have been significantly higher than it had been half a century before.

Table 5.1:
Relative Values of Fourteenth-Century Money

	Denomination	Monetary Value	Purchase Value	Rough $ Equivalent
Silver Coins	farthing (q.)	1/4 of a penny	1 loaf of bread	$1
	halfpenny (ob.)	1/2 of a penny	1 gallon of small ale	$2
	penny (d.)	20 (1/24 oz.) grams of 90% pure silver	1 lb. of butter	$4
	half-groat	2d. (2 pence)	1 day's earnings for an unskilled laborer	$8
	groat	4d. (4 pence)	1 day's earnings for a skilled laborer	$15
	shilling (s.)	12d. (12 pence)	1 day's earnings for a gentleman	$50
Gold Coins	quarter-noble, quarter-florin	1s. 8d.	1 lb. sugar or spice	$75
	half-noble, half-florin	3s. 4d.	1 year's rent for a floor in a townhouse	$150
	noble, florin	6s. 8d.	1 day's earnings for a lord	$300
Moneys of Account	mark (marc.)	13s. 4d., or 2/3 of a pound		$700
	pound (li.)	20s.	1 cart horse	$1,000

Table 5.2:
Sample Daily Wages

Bishop or Earl	6s. 8d.	Clerk	1s.
Baron or Banneret	4s.	Mason	5 1/2d.
Knight	2s.	Carpenter	4 1/2d.
Squire, Chaplain	1s.	Thatcher	4d.
Mounted Archer	6–8d.	Thatcher's Assistant	2 1/4d.
Archer	3–6d.	Agricultural Laborer	8d. at harvest, 3–4d. at other seasons
Page	2d.	Female Agricultural Laborer	2d.

Table 5.3:
Sample Yearly Incomes

Duke of Lancaster	£10,000	Petty Merchant	£10
Earl	£3,000	Abbot	£1,000
Knight	£40 or more	Craftsman	£5
Yeoman	£10	Husbandman	£4
Cottar	£1 from land	Laborer	£2

Governmental authorities tried to resist economic change, particularly change that benefited the poor at the expense of the rich. As early as 1349, Edward III issued an Ordnance of Laborers, seeking to fix wages at pre-Plague levels, and Parliament gave his decree statutory force in 1351 with a Statute of Laborers. Yet the effort was ultimately doomed, in spite of multiple supplementary laws issued over the following decades. Employers agreed that the rising cost of labor was unacceptable, but in the end they had to compete with each other in order to hire workers. Workers were required to swear obedience to the statute, but at Knightsbridge, outside of London, a carpenter who was engaged to make stocks to imprison those who refused to swear was himself paid at the illegal rate of 5 1/2d. a day.[3]

To gain an idea of the purchasing power of fourteenth-century incomes, one can compare them to the sample prices in Table 5.4.[4] Bear in mind that prices could vary drastically according to time and place (for example, city prices might be from 1 1/3 to 2 times as high as those elsewhere). Another important factor was the heavy reliance on secondhand wares. Most ordinary people could not afford to buy major items new, so used goods (especially clothing) constituted a large portion of the economy. Quality was also a factor: it is rarely possible to tell from a medieval account-book what quality of items the prices represent.

THE LIVING ENVIRONMENT

Medieval dwellings varied enormously, from the manorial complexes of the nobility to the hovels of the poor; yet to a modern observer even the most luxurious medieval home, however sumptuous, would probably seem short on comfort and convenience. Most medieval interiors would strike the modern observer as drafty, dim, and smoky, although medieval people took pride in their homes, decorating them according to their means and cleaning them regularly.

The Peasant Home

At the low end of the social scale, the typical peasant cottage had very few rooms—typically just one to three—and consisted of two or three bays,

Table 5.4:
Sample Prices of Goods and Services

Cow	9s.	Cart horse	20s.
Horse	40s.–70s.	Pig	3s. 2d.
Sheep	1s. 6d.	Hen	1 3/4d.
1 day's food for a lord	7d.	1 day's food for a squire	4d.
1 day's food for a yeoman	3d.	1 day's food for a servant	1d.
Ale, best quality (1 gal.)	1 1/2d.	Small ale (1 gal.)	1/2d.
Loaf of bread	1/4–1d.	Butter (1 lb.)	1d.
Roast pig	8d.	Roast hen	4d.
Eggs (10)	1d.	Leg of pork	4d.
Herrings (6–10)	1d.	Wine (1 gal.)	8–10d.
Pepper (1 lb.)	1s. 4d.	Oil (1 gal.)	1s. 4d.
Sugar (1 lb.)	1s. 7d.	Almonds (1 lb.)	3d.
Ginger (1 lb.)	2s. 3d.	Saffron (1 lb.)	14s.
Canvas (12 ells)	3s. 9 1/2d.	Linen (1 yd)	6d.
Wool, fine (1 yd.)	4s.	Wool, 2nd grade (1 yd.)	2s.
Breech	1d.	Gown	4–5s.
Russet gown	9d.	Kirtle and hood	1s. 4d.
Surcoat	2s.	Hose	20d.
Hood	4d.	Straw hat	6d.
Cap	7d.	Fustian shoes	6d.
Wax candles (1 lb.)	1s.	Tallow candles (1 lb.)	2d.
Eyeglasses	1/2d.	Stool	6d.
Knife	1 1/4d.	Wooden comb	1d.
Bible	£1-3	Ordinary book	2s.
Peasant house	£2-£7	Castle tower	£400
Rent for a craftsman's town-house	20s.	Rent for 1 acre (villeinage tenure)	3–9d.
Rent for 1–2 rooms	3–4s./year	Hire courier from London to Oxford	10d.

or framed construction units, measuring about 15′ × 15′ each. Longer versions of this house often sheltered not just the family but its livestock as well, albeit in the far end from the human occupants. An ordinary peasant cottage would have just two rooms for the inhabitants: a bedchamber serving as the private space of the household, and a multipurpose public room that served as workspace, kitchen, and eating area.

The frame of the peasant house was of joined timber, and the walls were commonly filled in with wattle and daub. In this technique, the spaces between the posts and beams were filled with wattling: long stakes fixed upright between lateral beams, with flexible sticks woven densely between them. The surface thus created was covered on both sides with daub: a mixture that combined clay for adhesion, sand for bulk, cow manure for elasticity, and straw or some similar fiber for strength. Alternatively, the walls might be made of turf (peat cuttings), cob (unbaked clay), or even stone, although this was beyond the means of the peasant except in places where building stone was locally abundant. Both the exterior and interior walls were typically coated in bright limewash: on the outside, the coating protected the daub from rain, while on the inside the bright walls helped brighten the room. The roof was thatched with reeds or straw, although wood shingles, tiles, or slate might be used if these were plentiful in the area. The house would typically have a floor of packed dirt or clay, and only one story; lofts under the rafters might provide additional space.

The ground on which a peasant house was built was called a toft, and for a well-to-do peasant household it might include a cobblestone courtyard and a few additional outbuildings for storage and housing for domestic animals such as horses, cows, and poultry. Behind the toft was a croft, a small plot of land used for the household garden and orchard, and for penning animals. Together the toft and croft were called a messuage.

Pillaging a house. Late fourteenth century (British Library MS Royal 20.C.VII, f. 41v). McLean.

The Village

In areas of woodland settlement, where land was held in compact units, the messuage might stand alone in the middle of the holding; but in champion lands a few dozen or more messuages clustered together as a village, usually with a parish church among them and perhaps a green. Surrounding the village were fields for agriculture and meadows for growing hay, and beyond them lay the uncultivated ground, often consisting of forested or marshy lands unsuitable for agriculture. Villages were mostly 400–600 people or less. Water was an important factor in making settlement possible, so most villages had a well or stream near the center, and households would have barrels or cisterns for storing the water they needed for daily use.

Homes of the Aristocracy

Toward the center of the village there might be a manor house belonging to the local lord. The dwellings of the medieval aristocracy varied as enormously as their incomes, but certain features were generally common to them all. Stone was the preferred material of construction, although the lesser aristocracy might have to be content with brick or even with a superior version of wattle and daub. The ideal roof was made of slate or tile, which was supported by wooden framing. The flooring might be of wood, tiles, or stone.

The central room of the aristocratic home was the hall, the most public space in the house. Here the members of the household interacted with each other and with the outside world: it was a place for transacting public business, for holding entertainments, and especially for eating formal meals. It was usually the largest room in the building and was often high as well, with no ceiling but open to the roof.

The hall had a high and a low end. At the high end was a raised dais that accommodated the high table used by the family and their favored guests. The area below the dais was for ordinary guests and servants. At the low end of the hall a wooden partition cut down on drafts; behind it were the main door to the outside and the doors to the service wing of the manor house (kitchen, larder, and other areas used by the household staff). Behind the dais there was access to the solar (a private room for the family) and other private chambers. These rooms might be located in their own wing of the building or above the hall. Below the main floor of the manor house there would often be a cellar serving as a cool storage area.

Although it was traditional for the family to eat in the hall, aristocrats increasingly chose to have their meals in the private section of the house. William Langland laments the trend in *Piers Plowman:*

> Desolate is the hall, every day in the week,
> Neither the lord nor the lady likes to sit there:

Now each rich man has a rule to eat by himself
In a privy parlor on account of the poor
Or in a chamber with a chimney, and leave the chief hall
That was made for meals, for men to eat in.[5]

The physical division of the aristocratic home by the hall dais was a major factor in organizing home life. The entire establishment was divided into the household (the public section of the house below the dais) and the chamber (the private section—the dais and beyond). Even for servants there was a distinction between the prestigious jobs of the chamber and the ordinary ones of the household.

Depending on the wealth of the owner, the manor house would sit at the center of a greater or lesser number of buildings grouped in a complex, often surrounded by a wall and perhaps a ditch. The complex included all the specialized facilities needed by the aristocratic household, such as bakery, brewery, stables, barns, cowshed, dovecotes, and granary. There might also be decorative gardens and peacocks to grace the grounds. There was often a pond stocked with fish for household consumption on fast days. The complex would normally have a well for water supply, and cisterns for storing water ready for use. Some manor houses had water catchment systems, with roof gutters to collect rainwater and a purifying apparatus to clarify it in the cisterns.

The Townhouse

The townhouse was different from both peasant and aristocratic dwellings. In construction the ordinary townhouse resembled the timber-framed peasant dwelling, commonly measuring about 12′ × 20′ with a garden of comparable size behind. Unlike the peasant house, it was at least two or three stories high, to economize on valuable urban land, and it was more likely to have a floor and a cellar as well as a wooden, tile, or slate roof— many towns forbade thatched roofs because of their vulnerability to fire.

If the house belonged to a craftsman or tradesman, the front door would lead into the shop. This shop might extend into the street during the day. Wares were placed on display out front, and some tradesmen actually did their work there—this was especially true of butchers, who were naturally disinclined to have the refuse of their work on the floor of their homes. The family lived in a room behind the shop or above it; upper floors could also be used for servants, apprentices, or tenants. The upper floors were accessible by stairs or ladders and sometimes projected over the street to make maximum use of limited urban space.

Most urban families probably lived in two rooms and a kitchen or less, and in many cases the building would be carved up among multiple tenants. Rich city-dwellers often had complexes comparable to condensed versions of aristocratic manor houses, consisting of several specialized buildings grouped around a courtyard, with a gateway leading to the street. It was also common for especially wealthy aristocratic families to have a permanent residence in London in addition to manor houses on their landed estates.

The Town

Townhouses were packed much closer together than peasant homes or manor houses; many were built as row housing. With multiple occupancy of a single building, urban density could be quite high. A large provincial town like Winchester had 29 people per acre within its walls and as many as 81 per acre in the center, greater than that of modern British cities. The largest town was London, with a pre-plague population that may have been as high as 80,000, though by the 1370s this figure had almost been halved. The next largest towns were Bristol with 9,500, York with 7,000, and Norwich with 6,000. Other towns all had fewer than 3,000 inhabitants.

The best streets were cobbled, often with a gutter running down the center. Lesser streets might be only of dirt and became very muddy in bad weather.

Water for cleaning and other non-consumption purposes could be drawn from rivers or streams flowing through the town. Drinking water was piped in from nearby sources and stored in cisterns and water towers. Town-dwellers might collect water from public fountains or purchase it from a professional water carrier, saving them the trouble of collecting it themselves. For a fee, they might have it piped directly to their homes, but this was expensive and only possible for those who lived close to existing water pipes.

Sanitation was a constant problem in spite of earnest efforts by town governments to regulate waste disposal. Numerous ordinances sought to restrict the dumping of rubbish in the streets, and official rakers had the job of carting rubbish and cleaning the streets, but these efforts were never enough to deal with the mass of waste produced in a medieval city. Consequently, the streets were often foul-smelling and littered with various sorts of waste.

Animals were another hazard. The animal population of a town was high, including horses for transportation and poultry for their meat and eggs. Pigs were a handy animal in a city, since they could be fed on household scraps, but they could also be downright hazardous: babies were occasionally bitten to death when a pig wandered into an unsupervised home.

Since townhouses commonly had gardens, there was a great deal of green space within a city. In addition, the division between a town and the country outside was not very great: even London measured only about half a mile by a mile and a half, and beyond its walls were fields. It was never a very far walk to the countryside. Many English towns were sur-rounded by walls, but by no means all—the custom was more common on the Continent, where the danger of war was always more imminent.

Domestic Interiors

All types of houses had windows to let in daylight. The wealthy cov-ered the window openings with paned glass, but the poor made do with mere shutters, open in daytime and closed at night. Some windows were constructed with glass in the upper part and shutters below. At night people relied on candles. The finest were made of beeswax, but most people had to be content with tallow, made of processed animal fat. Tallow was much cheaper than wax, as it was a by-product of meat consumption, but it burned less brightly and less cleanly. Candlesticks might be made of silver or of cheaper materials such as pewter, brass, or wood. Some were simple sockets on an angled spike, designed to be jammed into the timbers of the house. Candles were more complex to use than they are today: the wicks were not designed to burn up their own excess, as in a modern candle, so they had to be trimmed as they burned. Other sources of light included the rushlight—a rush steeped in fat and set alight—and the oil lamp, also generally fueled with animal fats. Lanterns were made with glass or horn windows, or pierced with many small holes.[6]

Fires were another essential facility in every house, since without them people could neither cook nor keep warm. Aristocratic and urban houses had fireplaces with chimneys, typically in the form of a smoke hood extending over the hearth, while peasant homes had only a raised firepit in the center of the room with a hole in the roof to let out smoke. Firewood was an important commodity for any household, although Londoners usually used charcoal. Mined coal was mostly restricted to industrial use, since its foul smoke makes it ill suited for use on an open fire.

At night, fires had to be either extinguished or banked—allowing the coals to smolder slowly so the fire could be easily relit in the morning. Banking involved reducing oxygen flow to the coals by covering them with ashes or with a curfew (cover-fire), a perforated ceramic lid placed over the coals. If the fire went out overnight, it might require a tedious rekindling with a flint and steel, although people generally preferred to ask their neighbors for some hot coals, carrying them home in a covered metallic firepan.

Interior walls were whitewashed with lime to brighten the room, and those who could afford it added a smooth layer of plaster. The homes of the wealthy were adorned with wall hangings, which served the double pur-pose of decoration and insulation. The very rich used tapestries for this pur-pose, but others contented themselves with painted cloths. Alternatively, decoration could be provided by wall paintings.

LONDON FIRE-SAFETY REGULATIONS, 1376

Precept was sent to each alderman to see that a large vessel of water be kept outside every house in case of fire, the season being very dry and hot, and further that ladders and hooks be provided and that thoroughfares be conveniently made.

Reginald R. Sharpe, *Calendar of Letter Books . . . of the City of London: Letter Book H* (London: John Edward Francis, 1907), 28.

The floor could be covered with straw or rushes, either loose or woven as mats. The wealthy often strewed the floor with sweet-smelling herbs and flowers. Interior surfaces were periodically dusted with canvas cloths, and washed down with hot water to kill fleas. The floors were swept with besom-style brooms made of birch or broom; even peasants swept their earthen floors, replacing the dirty straw with fresh.

Furnishings

Personal property for most people was very limited. A surviving inventory from a thirteenth-century butcher in Colchester lists a trestle table, two silver spoons, a cup, a tablecloth, two towels, a brass cauldron, a brass dish, a wash basin and ewer, a trivet, an iron candlestick, two beds, two gowns, a mantle, and two barrels, the total valued at £2 5s. 5d (this inventory was probably not entirely complete: since the butcher had a table, he probably also owned some benches or stools, and probably a lockable chest or coffer for his valuable silver spoons).[7]

By contrast, the inventory of a knight in 1374 lists the following items in the various parts of his manor complex:

Chamber: 7 full beds, 4 mattresses, a selection of blankets and bedspreads, a white coffer, two basins and a laver, a full set of plate armor for a man and war-gear for a horse, 3 habergeons, 4 ordinary helmets, a cloth sack and a leather sack.

Pantry and Buttery: Several silver bowls, a silver ewer, a collection of tablecloths, napkins, and towels, 3 canvas cloths, 12 barrels, 4 brass candlesticks, 2 tubs, 4 bottles, 4 leather pots.

Hall: 3 tables with benches, 2 basins with a laver, a brazier and a fire-fork.

Kitchen: Vessels and plates of pewter, brass bowls and plates, 3 iron spits, 1 cob-iron, a griddle and frying pan, a trivet, 2 hooks, a grater, 2 knives for the dressing board, 2 brass mortars and pestles.

Larder: a salting-trough, 30 pigs, 3 oxen, a salt-box, a table.

Bakehouse: a brewing vat, 3 leaden pots, 2 kneading troughs, a pail.

Lord's Chapel: a complete vestment with chalice, book, altarcloth.

Lord's Stable: 4 horses.

Cart Stable: 5 horses, 2 carts.

Cowshed: 12 oxen, 5 plows, 2 bulls, 19 cows, 10 steers and heifers, 5 calves, 1 cart, 78 pigs with boars.

Various Granges: 30 quarters wheat, 60 quarters barley, 90 quarters peas, 8 quarters rye, 40 quarters mixed grain and oats.[8]

The list is substantial yet still limited in comparison to a modern counterpart of such an aristocrat. Again, the inventory is not complete—no spoons or clothing are mentioned, for example.

The commonest item of furniture for storage was the chest. For greater usefulness, it might have removable shelves inside, a lock on the outside, or a small locked till inside at one end. Commoners relied on chests because they were simple, versatile, and relatively inexpensive. Aristocrats used them because their lives often involved travel from one residence to another, and chests could be readily transported. Storage was also provided by sacks and bags made of leather, linen, canvas, or wool. Clothes might be draped over horizontal poles when not in use. For seating, benches and stools were more common than chairs. Tables were typically boards set up on trestles, and could be taken down for transport or to open up floor space.

FROM A MANORIAL INVENTORY, 1352

Item, . . . in the chamber 2 benches, 1 shield. Item in the steward's chamber 1 bench. Item, in the larder, 2 troughs for salting meat, 1 block for cutting meat. Item in the chapel, 1 wooden altar, 1 superaltar, and 1 painted panel above the altar, 1 lectern, 1 bench. Item in the hall, 6 tables, 5 pairs of trestles, 4 benches, 1 worn bowl, 1 laver, 1 broken andiron. Item in the pantry 1 chest for bread, 1 vat, 2 canvases. Item in the buttery 2 casks . . . 2 pairs of trestles, 1 board for cups with trestles. Item in the kitchen, 3 brazen pots, . . . 2 worn pans, 1 cauldron . . . 2 tripods, 1 gridiron, 1 iron spit, 1 mortar with 2 pestles, 1 dressing-board, 1 flesh hook.

Item in the dairy, 1 bench . . . 1 table with 2 trestles, 1 table for drying cheese, 5 cheese vats, 2 pressing boards, 1 wooden bucket, 1 churn, 9 dishes, 9 plates, 12 saucers, 2 hanging tables, 1 press, 1 large jug, 1 broken tong.

Item in the bakehouse 1 tub for sifting, 2 hanging lead vats with wooden covers, 1 trough for pastry, 1 moulding board, 6 vats, 4 casks, 2 wide shallow tubs, 3 little troughs . . . 1 sieve for ale, 1 sieve for flour . . . 2 shovels for malt, 3 malt-stools, 1 bucket bound with iron for the well, 1 spout for the cistern, 1 leaded cistern, 2 hair cloths for the kiln.

Item in the granary, 2 wooden bushels bound with iron, 2 fans . . . 2 shovels for corn, 2 sieves, 4 sacks, 1 cloth for winnowing, 1 peck of straw, . . . 6 plows of which 4 are old, 6 coulters with 10 shares and 12 collar of leather, 3 pairs of traces, 4 pairs of plow wheels, 4 pairs of traces, 3 harrows.

From David Yaxley, *The Prior's Manor-Houses: Inventories of eleven of the manor-houses of the Prior of Norwich made in the year 1352 A.D.* (Derham, Norfolk: Lark's Press, 1988), 14–15.

Well-dressed people at a very simple table.
Italian, c. 1395 (TS Vienna, f. 45). McLean.

A young man lying on a rope bed is restored to life by the True Cross while the
emperor's mother and her ladies look on. From the Legend of the True Cross. Gaddi,
Agnolo 1385–1387 S. Croce, Florence. Photo Credit: Scala/Art Resource, NY.

Ms 1130 fol.83r Chastity and Poverty making a bed, from "Le Roman des Trois Pèlerinages" by Guillaume de Digulleville (vellum), French School, (fourteenth century)/Bibliothèque Sainte-Geneviève, Paris, France/Archives Charmet/Bridgeman Art Library.

The Chamber

One of the most important items of furniture in any house was the bed, which was not only a place to sleep, but might serve as seating during the day. A fully appointed bed had as its base a wooden bedstead, which might be hung about with curtains to keep out the chilly night air. On this was placed a mattress made of canvas or linen stuffed with wool or cotton and quilted to hold its contents in place. Next came a featherbed, which was another mattress (probably of linen) waxed on the inside and stuffed with feathers. Both mattress and featherbed might be white or colored—for example blue or red. Striped ticking was probably also used. Across the head of the bed was a long bolster, probably stuffed canvas or linen, covered with a headsheet of linen, and topped with feather pillows in pillowcases. The person sleeping lay between two white linen sheets, covered by blankets or quilts, and perhaps a decorative coverlet. From the waist down, the sleeper lay flat on the bed, with their back up on the bolster and the head almost vertical on the pillow. Cheaper beds had a mattress but no featherbed.

Nativity. Mary lies on a pallet, which the artist has taken the liberty of covering with a rich pattern of lilies, one of her symbols. A costrel, a medieval canteen, sits on the table at lower right. Joseph seems to be slitting the seam of his hose to make swaddling cloths. Melchior Broederlam (1381–1409) Antwerp, Belgium. Photo Credit: Erich Lessing/Art Resource, NY.

A poor person would at best have a simple pallet on the ground, equivalent to a mattress but stuffed with straw or rushes, or even furze or broom. Servants and children might sleep several together on a pallet, laying it out at night and gathering it up again in the morning to get it out of the way: their sleeping quarters might be on the floor of the householder's chamber, in the hall, or in the kitchen. A straw pallet might also go underneath a finer mattress for a bed of middling quality, and such pallets were even used by noblemen when they were on campaign.

Household Wastes

For urinating or defecating, people used ceramic chamber-pots, known as jordans, which could be used as needed and emptied when convenient.

A domestic scene. Italian, c. 1400 (TS Casanatense, f. cxliv). McLean.

A slightly more substantial device was the night-chair or close-stool, which enclosed the chamber-pot in an actual seat. Permanent privies were also in use, so called because they were actual rooms that afforded genuine privacy. In the town, several houses might share a common privy; there were even public privies in London.

Both urban and rural privies usually emptied into a cesspit, which had to be cleaned out from time to time. On a peasant farm this was done by the householders, and the refuse was carted out to the fields as fertilizer. In the city there were professional gong farmers (gong being the word for a cesspit) who cleaned cesspits for a fee. The best cesspits were lined with stone to facilitate cleaning and prevent leakage. Privies were sometimes located on an upper floor, either open to the ground below or having a pipe leading to the cesspit. For toilet paper people used a piece of cheap fabric, or an arsewisp, which appears to have been a small bundle of straw or some similar material.[9]

Other forms of household waste might be dumped into the cesspit as well. Alternatively they might be buried in the ground or dumped some place away from the house—the Thames River today is a rich archeological source for artifacts discarded from the homes of medieval London. However, many forms of waste matter had some residual economic value. Food scraps were fed to the household livestock, especially poultry and pigs. Other biodegradable waste, such as animal manure and old straw swept from the floor, could go to a muck-heap behind the home, where it

TOWN REGULATIONS FROM BRISTOL, c. 1350

It is ordained that henceforth all who have occupied the common streets and lanes in Bristol and its suburbs with manure and rubble are to have it removed within three days under a penalty of 40d. for each person. And also that no one presume to throw such ordure over the quay under the same penalty for each offence of which he should be convicted.

Translated by J. L. Forgeng from the Latin in *The Little Red Book of Bristol,* ed. Francis B. Bickley (Bristol: Hemmons; London: Sotheran, 1900), 2.31.

could be allowed to compost. Old shirts became rags; old rags were sold to the papermakers. Metals were also recycled, and when an old house was torn down, its timbers were often reused in a new structure.

HYGIENE AND HEALTH

Personal hygiene was something every medieval person learned as a child, although bodily cleanliness was understood chiefly in terms of avoiding visible dirtiness, rather than as means to promote health. People typically washed their face daily, and their hands several times a day. The ordinary wash involved pouring water from a water jug (called a ewer or laver) over the hands into a basin. A towel of linen or silk could be used for drying. Ordinary or French soap consisted of two-thirds lye and one-third sheep's tallow; more expensive was Saracen soap, which was made with olive oil instead of tallow and might be scented as well.

It was customary to wash one's hands before and after a meal, or after defecating. Washing the entire body occurred less frequently. This was probably less due to a lack of interest in bathing than to the problems that bathing entailed. There was a very real risk of illness, even death, when bathing in a cold climate and drafty home. The substantial effort involved in drawing and heating water was probably a factor as well. However, the pleasant medieval custom of eating and drinking during a bath, and the various comforts afforded by the public bathhouses (some of which were essentially brothels) afforded incentives to cleanliness. People bathed in wooden tubs, using water heated over a fire. Hair could be washed using lye and water.[10]

Medicine

The primary health care provider in any home was the woman of the house. Every girl would expect to learn basic medicinal skills from her mother as she was growing up, and the woman of a house would always have a garden in which she could grow at least a few essential herbs for medicinal as well as culinary purposes.

A doctor examining a patient. From the "Liber notabilium Philippi Septimi," by Guy de Pavia. Ms.334/569, fol.18. Italy, 1345. Location: Musée Condé, Chantilly, France. Photo Credit: Erich Lessing/Art Resource, NY.

At the professional level, medicine was a stratified activity with a range of practitioners at different levels of training and expense. At the top was the physician, who was primarily a theorist, educated at a university faculty of medicine. He was expected to have mastered the physiological learning passed down from the ancients about the workings of the body in sickness and health and the efficacy of diverse substances against specific illnesses. His primary skills were in diagnosis and in prescription of remedies. By examining the patient's appearance, taking the pulse, smelling the breath, inquiring after symptoms, and other forms of observation, the physician would attempt to analyze the problem and prescribe a remedy. Among his principal skills was uroscopy, the art of diagnosing patients' conditions from the appearance, scent, and even taste of their urine—because the senses of smell and taste are essentially rudimentary apparatuses for chemical analysis, the process can actually be compared to modern urinalysis.

The illness of John, Duke of Normandy, end of the fourteenth century. He lies in bed while a trio of doctors by his bedside study the contents of a urinal. From "Chroniques de France ou de Saint Denis." BL Royal 20 C. VII, f.78v, London. Photo Credit: HIP/Art Resource, NY.

Under the circumstances, it is hardly surprising that the physician's medical practice tended to be bookish. Like other mainstream intellectuals of the period, he favored authority over experience: medical learning was acquired by reading treatises by long-dead authors rather than by systematic analysis of observed phenomena. Chaucer offers a portrait of such professionals in the Physician of *The Canterbury Tales:*

> He knew the cause of every malady,
> Were it of hot, or cold, or moist or dry,
> And where they engendered, and of what humor.
> He was a true, perfect practicer. . .
> Well he knew the old Asclepius,
> And Diascorides, and also Rufus,
> Old Hippocrates, Haly, and Galen,
> Serapion, Razis, and Avicenna. (*CT* A.419–33)

Medieval understanding of human physiology was based on the Four Humors: Blood (hot and moist), Phlegm (cold and moist), Choler (cold and dry), and Melancholy (hot and dry). An individual's personality was thought to be based on the mix of humors in their body. Illness was typically attributed to an imbalance of humors, so the remedy was to be found by administering substances that would restore the balance. The Four Humors corresponded to the Four Elements of which the material world was thought to consist, and there was an elaborate scheme of correspondences between these and other aspects of the material universe and the human body, as laid out in Table 5.5. Careful manipulation of these correspondences, for example using medicines with the right hot-cold and moist-dry properties, or letting blood from the correct body-part, was thought to be the key to restoring health. The physician would make the recommendations, and refer the patient to an apothecary or surgeon as appropriate.

Manual work was considered beneath the dignity of a physician: any procedure like bloodletting that we might consider an operation was left to the surgeon. In fact, the surgeon's title derived ultimately from the Greek word for manual worker. Whereas the physician enjoyed the gentlemanly status of the professional, the surgeon was classed with artisans: instead of studying at the university, he learned his craft in apprenticeship to a master surgeon. All physical aspects of physiological care were the domain of the surgeon: this included not just surgery, but dentistry as well. The work of the surgeon was more practically oriented than that of a physician: as a craftsman the surgeon had to learn by experience, and in any case there were not many ancient authorities on surgery. Ironically, the less prestigious profession seems to have been more effective in healing and more fruitful in contributing to the understanding of human physiology. The distinguished English surgeon John Arderne successfully operated on certain kinds of cancerous tumors, and a number of ground-breaking surgical treatises were written in this period.

Comparable in status to the surgeon was the apothecary, who concocted the medications prescribed by the physician and who belonged to the

---

RECOMMENDATIONS FOR A SURGEON, c. 1376

After the prognosis has been given, if the patient adamantly wishes to be treated . . . let them agree on a fee, and of this fee—setting aside all excuses—let him take half beforehand, and then assign a day for the patient when he will begin. In the mean time, let the healer make ready his medicines and his instruments. Specifically, he should have two or three sponges at the least, and a razor or very sharp lancet . . . and silk threads, and linen cloths and bandages. . . . He must also have ready a styptic medicine and warm or luke-warm water. . . . In addition to all of this, it is best that he does not cut . . . when the moon is in Scorpio or Libra or Sagittarius, for then the cutting is forbidden by astronomers.

Translated by J. L. Forgeng from the Middle English in John Arderne, *Treatises of Fistula in Ano,* ed. D'Arcy Power (London: Kegan Paul, Trench, Trübner and Co., 1910), 15–16.

Table 5.5:
Humors, Elements, and Correspondences

Humor	Element	Qualities	Wind	Celestial Quarter	Time of Day/Gender	Zodiacal Sign	Part of Body	Planet
Blood	Air	Hot-Moist	South	West	Day/Male	Gemini Libra Aquarius	Shoulders, Arms Hands Lower Belly, Navel Shins	Mercury Venus Saturn
Choler (Yellow Bile)	Fire	Hot-Dry	East	East		Aries Leo Sagittarius	Head, Face Stomach, Muscles, Heart Thighs	Mars Sun Jupiter
Melancholy (Black Bile)	Earth	Cold-Dry	North	South	Night/Female	Taurus Virgo Capricorn	Neck/Throat Belly/Guts Knees	Venus Mercury Saturn
Phlegm	Water	Cold-Moist	West	North		Cancer Scorpio Pisces	Breast, Ribs, Lungs Genitals Feet	Moon Mars Jupiter

This table illustrates the system of correspondences between various aspects of the physical universe as understood by medieval science. The humors are the four substances which compose the human body; the elements are the substances which compose the physical world. Each of the humors and elements is defined by two pairs of opposing qualities (cold/hot and moist/dry). All of these substances and properties are integrated into an orderly scheme of associations, as shown above. For example, the Sun was said to govern the human stomach, and was associated with the zodiacal sign Leo, with daytime and the male gender, with the East, and with Choler and Fire.

powerful and wealthy guild of grocers. Surgeons and apothecaries occupied a position at the highest end of the artisanal spectrum: they were literate (even in Latin) and sometimes acquired considerable prestige and wealth.[11]

Below the surgeon in the hierarchy was the barber-surgeon. He belonged to the barbers' guild; he was less educated than the surgeon, although he might perform the same sorts of procedures. He might also offer haircuts and shaves. Despite their lower status, barber-surgeons were sometimes quite competent medical practitioners. Ordinary barbers (called barber-tonsors) also performed surgical procedures, particularly the simple ones such as pulling teeth or letting blood. In token of their surgical activities, the barbers had a red-and-white striped pole as their professional emblem. The cheapest medical professionals were uncertified healers practicing essentially folk medicine. They were known as leeches, and might just be part-time practitioners.

Access to medical care varied enormously. Most of the professional practitioners were in London. In other large towns there might be a few physicians and surgeons, but most people relied on barber-surgeons, barber-tonsors, and leeches. The countryside was served only by part-time healers, unless a patient was wealthy enough to import the services of a professional. Treatment by a highly skilled practitioner could be very expensive: Arderne recommended a fee of 100 marks for a great person, £40 for lesser people, and £5 as a minimum. In principle, medical practitioners were supposed to treat the poor free of charge, but it is unlikely that they devoted much of their valuable time to such charity.

Sickness

In a society that was generally poor, with a relatively primitive standard of living and very little understanding of the causes of illness, sickness, and disease were never far away. The situation was worst in the cities because of overcrowding and inadequate sanitation. The surgeon Arderne estimated post-operative infection to be as high as 50 percent. Remains of villagers found by archeologists have shown evidence of rheumatic diseases and gallstones. On the other hand, the rate of dental cavities among these villagers was relatively low—not surprising, given the near total absence of white sugar in their diet. The average height was 5′ 5″—slightly short by modern standards, but much taller than the stunted peasants we sometimes imagine today.

Health conditions were rendered worse by the omnipresence of vermin: rats were common, and fleas and lice were a perennial source of discomfort. Rats and fleas contributed disastrously to the spread of the greatest health risk of Chaucer's day—the Plague, or Black Death. This disease came to Europe from the Crimea in 1347 and reached England in 1348. The disease took two principal forms. Initially, it is carried by the flea

Xenopsylla cheopis, which lives primarily on rats. If the flea transfers to a human host there is the possibility of an outbreak of bubonic plague, which has a mortality rate of about 50 percent. If the disease enters the pulmonary system, it can become pneumonic plague, an even more deadly and virulent form of the disease that can be transmitted directly from person to person, and has a mortality rate near 100 percent.

The effects were devastating: within a few years the disease wiped out a third of England's population, and local mortality was sometimes much higher. After its first visitation the plague returned in several lesser outbreaks during the rest of the century, and it remained a health problem in England long after the end of the Middle Ages. It did not truly subside until the late 1600s, and it is still present in some parts of the world today.

Fourteenth-century Englishmen usually referred to the plague as the Pestilence or murrain. Both of these were fairly vague terms that might be applied to any epidemic, and it is entirely possible that other epidemic diseases played a part in the mortality that struck England after 1348—the early part of the century had seen several catastrophic outbreaks of disease in England's livestock population.

In general, it can be difficult to diagnose medieval sicknesses across the centuries—the characteristics we use to identify an illness today are not necessarily the same ones noticed in the Middle Ages. Among the ailments that afflicted fourteenth-century people, many were skin diseases—which is not surprising given the infrequency of bathing. Leprosy was one of these, although medieval people used the term for a broad and poorly defined spectrum of skin ailments; they also used the word measle for the same sorts of sicknesses, although for us measles has a much more precise and different meaning. The falling evil was another affliction, probably corresponding to what we would call epilepsy or apoplexy. There were various sorts of tumors and cancerous phenomena, known by such names as apostemes, fistula, cancer, and blains. Many afflictions were simply known as fever—the quotidian fever that occurred daily, the tertian fever that recurred on alternate days, and the quartan fever that recurred on every third day. At the most ordinary level, medieval people were also subject to the head cold, known to them as a pose.

NOTES

1. *A Collection of Ordinances and Regulations for the Government of the Royal Household Made in Divers Reigns from King Edward III to King William and Queen Mary* (London: Society of Antiquaries, 1790), 9; James E. Thorold Rogers, *A History of Agriculture and Prices in England* (Oxford: Clarendon Press, 1882), 1.282, 314, 322; 2.582–83.

2. Christopher Dyer, *Standards of Living in the Later Middle Ages* (Cambridge: Cambridge University Press, 1989), 147, 194. The landholder incomes are based on a per-acre yield of 4s. 6d.

3. David Farmer, "Prices and Wages,"in *The Agrarian History of England and Wales Volume 3 1348–1500*, ed. E. Miller (Cambridge: Cambridge University Press, 1991), 484n.

4. Rogers 1.348–50, 362–63, 451, 453–54, 593, 641, 2.584; *Middle English Dictionary* (hereafter *MED*) s.v. "brech"; Edith Rickert, *Chaucer's World* (New York: Columbia University Press, 1948), 29–30, 113, 237, 338; Earnest Savage, *Old English Libraries* (London: Methuen, 1912), 243, 248–49; C. Pendrill, *London Life in the 14th Century* (London: Allen and Unwin, 1925), 37, 177, 181–82; Dyer, *Standards of Living*, 80, 167.

5. William Langland, *The Vision of William Concerning Piers the Plowman*, ed. Walter W. Skeat (Oxford: Clarendon Press, 1886), B 10.94 ff.

6. G. G. Coulton, *Medieval Panorama* (New York: Macmillan, 1938), 312; *MED* s.v. "rishe"; John Trevisa, *On the Properties of Things. John Trevisa's translation of Bartholomeus Anglicus'* De Proprietatibus Rerum, gen. ed. M. C. Seymour (Oxford: Clarendon Press, 1975), 137, 1149; William Woods, *England in the Age of Chaucer* (New York: Stein and Day, 1976), 56a.

7. Coulton, *Medieval Panorama*, 310.

8. Summarized from G. G. Astill, "An early inventory of a Leicestershire knight," *Midland History* 2 (1974), 279–81.

9. John Russell, *The Boke of Nurture*, ll. 931 ff., in F. J. Furnivall, ed., *The Babees Book* (London: Trübner, 1868), 61–114.

10. John Russell, *Boke of Nurture*, ll. 975 ff.

11. Robert S. Gottfried, *Doctors and Medicine in Medieval England 1340–1530* (Princeton: Princeton University Press, 1986), 86–89. See also Charles Talbot, *Medicine in Medieval England* (London: Oldbourne, 1967).

6

CLOTHING AND
ACCESSORIES

Fashion

The latter half of the fourteenth century was a period of rapidly changing techniques and fashions in clothing. Prior to Chaucer's lifetime, clothing styles had been fairly static for centuries. Garments were generally cut on straight lines, which severely limited the possibility for variation. The fourteenth century witnessed the true emergence of the tailor's craft as clothesmakers began to experiment with curved seams, allowing garments to be more fully shaped. At the same time, buttons and laces began to be used to allow a closer fit—in previous centuries garments had to be loose enough to be pulled over the torso. The history of costume was precipitated into the age of fashion, which has continued ever since. In many ways, the transformation of personal fashion reflects the profound cultural changes at work during Chaucer's lifetime.

In *The Canterbury Tales*, the Parson comments bitingly on the new trends:

Superfluity of clothing . . . makes it most expensive, to harm of the people; not only the cost of embroidering, the elaborate notching of edges or ornamenting with strips, undulating and vertical stripes, folding or bordering , and similar waste of cloth in vanity; but there is also costly furring in their gowns, so much piercing with stamps to make holes, so much slitting with shears; also the superfluity in length of these gowns, trailing in the dung and in the mire. . . .

Upon the other side, to speak of the horrible disordinate scantiness of clothing, as be these "cutted slops," or "hainselins," that through their shortness cover not

Marital felicity. The rich red and patterned fabric of the man's gown, full lined sleeves of the woman's, the ample cut of both and the lavish display of belt mounts and fashionably pointed shoes all testify to the couples' prosperity. TS. c. 1395 Codex s.n.2644, f. 104v Vienna. Photo Credit: Alinari/Art Resource, NY.

the shameful members of man, to wicked intent. Alas, some of them show the bulging shapes and the horrible lumpy body parts, looking like the malady of the hernia wrapped in the hose; and likewise their buttocks go like the hinder part of a she-ape in the full of the moon. And in dividing of their hose in white and red, it seems that half their shameful privy members were flayed. And if they divide their hose in other colors, as in white and black, or white and blue, or black and red, and so forth, then it seems, by variance of color, that half the part of their privy members is corrupt by the fire of Saint Anthony, or by cancer, or by other such mischance.[1]

Of course, rapidly changing fashion mostly affected the aristocracy and wealthy townsfolk. The clothes of poorer people were simpler in construction and were sometimes 50 years behind the current styles. Indeed, as medieval garments were generally quite durable, used clothing worked its way down the social scale, being passed on to servants, used-clothes dealers, and ultimately the poor.

A PAYMENT BY THE COUNTESS OF ULSTER FOR CLOTHES FOR CHAUCER, 1357

To a certain paltock-maker in London for a paltock [doublet] purchased from him and given to Geoffrey Chaucer as a gift from the countess . . . . 4s. For a pair of black and red hose and a pair of shoes purchased in London and given to the same Geoffrey . . . . 3s.

Translated by J. L. Forgeng from the Latin in Martin M. Crow and Clair C. Olson, *Chaucer Life-Records* (Austin: University of Texas Press, 1966), 14.

Fabrics

The staple fabric of medieval clothing was wool. Woolen fabrics are versatile, durable, and elastic. They take dye well, resist water, and have good insulating properties. For all these reasons, wool was the most common material for the visible layers of the medieval wardrobe—even among the aristocracy, most of whom relied on wool for everyday use. Raw wool was England's principal source of commercial wealth. Some woolen cloth was produced in England, but the best woolen cloths were manufactured on the Continent, especially in the Low Countries and Italy.

Although outer clothes were generally made of wool, most people wore linen next to the skin. Linen derives from the fibers of the flax plant. It is easy to wash, quick to dry, and more comfortable against the skin than wool. It takes dye poorly, but white linen can be washed to quite a brilliance. For these reasons, linen was favored for undergarments of various sorts and was also used to line garments (in fact, the word "lining" derives from the same root as "linen"). Flax was grown in England to make linen cloth, but the best linens came from the Low Countries and northeastern France.

Another common fabric was canvas, a heavy and coarse material made from flax or hemp. Canvas was most often found as lining in garments that needed extra strength. Cotton, which had to be imported from the Mediterranean regions, was less common. Pure cotton cloth was rare, but cotton was sometimes used as stuffing and as a component in the relatively common fabric known as fustian, a blend of cotton and linen. Fustian was especially used in military undergarments such as doublets—the jupon worn by the Knight in the *Canterbury Tales* is made of this material. Both linen and canvas were sometimes treated with beeswax to enhance their resistance to water, making them more useful for outer garments.

The finest fabrics were made from silk. These were imported and very expensive. Fancy shirts were made of silken cloth, and rich fabrics such as satin, velvet, and taffeta were always based on silk.

The weave of most fabrics was of two principal sorts, plain and twill. In plain-woven fabrics, the threads alternate over and under in every direction. Plain weave was used for wool and linen. Plain-weave wool is very durable and sheds water well, so it was especially common among the lower classes. Plain-weave woolen cloth was normally heavily fulled, a washing procedure that produced a smooth outer surface akin to felt, making the fabric even more durable, warmer, and better at shedding water. As the fabric aged, parts of the felted layer would eventually be rubbed off—a threadbare fabric was a wool whose threads had once again become visible through the felted exterior.

In twill fabrics, the threads pass over and under two or more other threads at a time, giving twills their characteristic diagonal look. Twill weave was used for woolen fabrics and was particularly favored for fashionable garments, as it drapes more gracefully than plain-weave. There is also some evidence of knitting in England at this time, at least for gloves and caps; these would also be fulled.

The outer layers of clothing, such as mantles, gowns, hoods, gloves, and surcoats, were occasionally lined with fur for extra warmth or display. Many of the finest furs came from animals of the weasel family, notably marten, sable (which is dark brown to the point of black), and ermine (the winter coat of the stoat, which is snowy white save for a spot of black at the tip of the tail). Some fine furs came from various species of squirrel. Such quality furs were often imported from Scandinavia or Russia, where the cold climate produced especially rich pelts. Less expensive furs included fox, rabbit, lamb, kid, and even cat.

Colors and Dyes

The colors of fashionable clothes tended to be bold and bright; ordinary people's clothes were diverse in color but generally muted in tone. All dyes derived from natural sources, usually plants. Blue dyes were derived from the native plant woad and from indigo, imported from the East: both contain the operative chemical indigotin, although indigo has it in a more concentrated form. The native plant madder produced a warm brick-red, while imported kermes (made from a Mediterranean insect) dyed a rich scarlet. The plant weld was used for yellow, while other plant sources were used for purple and brown. Dyes could be combined to produce other colors—blue was overdyed with yellow to produce green, for example. Black was difficult to achieve with dyes of the period and was therefore expensive, although not beyond the means of a prosperous gentleman; its expense made it an especially fashionable color. Linen and cotton are more difficult to dye than wool or silk. Woad or indigo can dye linen or cotton a reasonably good blue, but European dyers of this period were unable to achieve bright and colorfast reds on these fabrics. Bold and long-lasting dyes were costly, whereas the cheaper dyes tended to fade fairly quickly. Since most people could not afford to replace their clothing very often, their clothes typically had a washed-out look.

FASHIONABLE STYLES, 1362

In this year and last year Englishmen have gone stark mad over fashions in dress. First came wide surcoats that reached no farther than the hips; then others that came clear down to the heels, not open in front as becomes a man but spread out at the sides to arm's length, so that when their backs are turned you think they are women rather than men. This garment is called a "gown" in the mother tongue . . . They also wear small hoods fastened right up under the chin in womanish fashion. Besides, they are embroidered all about with gold, silver, and precious stones. Their liripipes, dagged in the manner of fools, reach to their ankles. They have another garment of silk, commonly called a paltock, so handsomely adorned as to be suitable rather for ecclesiastics than for laymen . . . They also wear tight two-piece hose, which they fasten with latchets to their paltocks . . . They wear costly gold and silver belts . . . though they have not so much as twenty pence saved up. Their shoes, which they call "cracows" have curved peaks more than a finger in length, resembling the claws of demons rather than ornaments for human beings. Wearers of such attire ought to be considered players and worthless fellows than barons, actors rather than knights, buffoons rather than squires. They are lions in the hall and hares in the field.

Frank Scott Hayden, ed., *Eulogium Historiarum* (London: Longman et al., 1853–63), 3.230–31.

Coloration could also be provided by the wool itself. Some wools are naturally pigmented black, although they tend to produce a coarse fabric. Other wools are naturally brown or gray. Earth tones and natural tones were the least expensive and were generally worn only by the poor.[2]

Construction

Some garments were lined, but many seem to have been unlined except for silk, linen, or wool facing around the buttonholes. In many surviving unlined garments, neck and wrist openings are faced with a narrow linen or silk strip to cut down on chafing. Often the edges of wool garments were left unfinished, since the heavily felted wool resisted fraying, and hems at the bottom of an overgarment could actually collect rainwater. Raw edges of cuffs and collars were sometimes finished by tablet-weaving a fine braid directly onto the cloth, probably using a weft thread on a needle. Many rough openings that were not faced or finished with tablet-woven edging were turned back and trimmed with a narrow silk or linen ribbon folded over the edge. All these finishes helped prolong the life of the garment by protecting the areas that received the most wear. Silk and linen were the most common threads for sewing, with silk usually being used for buttonholes and finishing stitches on quality garments (although its use also seems to have been common among the lower middle classes).

Decorative fabric finishes were quite fashionable. The most common was probably the notching of edges, or dagging, that Chaucer's Parson

Women in simple but elegant kirtles. Italian, c. 1365 (Giovanni da Milano, "The Birth of the Virgin"). McLean.

found so distasteful. In this technique the edge of the garment was cut into decorative shapes. On well fulled wool, the cut edge could be left unfinished; on other fabrics, a contrasting lining added to the decorative effect. Such dagging might be found on the lower edge of a coathardie, hood, or mantle, or on the voluminous cuffs of a houppelande (all described later in this chapter).

Maintenance

The outer layers of clothing, made of woolen or silken fabric, did not generally wash well. Instead, they were brushed to remove dust and to protect against moths. Ideally, linen underclothes were to be washed once a week; evidence suggests that the upper classes may have changed shirts about twice a week, their servants once. Wrinkles might be pressed out with a heavy flat-sided object called a sleek-stone—like nineteenth-century irons, it may have been heated in a fire.

The Outfit

Medieval people had different ideas than we do of what it was to be properly dressed. The public was more likely to see a man's underpants than his naked elbows. Fourteenth-century men and women commonly wore multiple layers of clothing that could be adjusted in accordance with the temperature and context.

Imagine an ordinary fourteenth-century man getting dressed on a chilly spring morning. He might first pull his shirt over his head. Next he would pull on his breech (underpants) and tie or belt it in place. To this he would attach his hose. On top of these undergarments he might pull on a kirtle (the basic form of outer garment), over-kirtle, and hood. Aside from a change or two of shirt and breeches, this might well be the only outfit he owned. As the day warmed he might put aside his over-kirtle. Warmer still, and he might fiddle with his hood. Hoods are wonderfully versatile garments, and they can be worn in a variety of ways to achieve different levels of warmth: with the cowl raised to cover the head or pushed back onto the neck; tied around the head as a hat; or slung over the shoulder. If the weather was very warm, the man might unlace his hose and roll them down over his garters, or remove them entirely. Laborers in the fields in summer often stripped to

---

THE DESCRIPTION OF THE CARPENTER'S
WIFE ALISON IN CHAUCER'S *MILLER'S TALE*

A belt she wore, barred all of silk,
An apron also as white as morning milk,
Upon her loins, full of many a gore;
White was her smock, embroidered all before
And also behind, on her collar about,
With coal-black silk, within and also without.
The tapes of her white voluper [cap],
Were of the same trim as her collar;
Her fillet broad of silk, and set full high;
And surely she had a lecherous eye. . .
And by her belt hung a purse of leather.
Tasseled with silk, and pearled with latten,
In all this world to seek up and down,
There is no man so wise that could conceive
So gay a poppet or such a wench. . .
A brooch she bore on her low collar,
As broad as is the boss of a buckler,
Her shoes were laced on her legs high.

Translated by J. L. Forgeng from the Middle English in Geoffrey Chaucer, *Canterbury Tales*, in *The Works of Geoffrey Chaucer*, ed. F. N. Robinson (Oxford: Oxford University Press, 1974), A.3235–67.

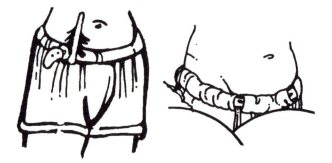

Breeches. The example on the left is from a woodcut
of c. 1410–1420; the belt is clearly visible (Anonymous
Bavarian Master, "The Martyrdom of St. Sebastian"). The
breech on the right is from a painted cloth of c. 1375. Note
the cords attaching the hose to the belt within the casing
of the breech ("Le Parement de Narbonne"). McLean.

their shirt and breeches. Aristocrats did not need to sweat as often, but even
young gentlemen playing at swords or handball might roll their hose down,
revealing their breeches below their short doublets.

Women also wore several layers for comfort and versatility, although
they had fewer options without offending contemporary standards of
decency. A complete outfit might include a shirt, short hose, a kirtle, an
over-kirtle (possibly short-sleeved), and headgear. The over-kirtle might
come off for warm weather or housework. Sometimes women would hike
the skirts of their garments for convenience and comfort. Like the men,
farm women in the fields at harvest time sometimes stripped to their
shirts, but you would not have seen naked elbows outside the bathhouses.
Except under exceptional circumstances, decent dress involved at least a
shirt and one other layer.

Underwear: Breech and Shirt

The innermost layer of a man's clothes was a pair of loose shorts, known
as a breech, which served the double purpose of helping to concealing his
private parts (if he was wearing one of the fashionably short garments
of the age) and providing support for his leggings. The clearest illustrations show breeches held up by belts, which may have passed through a
channel in the top of the breech, or the tops may simply have been folded
around the belt. Alternatively, they might have been held up by a drawstring, particularly if a doublet supported the hose. The belt sometimes
supported a purse—it was, after all, a relatively secure location for one's
money. Breeches were normally made of white linen.

Women did not wear breeches. Evidence regarding women's supporting garments is predictably scarce, but a few texts of the period refer to

a breast-girdle or breast-band, which may have been some sort of linen band that served the function of a modern bra.[3]

The next garment for a man, and the first for a woman, was the shirt, again typically made of white linen. The shirt was considered underwear. People were not normally seen in public wearing nothing over their shirts unless they were engaged in some particularly strenuous activity. In fact, a person wearing only a shirt was said to be naked. The medieval shirt was characteristically cut with straight seams and was pulled over the head.

The pattern shown here is that of the thirteenth-century shirt preserved at Notre Dame cathedral in Paris and reputed to have belonged to Saint Louis. It is one of very few surviving medieval European shirts. It illustrates the value of fabric in the Middle Ages: the design of the shirt keeps waste to an absolute minimum. The cut of this shirt is long, designed for the long kirtles of the 1200s; shirts of Chaucer's day would be no longer than the overgarment on top of them. In the fifteenth century, three yards of fabric were reckoned enough to make a shirt, some two feet less than the St. Louis shirt.[4] The triangular gores inserted at front and back allowed greater ease of movement. Shorter shirts in the fourteenth century might

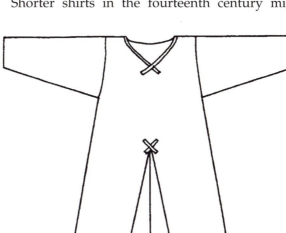

The St. Louis Shirt (1200s). It is shown above inside-out, revealing its reinforcing tapes. The cutting pattern on the left illustrates how carefully the fabric is used. McLean, after Burnham.

achieve the same effect with open side seams from the waist down. Shirts had necklines roughly matching those on the outer garments: the triangular neckline on the St. Louis shirt is again a thirteenth-century feature.

The female equivalent to the man's shirt was called a smock. It is possible that, as in later centuries, the smock was distinguished from a shirt by having the gores inserted into the side seam rather than in front and back. A smock could be decorated with embroidery about the collar.

Hose

To cover their legs, both men and women wore a pair of cloth leggings known as hose. These were typically made of wool, cut on the bias (diagonally) for extra elasticity. Still, being of woven cloth rather than knitted, they tended to be baggy (unlike the tights we see in today's movies). Medieval hose were often brightly colored, striped, or even of contrasting colors for each leg. Sometimes they were lined with plain white linen. Hose could also be made of leather; sometimes just the soles were made of leather, so the hose could be worn without shoes.

The length of the hose was determined by the length of the upper-body garment. Men's hose covered the entire leg and had cords or laces called points attached to the top, with which the hose were secured to the breeches-belt, breeches, or doublet. Since women's legs were already covered by their kirtles, their hose reached only to the knee, where they were secured with garters. Men might also wear short hose with longer garments. Sometimes they rolled their long hose down to their knees in hot weather.

More fashionable men's hose were cut high enough to lace to a short upper-body garment (called a doublet or pourpoint) at front, side, and back. This restricted the wearer's range of motion, and contemporary illustrations often show the rear and/or side points unlaced to allow extra freedom of movement for difficult tasks.

Kirtles

The usual form of outer clothing for ordinary people was the kirtle, a garment worn over the shirt, usually of wool, occasionally of linen. In its simplest form it was similar in cut to a shirt: the body was made of a single piece, with gores in the front and back or sides (usually both), and straight-cut sleeves. A kirtle of this sort was found in a bog at Boksten in Sweden. Kirtles reached to the knee or calf for men; for women they were cut longer, stretching to the ankle or foot. A kirtle could be lined and might be adorned with braided lacing, which also served to bind loose edges. Several layers of kirtles might be worn, and men's over-kirtles sometimes had slits in front for riding. Over-kirtles might have short sleeves to reveal the layers underneath, but the main kirtle was always long sleeved.

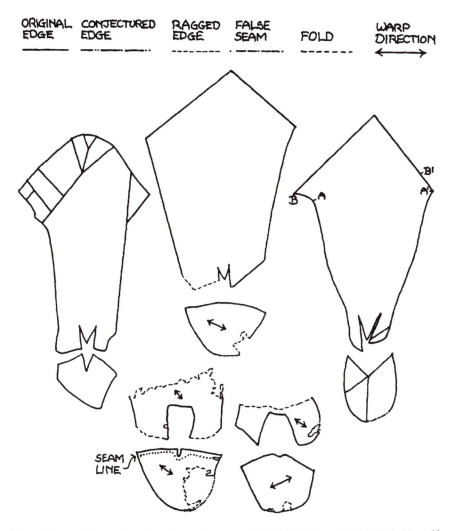

ORIGINAL EDGE — CONJECTURED EDGE — RAGGED EDGE — FALSE SEAM — FOLD — WARP DIRECTION

SEAM LINE

Hose. Top (left to right): Hose from Bremen (1200s), Boksten (1300–1350), Herjolfsnes (probably 1350–1400). Bottom: Late fourteenth-century hose fragments from London—the heel and foot on the right are probably not from the same hose. All are for the right foot except the Herjolfsnes hose (uncertain) and the London foot piece at bottom right (probably left, but reversed here for easier comparison). The complete hose all have a triangular extension of the leg over the instep, overlapping the foot piece in the case of the Boksten hose. The overlap at the top of the Herjolfsnes hose reduces the strain on the seam. The piecing probably served to economize on fabric. Leather straps to hold up the hose were attached at three points at the top of each leg of the Boksten hose. McLean: Bremen and Boksten hose after Lundwall, Herjolfsnes hose after Norlund, London fragments after Unwin.

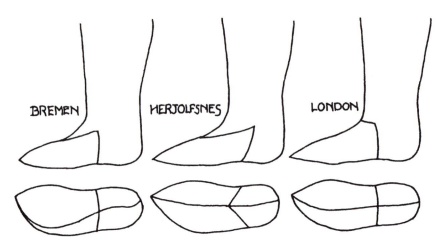

Assembled hose. Note how the seam on the bottom curves to avoid the ball of the foot. McLean.

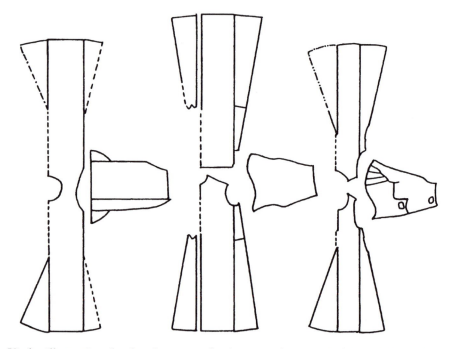

Kirtles illustrating the development of tailoring techniques (left half, 1/30 scale): Boksten (c. 1300–1350), Moselund (?c. 1350), Herjolfsnes no. 43 (?c. 1340–1400). McLean.

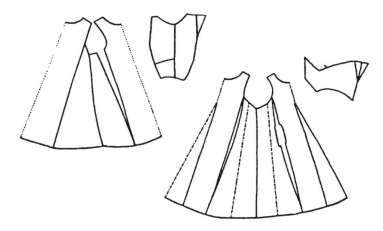

Loosely fitted kirtles from Herjolfsnes (nos. 33 and 45, right half and left sleeve, 1/30 scale). Norlund.

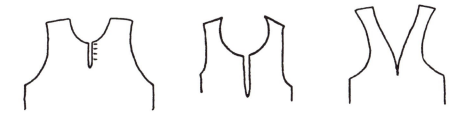

Additional necklines from Herjolfsnes (nos. 60, 43, and 58, 1/15 scale). Norlund.

The fourteenth century witnessed a turning point in the history of costume, with the introduction of curved seams, which allow garments to be more fully shaped. This development significantly changed the design of kirtles. A transitional style is found in the Moselund kirtle, another Scandinavian bog-find. It is partially tailored and probably somewhat later in date than the Boksten kirtle: most of the seams are straight, but the front and back pieces are separate, the top of the front piece is angled to fit the shoulders better, the side gores extend to the armholes, and the armhole edge of the sleeves is curved in essentially the same shape as a modern sleeve.

The next development from this type of garment was the fully tailored kirtle, of which quite a few have been excavated from Scandinavian graves at Herjolfsnes in Greenland. The shoulder seams are angled in both the front and back. The side gores, stretching right up to the armholes, have become fully tailored pieces rather than simple triangles. In several cases they are shaped to give a narrow waist and a broadly flaring skirt. The necks are often close-fitting, with a slash to allow them to be pulled over

Closely fitted kirtles from Herjolfsnes (nos. 38, 41, and 39, left half and left sleeve, 1/30 scale). Nos. 38 and 39 have been identified as women's kirtles on the basis of their length: their cut does not differ from those of male kirtles. Norlund.

the head, and are fastened with buttons, a lace, or a brooch. In some cases the sleeves are quite tight, and are designed to be fastened with buttons or sewn up at each wearing. The Herjolfsnes kirtles show the highly pieced construction that is typical of medieval garments, by which the makers conserved precious fabric. Several have pocket slits, probably giving access to a purse worn underneath.

Women's kirtles were not substantially different from those of men, save that they were cut longer. Two examples have been identified from Herjolfsnes.

By the latter half of the 1300s, the kirtle was considered an ordinary sort of garment and by no means particularly fashionable. Tailored kirtles fitted better than their straight-cut predecessors, but they still had to be pulled over the head and could not be very closely fitted. The fourteenth century witnessed another major development with the use of buttons or lacing to allow a closer fit. A garment that buttoned in front did not have to be pulled over the head, and could be tailored more closely to the body. In fact, the truly fashionable styles for the first half of Chaucer's lifetime were extremely tight fitting. Since such garments appeared at almost the same time as the suit of armor, there is reason to believe that the fashion imitated the new style of padded military undergarment, which had to be carefully tailored to fit under a knight's body protection.

The characteristically tight-fitting garment of the period is known today as the coathardie, although contemporary terminology was nowhere near this precise, and the name was rarely used in fourteenth-century English: other names applied to garments in this class included coat, doublet, jupon, and paltock. Such garments were worn by both men and women. They were closely fitted about the waist, and sometimes about the hips too, although they might have a flaring skirt. On men they were shorter than a kirtle, sometimes reaching as far as the tops of the knees but often only to the upper thighs. The female version was probably still known as a kirtle: like more old-fashioned kirtles, it reached to the ankles or feet. The sleeves might be embellished with decorative strips of cloth hanging from the upper arms.

The distinctive feature of these garments was the opening for putting them on. The male version usually opened from neck to hem in front, buttoning all or most of the way. Occasionally the front opening laced shut. Some pictures of quite tightly fitted male coathardies show no signs of a front opening; these may have laced under the arm. The female version usually opened to the waist in front and was secured with buttons or lacing; alternatively, it might lace up the side under the arm. The coathardie might also have buttons at the lower sleeves to allow for a very tight fit. Buttons were small and might be unevenly distributed, with more buttons at points of greater strain such as the midriff. Coathardies became less fashionable in the latter part of the century, when they were likely to be covered by looser outer garments.

Versions of the coathardie were worn as undergarments, either for warmth or as a foundation layer under armor; such a garment might be called a doublet or pourpoint. One of the essential purposes of these garments was to hold up hose (hose returned the favor by keeping the doublet from riding up). By fitting as tightly as a belt at the natural waist level, the doublet could anchor the hose to the waist just as a belt does for modern trousers. Although it had to fit snugly at the waist, a doublet could fit more loosely above that point. Such garments might well be loose from the bottom of the ribs upwards. The difference in fit might

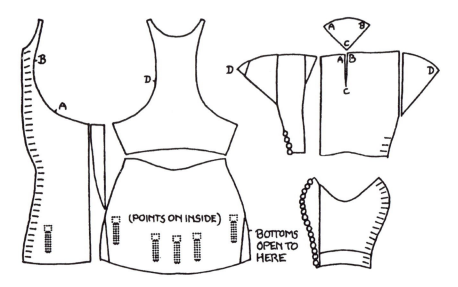

The Charles of Blois doublet. For a reconstruction, see the chapter on Arms and Armor. McLean, after Zylstra-Zweens.

be emphasized by using larger buttons above this point or buttons above and laces below. The wasp-waist effect could also be emphasized by padding. A doublet worn beneath armor was padded most heavily on the shoulders. Garments worn over the doublet, such as the coathardie, often followed the same cut.

Perhaps the only surviving garment of this sort is the doublet associated with Charles of Blois, dating to 1360–1400. It is elaborately tailored, fitting closely at the waist and hips and more broadly at the chest. It has very large armholes, with a seam across the elbow; a garment like this might theoretically be worn under armor, so the design is intended for maximum flexibility and a good fit. Again, the highly pieced construction illustrates how precious fabric was, even for a nobleman like Charles of Blois. The doublet is made of ivory-colored silk brocaded with gold, lined with fine linen canvas, and interlined with cotton wadding; it is quilted with horizontal rows spaced at 1 1/2 inches. There are points (laces) sewn in for attaching hose. The points are of linen, except for those at the center back, which are of kid leather. The separate triangular piece shown for the sleeve seems to have been added last, to allow for precise fitting. The cut of the arms provides for ample arm movement, suggesting military use, but other characteristics make this unlikely. The buttons, especially those up the length of the arms, are large enough to interfere with armor, there are no attachment points for arm harness, and the fabric seems too delicate (and well preserved) to have been worn under mail or plate. It might have been worn *over* armor, but its very tight tailoring suggests it was not. It

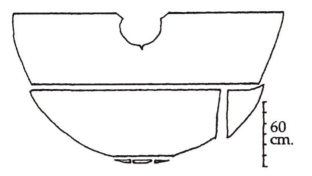

The Boksten mantle. McLean, after Lundwall.

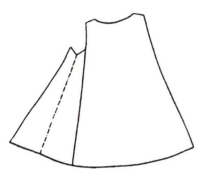

Incomplete garment, perhaps a surcoat, from Herjolfsnes (1/30 scale). Norlund.

is more likely a top-quality coathardie designed in a military style, although a more robust version of the same garment would serve well as an arming doublet.

Outer Garments

England has never been an especially warm country, and the climate of the fourteenth century was actually a bit cooler than it is today. For this reason, and for reasons of fashion, people usually wore several layers of clothing. A variety of outer garments were in use. The simplest of these was the mantle, of which an example was found in a bog at Boksten in Sweden. The right shoulder is sewn together rather than buttoned, and the neck opening is large enough to slip over the head. It is cut with a dart over the left shoulder for a better fit. This style of mantle, opening on the side, seems to have been a male fashion; women's mantles (as well as many for men) opened at the center front. The mantle might fasten with a brooch or with buttons. A mantle might have a lining, which could be shorter than the outer shell and not sewn directly to it at the bottom—like the lining of a modern raincoat, the design kept water from collecting in the hem.

Over a close-fitting garment people often wore a sleeveless surcoat. The fashionable woman's version of this garment was distinguished by deeply cut arm-holes, which allowed the kirtle underneath to be seen, showing off the shape of the body.

An even warmer overgarment was the gown. One of these was among the archeological finds at Herjolfsnes in Greenland. This loose garment covered most of the body and was open at the front, fastening with buttons.

The Herjolfsnes gown (1/20 scale). Norlund.

Man and woman in fashionable houppelandes from the end of the century. Ashdown.

The latter part of the century saw the emergence of the houppelande as the most fashionable garment for both men and women. The houppelande was a loose gown made to fit only at the shoulders. It might be belted—above the waist on women and below the waist on men. It was usually quite long and ostentatious in its liberal use of fabric, although men's houppelandes were sometimes cut short to show off the legs. The sleeves, long and loose, were frequently cut with dags and lined with fur or silk. Sometimes the full sleeves narrowed to a cuff at the wrist. The collar came up to the middle of the back of the head and buttoned up to the chin at the front. Often the collar was turned down, leaving the top few buttons undone. Men's long houppelandes were generally open from the hem to the knee.

Hoods, Hats, and Other Headgear

The characteristic headgear for a fourteenth-century man was the hood, of which many original examples survive. Like other outer garments, the hood was normally made of wool. The typical hood sported a tippet, or tail, at the back, which could be quite long on fashionable hoods. Young gallants sometimes used it for storing knickknacks—the Friar in *The Canterbury Tales* has his tippet "ever stuffed full of knives/And pins, for to give fair wives." The Herjolfsnes hoods also have a slight peak at the top of the face opening, improving the fit when the hood was folded back away from the face. Some fancy hoods had elaborate dagging cut into the hem of the cape.

There were two distinct styles of hood. One form had a small shoulder cape, with a gusset inserted into the shoulder. The other had a larger cape with a gusset inserted at the front, and sometimes one at the back as well. The front gusset allowed the selvage of the fabric to run along the edge of the face opening, permitting a more durable and easier finish for that edge, which was not always hemmed or lined. No lining survives on any of these hoods, but paintings of the period often show contrasting linings.

One fashionable way to wear the hood was as a hat, with the face opening going over the head and the cape and tippet draped to the side or back. The edge of the face opening could be rolled back to control the fit, and sometimes the tippet was wrapped around the head and tucked into itself to secure the hood in place.

Women could also wear hoods; theirs typically buttoned or tied under the chin. Illustrations often show women's hoods with a relatively short shoulder cape, and frequently worn unbuttoned. Sometimes these hoods appear to be designed so as not to close at all; they only vestigially preserve the shape of a hood that could be buttoned. Other illustrations show women wearing hoods with shoulder capes that almost reach to

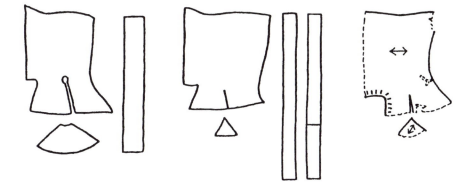

Side-gusset hoods (1/15 scale): two from Herjolfsnes, one from London. Left and center: Norlund; right: McLean, after Unwin.

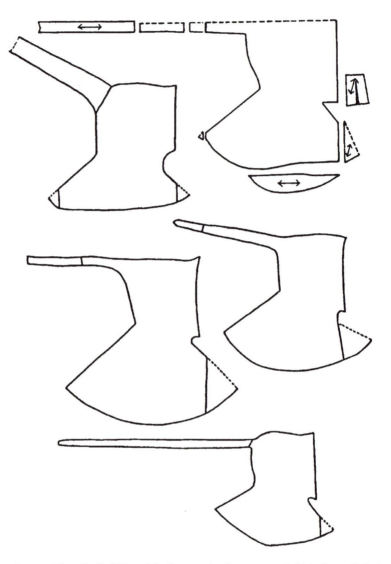

Front-gusset hoods (1/15 scale): the one in the upper right is from Boksten (Sweden), the others are from Herjolfsnes (Greenland). Upper right: McLean; others: Norlund.

their elbows, worn with the hood thrown back. A few seem to show hoods worn as hats in the masculine style, with the top of the head inserted into the face opening.

For women, the characteristic headdress of the early fourteenth century was the veil and wimple. The veil was typically a rectangle of white linen or silk worn draped over the head, trailing in back. The wimple was a similar piece of fabric arranged to fall in folds under the chin and around the neck—some wimples only covered the front, others surrounded the neck completely. Both veils and wimples were held in place with straight pins, anchored to a headband.

Later in the century, fashionable women ceased to cover the neck and chin, preferring only the veil. These veils were often fastened to a narrow fillet that circled the brow. The fillet also served to support the hair, which was braided, made into two bundles at the side of the face, and wired into place. The fillet might be tablet-woven or of more expensive jeweler's work. The veil might have a frilled edge, and it was often folded so that several layers of frilling framed the face and hair.

Older women, as well as the less fashionable, wore the plainer veil. Servants, peasants, and those performing arduous tasks often wore a simple veil or cloth tied about the head in some fashion to keep it from shifting and to keep the hair covered and out of the way.

In addition to their hoods, men often wore a coif made of linen or leather; this could be padded for military use. Hats were also popular. Ordinary hats were made of wool felt. They might be broad-brimmed with a low round crown or high-crowned with a small brim; the brim was sometimes folded up in front or in back. Men's hats were occasionally adorned with a hat-band and feathers. Both men and women wore straw hats in hot weather. Some hats were fitted with laces so they could hang from the neck. Unlike other head coverings for women, hats seem only to have been worn for outdoor pursuits, and they were often worn over a veil and wimple.

Fashionable women and men might adorn their hair with chaplets—wreathes made from flowers or greenery, or fabric cut to imitate those ephemeral materials, or from jeweler's work. At the end of the century thick, padded rolls of fabric began to appear on fashionable heads; these were to become very popular in the fifteenth century for both sexes.

Hair and Grooming

Some women wore their hair uncovered, particularly if they were young and unmarried. Various arrangements of braids were typical, or the hair might be worn in long tresses or gathered behind. Hairnets, which had gone out of fashion during the middle of the century, re-appeared toward the end with a more open and conspicuous mesh. Uncovered and undressed hair is sometimes seen in contemporary illustrations, but it was unusual. Most often women's hair was cut rather long, but a few contemporary illustrations show modern-looking cuts no longer than neck length.

Men wore their hair fairly long—to or past the collar, though not long enough to braid. Beards were common, except for churchmen, who were obliged to be clean shaven. Moustaches had fallen out of fashion after the Norman Conquest, and were very rare at this time, although not wholly unknown. Shaving involved a straight razor and basin, in a manner that remained essentially unchanged until the rise of the safety razor in the twentieth century; the process is tricky, not to say dangerous, and gave employment to a legion of professional barbers.

Hair was groomed with a comb—brushes were apparently used only for clothes. Medieval combs had two sets of teeth, one broad to deal with the larger tangles, the other fine to finish up. Ordinary combs were made of wood or horn; expensive ones were made of ivory. Then as now, curly hair was fashionable among women, who sometimes used curling irons to achieve this effect. The best mirrors were made of glass; a cheaper version consisted of polished metal; all were hand-held. Cosmetics were also used by fashionable women, although moralists condemned the practice as pure vanity.

Shoes and Pattens

Shoes in Chaucer's day were normally made of leather. The soles were flat, without heels, typically made with heavy sole leather to protect the underside of the feet. In some cases the need for shoes was circumvented by using leather for the soles of the hose.

A variety of shoe types were in use. Archeological evidence from London suggests that most were cut below the ankle, fastening either with a buckle, a latchet (a split leather strap passed through a pair of holes), or a leather lace. The next most common appears to have been ankle shoes, extending up to the ankle or a bit beyond. The least common were boots. Both ankle shoes and boots typically fastened up the front with laces. In the middle of the fourteenth century a round toe was favored, but by the later part there was a definite trend toward pointed shoes. Side-laced, front-laced, or ankle shoes had modest points, and were probably everyday wear or working-class shoes. Shoes with longer points, known as poulaines or cracows (Polish or Krakow shoes), were cut low over the instep and had an

Low shoe. Vernier, after Mitford.

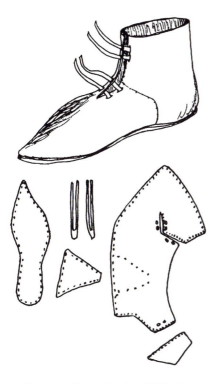

Ankle shoe. Vernier, after Mitford.

ankle strap secured with a buckle or latchet. The point on these fashionable shoes could reach four inches, but most were shorter. The extended toes could be stuffed with moss or hair to retain their shape. Buckled shoes seem to have been worn by men, whereas front latchets and laces were worn equally by both sexes.

An older method for making shoes involved a one-piece upper, with the seam on the inside of the foot. This method remained in use in the later fourteenth century, but poulaines, which required more leather, were usually made with two-piece uppers consisting of a vamp (front) and quarters (rear). The soles of poulaines were often of two pieces as well, joined at the arch of the foot.

Shoes for ordinary use were plain, but others might be decorated. One style of ornamentation was openwork, in which small holes were punched out of the leather in a pattern. This could simply be a design around the upper part of the vamp or could cover the entire vamp and quarter. The second style involved engraved lines and shapes cut or scraped on the surface of the leather. Incised latticework or engraved leaf motifs were both popular.

Because medieval shoes lacked heels and were not particularly durable or waterproof, people often wore pattens, the medieval equivalent of modern overshoes, for walking in rain and mud. Pattens resembled sandals. The sole was usually made from a soft wood such as alder, poplar, or willow and had leather straps to hold it onto the feet. There were three basic types: the platform patten, the flat patten, and the leather patten. Platform pattens were typically carved from a single piece of wood and held the feet off the ground on stilts or wedges. Flat pattens, also of wood, were hinged to follow the movement of the foot. Leather pattens were made by sewing together five to seven layers of thick leather to form the sole. The straps were sometimes adorned with stamped decoration.

Laces, Buttons, and Garters

Laces called points were widely used for securing garments in place. The laces might be woven or braided threads, or leather. They had metal ends known as tags or aglets, which made it easier to push them through lacing eyelets. Points were generally tied in a half bow.

Most buttons were made of fabric stuffed with fabric scraps. Others were discs or domes of wood or horn, also covered with cloth. Wealthier people could afford metal buttons of tin, pewter, latten, or brass. The rich might have buttons of silver or gold, or even set with gems.

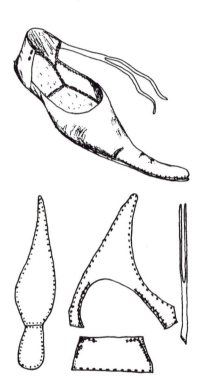

Buttons were essentially of the shank variety rather than pierced like modern shirt-buttons. Examples found in London range from about 1/8 to about 1 1/4 inches in diameter. Buttons were generally sewn to the garment at the very edge, not set in from the edge as on modern clothes.

Garters were essential to keep up a woman's hose and were sometimes worn by fashionable men as well. They tied just under the knee. The simplest ones were probably plain strips of tablet-woven cloth, but fashionable men and women wore garters of leather with buckles and sometimes painted decorations or mottoes. The most famous example was worn by members of the Order of the Garter; it can still be seen on the British royal coat of arms.

Pins were another important fastener, and were used extensively to hold clothing in place, particularly

Poulaine. Vernier, after Mitford.

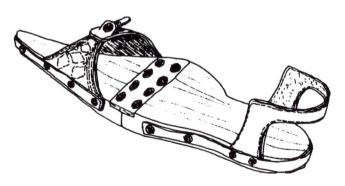

A flat patten. Vernier.

women's headgear. The simplest type was made by hammering the end of a piece of wire to make a head, and sharpening the other end. The wire-making itself was a time-consuming process: a piece of metal had to be first hammered thin, then drawn through a series of successively smaller holes to make it wire-shaped.

Accessories

Belts were a most important accessory, used to carry pouches, knives, and other essential items. The belts of the rich might be made of metal plaques hinged together—richly ornamented discs, squares, quatrefoils, or other shapes, often gilt or made of some precious metal. Sometimes the plaques were riveted to leather or fabric belts. More utilitarian belts were made of leather, fastened by a tongued buckle. Those who could afford them wore belts with strap ends, buckle mounts, and grommets of metal, and the strap itself might be decorated with appliqué or with rosettes of tin or brass. Tablet-woven belts were also worn; these were made of wool or linen for ordinary folk, or of silk for the rich.[5]

The belt supported a purse or belt-pouch, a crucial part of everyone's attire, since medieval clothes did not incorporate pockets. This might be a purse made of sturdy leather with a flap and buckle, or a pouch made of supple leather or fabric that closed with a drawstring, sometimes heavily embroidered. Such pouches were also kept inside a belt-purse as a handy way to store coins.

A knife was another essential item of personal gear—in fact, people were often expected to provide their own knives at the table. Knives were carried by all classes of people and were quite different from daggers, being designed for peaceful rather than violent uses. They were smaller than daggers, the blade was sharp on only one side, and there was no handguard. The typical knife was of steel with a wooden or bone handle; it might have iron or brass fittings. Often the sheath tied onto the back of a purse.

Both gloves and mittens were used in the fourteenth century; to judge by visual evidence, gloves were generally worn by people of social pretensions, mittens by commoners. As a mark of social status, gloves were as likely to be worn for display as for warmth. Both gloves and mittens had characteristically long gauntlets extending well past the wrist.

Eyeglasses were a relative novelty in Chaucer's day and were used only for reading, being essentially magnifying lenses comparable to modern reading glasses. They were similar to the pince-nez style, having no temple-pieces but hinging in the middle to rest on the nose.

Handkerchiefs were not unknown, but they were apparently a rarity—sleeves presumably suffered for this omission.[6] Travelers often carried drink in leather bottles, gourds, or miniature wooden barrels bound with iron.

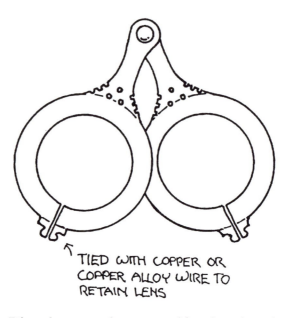

TIED WITH COPPER OR
COPPER ALLOY WIRE TO
RETAIN LENS

Fifteenth-century glasses, carved from bone (actual
size). McLean.

Jewelry

The upper classes delighted in jewelry. Brooches were especially fashionable, sometimes in the shape of letters or bearing mottoes. One example is the brooch worn by Chaucer's Prioress, on which was written *Amor
Vincit Omnia* (Love Conquers All). In many cases brooches served a practical function, being used to fasten a mantle or the neck-opening of a kirtle,
or to attach points to the hose. Rings were also popular. They were a common love token, and a man placed a ring on his bride's finger as part of
the marriage ceremony. Necklaces made of gold or silver were sometimes
worn by both men and women.

Faceted cuts were very rare on fourteenth-century gems, and those few
that do exist are much simpler than the faceting on most modern gems.
The vast majority of fourteenth-century examples are cut *en cabochon*,
shaped like a smoothly rounded pebble. Then as now, imitation gems of
glass were used in cheaper jewelry.

For those who wished to look fashionable but could not afford it, there
were brooches and rings of pewter, made in imitation of costly jewelry,
complete with raised domes where one might expect gems or pearls—
these domes may originally have been painted to contribute to the illu-
sion. Pilgrim badges were another form of jewelry that enjoyed wide
popularity. These were typically small badges of cast pewter in the shape
of an image relating to the holy shrine where they were sold—an early
version of the tourist's souvenir.[7]

CLOTHING PATTERNS

The instructions in the following pages are designed to allow you to make a complete set of simple fourteenth-century clothing. Unlike most costuming books, the patterns given here are as close to the originals as possible. Just how far you choose to take the authenticity will depend on the purpose of the clothing you are making. Dedicated living history groups like to be accurate even down to the kinds of stitching used on their garments, but if you are making costumes for a school pageant you won't want to worry about such precision.

By cultivating the characteristically layered look of medieval clothing, you can get the maximum mileage out of a few well-chosen, well-made garments. An ankle-length gown or kirtle is a good first garment for a man, since it can conceal shortcomings in the rest of the outfit. Hoods are versatile garments for both sexes. Linen, silk, and summer-weight wool are good choices if you expect to have to wear your clothes in hot weather. A hat, particularly a broad-brimmed straw one, will add a great deal to your comfort in summer.

The instructions describe each of the garments as being made of linen or wool—whether you actually use these fabrics will depend on your goals. When buying your fabrics, we recommend at least looking at the real linen and wool. Even if you plan to use another fabric, a glance at the real thing will give you some idea of the look of the original garments.

Medieval wool was often heavily fulled and therefore quite resistant to fraying. Dagging was often cut into the edge of the fabric without any further finish. This might work well with coat-weight modern wool, or you might try fulling a lighter-weight wool yourself. Do-it-yourself fulling can be accomplished by washing the wool in hot soapy water in the washing machine (this tends to shrink the center of the fabric more than the selvages); toss in a tennis shoe with it, as the pounding action is an essential part of the process. Fulling can also be done by hand in a tub by folding the fabric back and forth on itself and treading or pounding it in the water. The wool may shrink as much as 60 percent. In the Middle Ages, this shrinkage was moderated by stretching the cloth over wooden tenter-frames while it was drying after being fulled. Iron hooks called "tenter-hooks" gripped the fabric.

Choosing the correct colors will greatly enhance the authenticity of any attempt at medieval clothing. Many colors available today—bright purple or vivid lime green, for example—were impossible to obtain with medieval dyes. The best way to gain an idea of the colors of medieval clothes would be to look at modern wools left undyed or dyed with natural dyes (a good knitting shop might be a place to try, and textile suppliers will often provide sample swatches).

Many of the following patterns are simple and geometric and should be easy to scale up. For those that aren't, you can use an enlarging photocopier or lay a grid on the pattern and transfer it to a grid where the squares are larger by the proportion that you want to expand the pattern.

When cutting out any of the clothes described, remember to add an extra 1/2 inch to the seam allowance unless otherwise noted. With the more complex patterns, it is advisable to make a mock-up, or fitting, of inexpensive material first—muslin is a good choice. You can make the necessary adjustments to this fitting and proceed to the better fabric when you are satisfied with the fit.

Unless you are determined to make your clothing fully authentic, you will probably want to machine-stitch invisible seams. If you do the finishing stitches by hand, the clothes will still look quite accurate except under the closest scrutiny. Linen or silk thread is the most authentic.

For further information on the techniques of sewing, we suggest you consult an experienced seamster; another useful source is *Singer Sewing Step-by-Step*, which has brilliant instructions and illustrations to assist the home sewer.[8]

A Note on Gussets

Since medieval tailoring often involved inserting a gusset into a slit, we have included the following set of instructions for dealing with them.

Assume you are using a 1/2 inch seam allowance, and want to insert a gusset in the front of a kirtle. The same technique was also used on hoods and sleeves (as in the cases of the side-gore hoods and the Charles of Blois doublet).

Find the spot near the tip of the gusset where it is one inch wide, and put a dot in the middle of that inch (i.e., 1/2 inch from either edge). Mark the wrong side at the corresponding point. Still on the wrong side, draw a chalk line on the gusset seamline (1/2 inch from right edge). This line will pass through the point you just marked. Draw another chalk line on the fabric you want to set the gusset into, at the place you want the gusset to go. Don't cut yet.

Pin the gusset to the kirtle, right sides together. The bottom right corner of the gusset should line up with the bottom of the kirtle and the line you drew on it. The gusset itself will be off center with respect to the line. Now sew along the line you drew on the gusset from the dot near the point to the bottom. Be sure to fasten your stitching with a knot or backstitch at the point. Cut along the line drawn on the kirtle until about three inches away from the point. Move the gusset seam allowance out of the way and carefully cut along the line right up to, but not through, the point where you started. Be careful not to cut the stitching at that point. You will see that while the seam allowance on the gusset is 1/2 inch throughout, on the kirtle it will taper towards the point.

Open out the gusset, flip over the kirtle, and match the unsewn side of the gusset to the other side of the cut line, right sides together. Line up the bottom corners as before, and you will see that once again the kirtle side of the seam allowance tapers towards the point, with the kirtle side on top. You want this seam to look like a mirror image of the last one. Pin in place, and stitch 1/2 inch from the side of the gusset, sewing from the dot to the bottom, again anchoring your stitching securely at the dot. Be careful not to stitch over the rest of the kirtle or gusset, or anything but the seam.

Breech

Breeches were worn only by men. No medieval examples of breeches survive, so this design is purely conjectural, based on the evidence of medieval artwork. They would usually have been made of white linen.

The pattern is scaled to a men's medium, with a 1/2 inch seam and hem allowance and a 3/4 inch casing at the top for a drawstring included in the cutting diagram. The waist size should be enough to put your hips through. Since they are made from inelastic fabric, the correct size will probably look much larger than you might expect, based on your experience with modern underwear.

Cutting (Cut one of each piece)

G-F = **G'-F'** = half of (hip measurement plus 2–3 inches for ease and seam allowances)

G-H = **G'-H'** = waist to upper thigh along outseam

A-E = **A'-E'** = **D-H** = **D'-H'** = half of (the circumference of the thigh plus 2–3 inches for ease and seam allowance)

A-B = **A'-B'** = **C-D** = **C'-D'** = 2 inches along straight section of the inseam

Sharp corners at **B, C, B',**and **C'** are a source of weakness. The cutting line between **B** and **C** should be a semicircle of about 1/2 inch radius on size medium and the corners at **B'** and **C'** similarly rounded.

B'-C' = 3 1/4" measured across the highest points on the straight sections of the inseams

Sewing

Place the two pieces right side together and stitch the side seams together (**G-H** and **E-F**). Then stitch **A-B** to **A'-B'** and **C-D** to **C'-D'**. Ease **B'-C'** to **B-C** and stitch, forming a pocket for comfort. Hem the leg cuffs. Hem back 3/4 inch at the top to make a channel for the drawstring. Make two round or vertical buttonholes at I and J, to thread the drawstring through. The drawstring should double past itself in front within the casing, so that the ends of the drawstring point away from each other. This will help draw the fabric into a pouch in front. If you wish to use the drawstring to

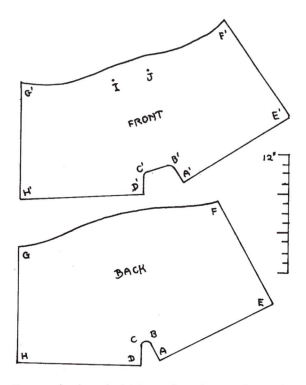

Pattern for breech. McLean, based on a design by
Robert MacPherson.

support hose, make two more holes just below the drawstring, one above
the center points of each thigh, to tie your hose to: the points will pass
around the drawstring on the outside of the casing.

This design can be adjusted to allow for a belt instead of a drawstring.

Hose

This pattern is a composite based on the surviving medieval hose shown
earlier. It is for the right leg—reverse it for the left. The scale is 1/9 full
size for a 6′2″, 210-pound man with size-13 feet. Note that this pattern
includes a 1/2 inch seam allowance. You will need to adjust for your size,
build, and the elasticity of your fabric. You may wish to try a mock-up of
inexpensive fabric first. The best final material is wool, since it affords the
most stretch. Remember to cut on the bias to allow the hose to stretch.

Cutting

Short hose should come just above the knee before you fold the top
over your garter. For long hose, **A-E** should be a few inches less than the

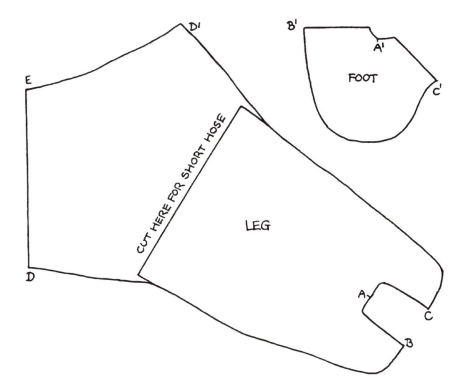

Pattern for hose. McLean.

distance from the top of your instep to your belt to allow for the stretch of the fabric when you tie it up. **D-D'** should equal the circumference of your thigh just below your buttocks, plus 2″. For **B'-C'** measure around your foot at the highest point of the instep and under your arch and add 1 1/2 inches. The narrowest point on the ankle should leave you just enough room to force your heel through with your toe pointed. A pair of jeans that fit you well can be a helpful starting point.

Put right side to right side and sew leg and foot together. You may get the best results by sewing out from the center, sewing from **A** to **B** and then **A** to **C**. Press and finish the seam. Now line **B** up against **C** and sew sole seam forward to the toe. Now sew from **B-C** up the back of the leg to the top of the hose. **B-C** should fall under the arch of the foot, and the sole seam should curve slightly to avoid the ball of the foot. Press and finish this seam. Finish the top of the hose.

For long hose, you will need to make some arrangement to attach the points. This may be a button sewn to the top, or you may instead reinforce the top with canvas or other fabric and let in holes or slots through which the points can pass. You will need an attachment point at **E,** and you can include additional points at the side.

Shirt

A shirt is an important part of a complete medieval outfit. It adds comfort under wool, absorbs sweat and keeps it away from your outer clothes, and gives you the option of dealing with hot weather, like a medieval person, by stripping off your kirtle. In addition, it enhances the general historical experience to be dressed medievally to the skin.

The design here, for both men and women, is a modified version of the thirteenth-century St. Louis shirt. The normal fabric would be white linen. To assemble the shirt, draft and cut your pieces as shown. Stitch the sleeves to the body, stitch up the side seam and sleeve seam, stitch in the gores in the front and back, hem the cuffs and bottom edge, and either hem back the neck opening or finish it with seam binding, braided lacing, or some similar material.

Cutting

Width of Body = 1/2 chest measurement + 2 inches or more.

Length of Body = 2 × distance from shoulder to hem. Men's shirts ranged from crotch-length to mid-thigh. Women's were calf-length or longer.

Gusset Width = about 4/10 height. The gussets can be omitted on a man's shirt. Gussets run from the bottom of the sleeve to the hem.

Sleeve Length = distance from shoulder to first knuckle with elbow bent.

Sleeve Width at Cuff = circumference of fist + 1 inch.

Sleeve Width at Shoulder = 1 2/3 width at cuff.

Sewing

Stitch sleeve to body. Sew bias edge of gusset to body section so that selvage or warp edge will form a side seam (this is important for the garment to drape properly). Stitch up the sleeve and side seam. If making a man's shirt without gussets, leave the side seam open from hips down. Hem cuffs and bottom edge and finish neck with hem, seam binding, or similar material.

Kirtle

The simplest kind of male or female overgarment to reproduce is the Boksten-style kirtle. The ideal fabric is wool.

Cutting

Width of Body = 1/2 chest measurement + 2 inches or more.

Length of Body = 2 × distance from shoulder to hem. Hems ranged from slightly above the knee to just above the ankle for men, ankle to floor-length for women. The pattern is drafted for a kirtle slightly below the knee.

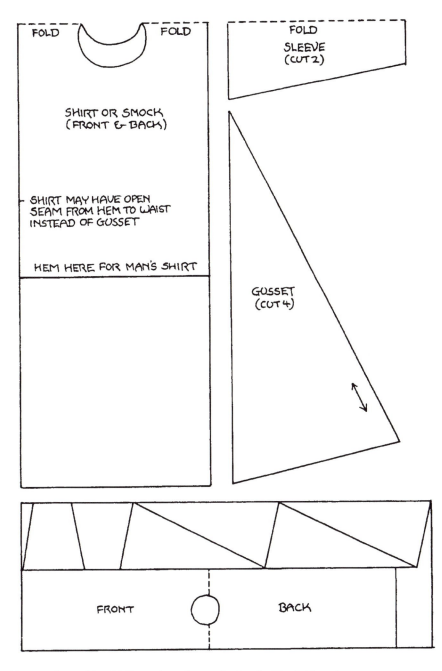

Pattern for a shirt. McLean, based on a design by Daniel Jennings.

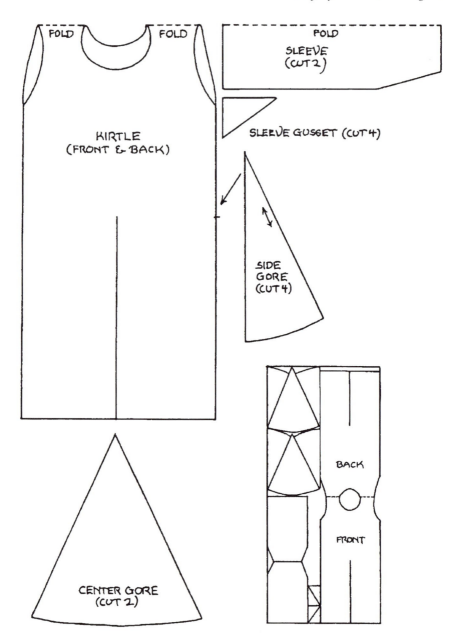

Pattern for a kirtle. McLean

Slits run from hem to 3 inches below the sternum.

Center gores are as long as slits and 1/2 to 2/3 as wide as their height. Side gores (cut 4) are half as wide as center gores.

Sleeve Length = distance from shoulder to first knuckle with elbow bent.

Sleeve Width at Cuff = circumference of fist + 2 inches.

Sleeve Width at Shoulder = 1 1/3 × width at cuff.

Sleeve gussets are right triangles measuring about 3 inches on each leg.

Sewing

Stitch the sleeve gussets to the sleeves. Stitch the center gores into the slits. Stitch the sleeves to the body. Sew the bias edge of the side gores to the edges of the body section, so that the selvage or warp edge will form the center side seam (as with the shirt, this is important if you want the garment to drape properly). Stitch up the sleeve and side seams. Hem the cuffs and bottom edge and finish the neck as with the shirt.

Men's Headgear

The hood is the distinctive masculine style of headgear, and it is easy to reproduce. The design is based on hood no. 70 from Herjolfsnes. In scaling the pattern to fit, the most critical dimension is the circumference of the neck (at **A-B**), which must be just great enough to go over your head. Scale this pattern up so that **A-B** = 1/2 inch + 1/2 the circumference of your head (adding your preferred seam allowance).

Wool is the best material for the hood. Cut two of the head piece and the tail, and one gusset. You can eliminate the gusset by extending the shoulder cape as shown, but the gusset saves fabric and lets you put the face opening along the selvage for a simpler, more durable finish.

Placing right side to right side, sew the tail pieces to the head pieces. Sew the gusset to the front of one of the head pieces. Press the seams. Put the two halves together right side to right side and sew them together from the front of the head to the back of the cape. Sew the front seam, working from the face down. Turn right side out. A dowel is useful for pushing the tippet through.

You can either finish the seams and hem the cape and face opening, or add a lining. A lining is durable, fashionable, and in many ways no more difficult than hemming and finishing seams, but it is not essential.

A man might also wear a coif for additional warmth or protection. Cut two pieces of linen as shown, stitch up the top and back, and add ties at the bottom front. The coif could also be made of leather.

Women's Headgear

The distinctive female headgear of the period is the veil and wimple, and it has the added advantage of being an easy way to cover up a modern hairstyle. The band should be a tightly woven linen that will not stretch, or else a woven band of trim, long enough to reach all the way around your head from the top, under the chin. For the veil, cut a

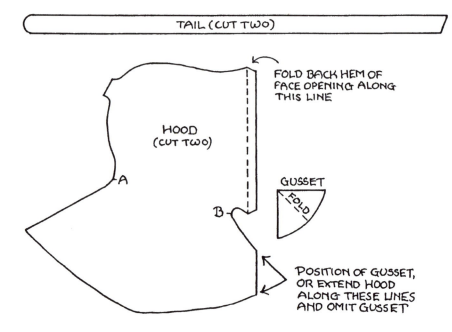

Pattern for a hood. McLean.

Pattern for a coif. McLean.

rectangle of very light linen or silk: the long dimension should reach from your forehead across the top of your head to the base of your shoulder blades, the short dimension from shoulder to shoulder across the head (it can be even larger if you like). For the wimple, cut a rectangle of the same fabric and about half the size. Both the veil and wimple will need to be hemmed. Wrap the band under your chin and over the top of your head, pinning it tight. Pin point **A** on the wimple to the band just above your left ear, and pin point **B** just above your right ear. Place the veil on top of your head, and pin it to the band at the sides of your head. Add any additional pins to achieve a drape which pleases you (have a look at the illustrations in this chapter to get an idea of what it might look like).

Shoes

An easy ersatz medieval shoe can be had in the form of Tai Chi slippers, especially the sort with a buckle. However, it is not particularly difficult to make a fourteenth-century turnshoe. The easiest way is to make

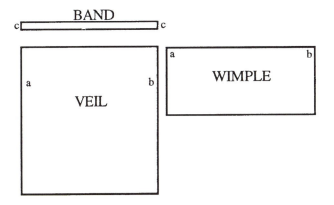

Pattern for a wimple. Forgeng, based on a design by Karen Walter.

a paper pattern, cut according to one of the patterns illustrated earlier in this chapter, but fitted to a cobbler's last in your size (if you cannot obtain a last, you can fit the pattern directly to your foot, although the fit will not be as good). Sew up the shoes inside out using an awl or a glover's needle and heavy waxed thread, first assembling the uppers, then attaching the soles. Be sure to leave the tip of the toe loose (the toe will otherwise be very difficult to turn), with long thread ends left on what will become the outside of the toe. Using these threads, turn the shoe inside out, then tighten the toe threads and sew up the toe from the outside. You may wish to glue or sew on an extra sole of thicker leather for heavier use.

Buttons, Holes, and Garters

To make a cloth button, cut a 1 1/2 inch diameter circle, then sew a gathering stitch around it. Gather the stitch to make a kind of purse; flatten the purse into a bulging disk, with the opening in the center of the top; then sew opposite points on the edge of the disk to each other to make the button. An easier, if less authentic, way to reproduce a cloth-covered button is with a kit, which is available at most fabric stores.

To make eyelets, thrust a pointed object through the weave of the fabric, spreading the weave (this will rip fibers, but don't worry about it), or use an eyelet punch. The eyelet is then stitched in a simple buttonhole stitch, drawing the overcasts tightly to open the hole, with the stitching cast in two layers before moving on to the next eyelet. Medieval buttonholes were constructed similarly to eyelets, the difference being that the buttonhole was first cut into the fabric and was not enlarged appreciably by the subsequent stitching.

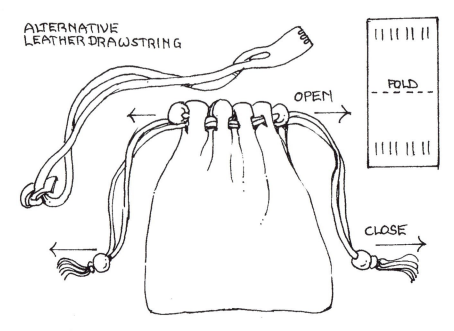

Reconstruction and cutting diagram for a pouch. These often had a separate suspension strap, not shown here, which could attach to the purse at the top where the drawstrings exited, and might be long enough to allow the pouch to hang inside the outer garment just above its hem. McLean.

To attach buttons, fold the edge of the garment under and secure the buttons by stitching with stout thread through the folded fabric. The loose edge of the fabric can be secured with top stitching.

Garters can be easily made of a strip of fairly elastic fabric from about 1 to 2 inches wide and long enough to tie in a bow just below the knee.

Belt, Purse, and Pouch

For a belt, the ideal would be a leather belt 1–2 inches broad, with a buckle and a tongue. Higher quality belts would have metal strap ends and buckle plates.

The easiest means of making a pouch is with a piece of leather or cloth roughly 6 × 12 inches. Fold it in half the short way, sew up the two sides, turn it inside out. If using cloth, fold the top edge in and sew it down to make a drawstring channel; open holes into the channel on each side, and thread a drawstring through. If using leather, simply punch holes in it for the drawstring. If the purse is made of fabric, it will be necessary to let in eyelets to avoid fraying. Purses frequently had a double drawstring, allowing them to be easily closed or opened by pulling the drawstring ends from both sides.

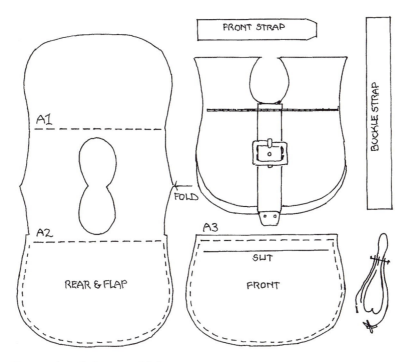

Pattern for a belt purse. McLean.

To Make a Belt Purse

Place outside to outside and sew the front of the compartment to the rear at bottom and sides. Turn right side out. Fold down the flap and stitch along A1 through A3 and A2, (three layers). A strap may be sewn to the front and rear of the purse with the same line of stitching. Leather binding was often used for this seam instead of thread.

Purses of this type excavated in the Netherlands typically ranged from 7 to 10 inches in width. This is a relatively simple design: belt purses frequently had two compartments, pouchlets sewn to the front of the rear compartment, or both. *Purses in Pieces* by Goubitz is an extensive guide to many of the possible variations.

MAKING A MEDIEVAL LACE

A medieval outfit often involved heavy use of lacing (comparable to modern shoelaces) for such purposes as fastening shoes, holding up hose, or adorning the edges of a kirtle. By a remarkable stroke of luck, a manuscript of the early fifteenth century actually preserves a collection of very clear instructions for making this kind of lace. As these laces are useful in reproducing clothes and are also a fun and easy medieval craft, we have included a sample here. The text in italics is the original, with the language somewhat modernized.[9]

In the manner of making laces, you shall understand that the first finger next the thumb shall be called A, the second finger B, the third C, the fourth D. Also, sometimes you shall take your bows reversed and sometimes unreversed. When you take your bow reversed, you shall take with the one hand the bow of the other hand from without, so that the side that was beneath on the one hand before is above on the other hand. To take unreversed, take with one hand the bow of the other hand from within so that the side that was above on the one hand is above on the other hand. . . . And sometimes you shall raise your bows, and sometimes you shall lower them. To raise them, take bow B and set it on A, and set bow C on B, and set bow D on C. And to lower them, take bow C and set it on D, set bow B on C, and set bow A on B.

To Make a Broad Lace of Five Bows

Set 2 bows on B and C right, and 3 bows on A, B, and C left. Then shall A right take through bow B of the same hand bow C of the left hand reversed. Then lower the left bows. Then shall A left take through B of the same hand bow C of the right hand reversed. Then lower the right bows, and begin again.

To Make a Round Lace of Five Bows

Put five bows on your fingers as you did in the broad lace. Then shall A right take through B and C of the same hand bow C of the left hand reversed. Then lower the left bows. Then shall A left take through B and C of the same hand bow C of the right hand reversed. Then lower the right bows, and begin again.

To Make a Baston Lace

Take five departed bows, that is to say that one side of each bow be of one color and the other side of another color. Set them on your hand as you did with the round lace, so that the color that is above on the right hand is beneath on the left hand, and the work in the manner of the round lace.

To set up, take five pieces of thread, each at least two feet long—embroidery floss works well. Tie each one into a loop. Next you will need a thin but solid handle to attach them to—a drawer handle or something comparable, provided it is not very thick and can be kept motionless. Take one of the loops, pass it around the handle, and then pass one end of the loop through the other. Tighten it around the handle such that the knot is at the handle. Do the same with the other five loops.

Hold your hands as illustrated in Step 1 of the diagram. To make the broad lace, place one loop on the index finger of the left hand, one on the middle finger, and one on the ring finger; and place one loop on the middle

Setting up a loop. McLean.

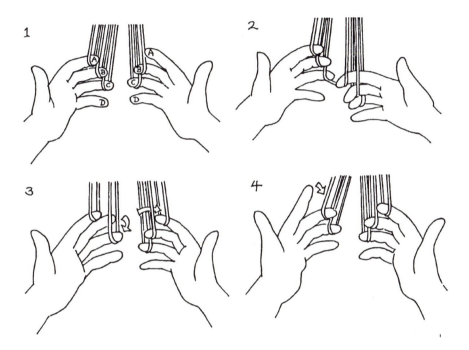

Weaving the lace. McLean.

finger of the right hand and one on the ring finger. Pass the index finger of the right hand through the middle loop on the right hand and hook the loop on the ring finger of the left hand, with the index finger pointing in the same direction as the ring finger it takes the loop from (this position is called reversed; Step 2 in the diagram). Take this loop off the ring finger and bring the index finger back to its original position (this will bring the loop through the middle loop of the left hand; shown on the right hand in Step 3 in the diagram). Pull the loops to make the lace tight, but not too hard.

Now shift all the loops on the left hand down one, the loop on the middle finger going to the ring finger, and the loop on the index finger going to the middle finger (shown on the left hand in Steps 3–4 in the diagram).

Do with your left index finger what you just did with the right, in mirror image, and shift the loops on the right hand as you did on the left. Then start over again. When the loops are too short to go any further, knot the free end to keep it from unraveling, then cut if off the handle and knot that end.

To make the round lace, the index finger passes forward through the first two loops on the same side before hooking the loop from the opposite ring finger; otherwise everything else is the same. The baston lace is the same as the round lace, except that the loops that start on one hand are of one color and the loops on the other hand are of another color.

NOTES

1. *CT* I.415 ff.

2. E. Crowfoot, F. Pritchard, and K. Staniland, eds., Medieval Finds from Excavations in London. Vol. 4: Textiles and Clothing (London: HMSO, 1992), 19–20, 199–200.

3. *MED* s.v. "brest."

4. Norman Davis, ed., Paston Letters and Papers of the Fifteenth Century (Oxford: Clarendon Press, 1971), 1.351. The shirt pattern is after Dorothy Burnham, Cut My Cote (Toronto: Royal Ontario Museum, 1973), 12.

5. For examples, see G. Egan and F. Pritchard, eds., Medieval Finds from Excavations in London. Vol. 3: Dress Accessories (London: HMSO, 1991), 35.

6. G. G. Coulton, Medieval Panorama (New York: Macmillan, 1938), 311.

7. For jewelry, see Crowfoot and Pritchard, Accessories and Jonathan Alexander and Paul Binski, eds., Age of Chivalry: Art in Plantagenet England 1200–1400 (London: Royal Academy of Arts, 1987).

8. Cy DeCosse Incorporated, Singer Sewing Step-by-Step (Minnetonka MN: Cy DeCosse, 1990).

9. The original Middle English text was edited by Eric Stanley as "Directions for making many sorts of laces" in B. Rowland, ed., Chaucer and Middle English Studies in Honour of Russell Hope Robbins (London: Allen and Unwin, 1974), 95–103. For a study of this text, see Elizabeth Benns, "'Set on Yowre Hondys': Fifteenth-century Instructions for Fingerloop Braiding," in Medieval Clothing and Textiles 3, ed. Robin Netherton and Gale R. Owen-Crocker (Woodbridge: Boydell Press, 2007), 135–44.

7

ARMS AND ARMOR

England in the fourteenth century was enjoying a period of relative peace. The civil wars of the 1200s were far in the past, and the Wars of the Roses of the 1400s had only a brief prelude in Henry Bolingbroke's seizure of the throne in 1399. Aside from occasional Scottish incursions in the north and French raids on coastal towns in the south, few military actions were fought on English soil.

Yet combat was never very far from daily life in the Middle Ages. Many people had either done military service in person, or had friends or relatives who had fought in the wars against Scotland and France. Even men who stayed home were subject to service in the militia: according to the Statute of Winchester, issued in 1285, men over age 15 were required to own arms in accordance with their income, and commoners were by law supposed to practice the bow regularly to ensure the king had a ready supply of skilled archers. At a fundamental level, military structures pervaded medieval society—the entire feudal network was theoretically a form of military organization.

Even in civilian contexts, violence and the tools of combat were always present in people's awareness. In a world where the structures for law enforcement were comparatively weak, nighttime lighting was feeble, and the roads between one town and the next were long and lonely, individuals often had to rely on themselves for self-defense. Perhaps most important of all, the use of violence did not necessarily carry social stigma in Chaucer's world—it was, after all, the prerogative of the upper class. At all levels of society, there was a potential advantage in being regarded as

**ARMS AND ARMOR REQUIREMENTS
IN LONDON, 1380**

Precept was sent to each alderman to see the men of his ward suitably armed
with basinet, gauntlets of plate, habergeon, sword, dagger, and hatchet,
according to their estate, and inferior men arrayed with good bows, arrows,
sword, and buckler.

Reginald R. Sharpe, *Calendar of Letter Books . . . of the City of London: Letter Book H* (London: John Edward Francis, 1907), 153.

a physically dangerous person, whether as a brawler in the streets, or as a
knight ready to avenge any insult with the sword.

For all of these reasons, several of Chaucer's pilgrims set off for Canterbury equipped with arms and armor: the Knight wears his jupon, stained
with the rust from his mail coat; the Yeoman carries bow and arrows, dagger, sword, and buckler; the Shipman carries a dagger; the Miller carries
a sword and buckler; the Reeve carries a rusty sword. Like the pilgrims'
clothing, their choice of arms tells us something about who they are and
how they wish to be perceived.

THE FOURTEENTH-CENTURY ARMY

The fourteenth-century army consisted of various types of soldiers, with
sharp distinctions of class and income among them. At the top of the military hierarchy was the man-at-arms, a horseman armored from head to
foot, who formed the backbone of the English army in the period. The
man-at-arms was by definition a man of means. He was expected to provide his own equipment, and this equipment was expensive. A full harness,
or set of armor, cost upwards of £2, as much money as a laborer made in
a year. An ordinary warhorse cost £5, and a good one could cost ten times
as much. The man-at-arms' pay was correspondingly high—at 12 pence a
day, his service cost four times as much as that of a common footsoldier.
Men-at-arms on foot were sometimes assigned to garrisons: because garrison duty did not require an expensive horse, they were paid only 8 pence.

The mounted man-at-arms typically carried a lance for delivering an
initial attack at the charge. After the charge, the lance might be discarded
in favor of a more maneuverable weapon such as a sword. The man-at-arms also carried a dagger for close combat. If fighting on foot, he might
go into battle with a staff weapon specialized for foot combat, such as a
short spear or pollaxe.

The English man-at-arms rode a horse to battle, but he usually fought on
foot. Early in the century the English had discovered that they could win
battles by dismounting their men-at-arms. Other things being equal, in a
face-to-face contest properly trained and equipped men on foot have the

Men-at-arms in combat on foot, c. 1400, armed with the usual high proportion of axes, spears, and war-hammers (BL Royal 20 C. VII). McLean.

advantage against an equal number of comparably equipped horsemen. Men on foot can hold a denser formation, outnumbering mounted opponents at the point of impact; and if well disciplined, they are much less likely than horses to whicker nervously and edge away once the yelling and shouting starts. Even if footsoldiers break formation, they can often be rallied, but once mounted troops start riding from the field, they can be almost impossible to regroup. Above all, footsoldiers defending a well-chosen position have a tremendous advantage over their attackers—and the French, England's principal opponents during the period, could usually be counted on to take the offensive in battle.

The chief disadvantages of dismounted men-at-arms were their limited mobility and their cost relative to other sorts of footsoldiers. The limited mobility was less disadvantageous as long as the battle plan was defensive. The cost might have been a drawback if the French had devoted their military resources to fielding large numbers of well trained but cheaper infantry. Fortunately for England, this was not the case. French military leaders of the period saw the men-at-arms as the principal fighting force of their army.

In many cases, French battle tactics involved hurling the mounted men-at-arms against dismounted English men-at-arms who were supported by archers. This was rarely successful, and resulted in the disastrous defeat at Crécy in 1346. An alternative approach was to dismount the men-at-arms to march against their English counterparts, leaving only a small force of mounted troops to support those on foot. This could leave the French men-at-arms weakened from their advance and from arrow fire by the time they reached the English line, as happened in the French defeats at St.-Pol de Léon in 1346, Taillebourg in 1351, and Poitiers in 1356. However, at Cocherel in 1364, the French successfully used this tactic to draw the English out of their defenses. The dismounted French men-at-arms began to withdraw before the strongly positioned English line, provoking their opponents to attack: the English advanced, losing their defensive advantage and the battle.

A substantial social gulf separated the man-at-arms from other sorts of soldiers. Hobelars, less heavily armored horsemen on lower-quality horses, also served in Edward III's armies, but were increasingly replaced by mounted archers in the second half of his reign. English tactics increasingly needed highly mobile mounted infantry rather than second-class cavalry. Hobelars were paid 6 to 8 pence a day.

The distinctive feature of English armies was their reliance on archers: Edward III's army on the Crécy campaign has been estimated at 2,700 men-at-arms, 3,250 mounted archers and hobelars, 7,000 foot archers, and 2,300 other footsoldiers. An archer on foot received from three to six pence a day. His main weapon was his longbow and sheaf of two dozen arrows, but he would also typically carry a sword and perhaps a buckler for close-quarters combat, and he might wear some light armor for personal protection. Archers could be used very effectively in conjunction with the men-at-arms, weakening the enemy sufficiently for the men-at-arms to break them. They were often mounted so they could keep up with the men-at arms in a fast moving strike force. Mounted archers were paid at the same rate as hobelars.

The infantry in English armies overseas were overwhelmingly archers, but footsoldiers armed for hand-to-hand combat were common in English militias for home defense, as well as playing a part in armies on the continent or in Scotland. Such infantry carried spears, axes, and other staff weapons, with swords as secondary sidearms. This sort of soldier was often expected to have a habergeon, helmet and gauntlets, and could have plate protection for their torso and arms. Leg harness was expensive and tiring to march in, and marching infantry rarely wore it.

At the base of the military hierarchy were irregular troops called ribalds or pillars. Often their only weapon was a long knife. They stayed out of the front lines but generally made themselves useful by foraging, skirmishing, pillaging, and finishing off the wounded. There were also servants whose duties included camp chores and holding the horses of the dismounted men-at-arms. Such servants sometimes made a useful contribution to the fighting—as at Otterburn in 1388, where they defended the Scottish camp as their masters armed themselves. However, they were equally likely to panic and run off with the horses.

In battle, troops of the same type usually fought together; but for purposes of recruitment, muster, and pay they were organized as retinues comprising all these sorts of troops (sometimes containing only a few men), each troop under the command of the man-at-arms that raised them.

Changing English armor in the fourteenth century. From left to right, Sir Hugh Hastings, 1347, Sir Miles de Stapleton, 1364, and Sir John de St. Quintin 1397. Foster, Stothard, and Ashdown.

ARMOR

The status of soldiers in the field was instantly recognizable from the armor they wore. Surprisingly little medieval armor has actually survived, and even less from before 1400. The fighting equipment of the medieval man-at-arms tended to get broken, rusted, or recycled. The suits of armor seen in museums, which shape the popular image of the medieval knight, generally date to the late 1500s. It has survived precisely because it was made when armor was losing its importance on the battlefield and was less likely to be destroyed in use.

The latter part of the fourteenth century was a time of rapid evolution in armor; it might even be considered the first and last period of major revolution in armor technology. Before 1300, knights were still armored very much like the men who fought for William the Conqueror in 1066, protected primarily by an iron helmet and clad in mail, a fine mesh of riveted iron rings. This was increasingly supplemented by solid plates of iron or "cuirbouilli" (hardened leather) to offer better protection at critical points such as the joints or vital organs. During the course of the fourteenth century, solid steel plates became the principal component of the best armor; the plates were carefully shaped, and articulated with each other by systems of rivets and leather straps that allowed the body to move freely. The finest harnesses came from Italy, which had the technological lead in producing plate steel armor with higher carbon content and hardened by heat treatment.

The Suit of Armor

Modern people, who are likely to see armor only from the outside, tend to forget that it was in many ways just an elaborate form of clothing. Like clothing, it was worn in layers, each of which had to be put on and fastened in succession. The following pages offer an idea of what it was like to wear a knight's full harness, with some additional information on the sorts of protection used by ordinary soldiers.

The knight preparing for battle wore ordinary civilian clothes as his innermost layer: breech, hose, and shoes. He might also wear a shirt, although a fifteenth-century set of instructions for arming, *How a Man Shall Be Armed*, recommends omitting the shirt, probably to avoid the discomfort of the shirt bunching up within the doublet. He might also wear a padded coif on his head. This had been common in the thirteenth century, but as the fourteenth century progressed such coifs were less used by aristocratic warriors, although they were still worn by more ordinary soldiers.

Next came the innermost protective garment for the torso, variously called a doublet, aketon, gambeson, jupon, or pourpoint—the terms were not fixed, and they might also be used to designate a similar garment worn *outside* the armor. The military doublet was essentially a sturdier version

---

SIR GAWAIN DONS HIS ARMOR IN *SIR GAWAIN AND THE GREEN KNIGHT*, c. 1390

He dwelled there all that day, and dresses in the morn,
asks early for his arms, and all of them were brought:
first a Toulousan tapestry extended over the floor,
and grand was the gold that gleamed upon it;
the stout man steps onto it, and the steel he handles;
adorned in a doublet of dear Tarsian silk,
and then a well crafted *capados* [a kind of cape], cut close above,
that was bound inside with a bright pelt lining,
then they set the sabatons on the man's feet,
lapped his legs in steel with lovely greaves,
with poleins affixed to them, polished full clean,
attached to his knees with knots of gold,

comely cuisses that cunningly enclosed
his thick-muscled thighs, attached with thongs,
and then the linked byrnie [mail-coat] of bright steel rings
enwrapped that man with wondrous material,
and well burnished bracers upon both his arms,
with good and gay couters, and gloves of plate,
and all the goodly gear that should help him that time,
with a rich coat-armor;
his golden spurs he strapped on with pride,
girt with a sword full sure,with a silken cincture about his sides.

Translated by J. L. Forgeng from the Middle English in *Sir Gawain and the Green Knight*, ed. J.R.R. Tolkien and E. V. Gordon (Oxford: Clarendon Press, 1936), ll. 566–89.

of the civilian doublet or coathardie of the period. In fact, civilian coathardies probably imitated the cut of military doublets: the close-fitted look that became fashionable in Chaucer's day probably developed because a man-at-arms in plate armor needed a closely tailored garment that would fit under his plate harness.

The doublet was made of a sturdy, washable fabric like linen or fustian, a cloth made of both linen and cotton fibers. A full suit of armor is heavily insulating, so the doublet helped absorb sweat, and it was padded to provide comfort and protection. Lacing holes at the legs and arms served for attaching armor. Military doublets commonly laced up the front, giving a tightly trussed fit over the abdomen that helped distribute the weight of the leg harness.

Man in an arming doublet, a reconstruction based on the Charles de Blois doublet. To illustrate its use, he is shown with some leg and arm harness attached. Vernier.

Leg Harness

Once the soft garments were in place, the armor itself was strapped and tied on, working from the ground up, an order dictated by the way in which the various components overlapped. First came foot pieces called sabatons. These were essentially armor overshoes made of a series of

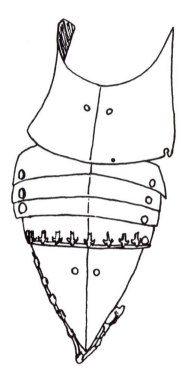

Remains of a sabaton. Vernier.

articulating plates, pointed at the toe to match the shape of the shoe; another plate at the back wrapped around the heel. The sabatons laced to the shoe itself. Less expensive versions were made from hardened leather. Some men-at-arms went without sabatons, skimping on protection for a little less encumbrance.

Next came the shin-guards called greaves. These flared over the foot and at the ankles for ease of motion, arching over the foot to reach close to the ground on each side. The greaves strapped directly to the shins and could lace to the sabatons.

After the greaves came the cuisses, which protected the thighs. These might be made of steel plate, but earlier in the period they were often made of leather or fabric with steel splints riveted lengthwise inside. Below the cuisses were knee pieces called poleines, which were half round or slightly pointed in profile, usually with a spade- or kidney-shaped wing on the outside to protect the back of the joint. Articulated at the base of the poleine was a demi-greave, a small plate that lapped over the top of the greave.

The cuisse, poleine, and demi-greave were often a single unit, attaching like contemporary hose by laces to the bottom of the doublet. A leather tab with holes was riveted to the top edge of the cuisse for this purpose. An additional strap or two held the cuisse to the thigh; another secured the poleine, and another the demi-greave. The cuisse, poleine, and demi-greave connected to each other via intermediary lames like the segments of a lobster's tail, allowing more flexibility than if they were joined directly to each other. The entire leg assembly could flex to a little less than a right angle—enough to kneel in, but not enough to squat. Alternatively, the entire leg might be protected with chausses, leg-coverings of mail similar to civilian hose. These were especially common earlier in the century.

Torso Armor

Next came the main body protection. A mail shirt called a habergeon or hauberk was usually worn on top of the doublet; a typical shirt might weigh about 20 pounds. The habergeon was waisted, and surviving examples show sophisticated tailoring. The tailoring not only addressed the concerns of the fashion-conscious warrior but also made the garment more practical, because the close-waisted design helped distribute some of the shirt's weight to the hips and fit better under the body armor. The sleeves could be full-length, tailored to a narrow cuff, half-sleeves ending just above the elbow, or three-quarter sleeves that protected the inside of the elbow but left no unnecessary bulk on the forearms. The cuff, collar, and skirt edges of the habergeon were often made with a few rows of brass links to give the effect of a golden border, and they might be dagged for additional style.

A jesseraunt was a mail shirt covered and perhaps lined with fabric, and could fill the same function. A separate mail collar, called a pisan or standard, could be worn in addition to protect the neck.

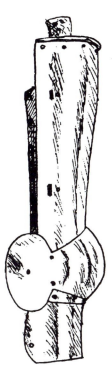

Leg harness consisting of cuisse, poleine, and demi-greave. Vernier.

In previous centuries the mail shirt had been considered adequate body protection, but by the fourteenth century it was supplemented with solid iron plates. The move towards plate body armor began with the "coat-of-plates," which fourteenth-century Englishmen probably called a "jack," "plates," or "a pair of plates." There were many variations on the coat-of-plates, but most were constructed of rectangular iron or steel plates riveted inside a cloth or leather "coat." The coat itself was either sleeveless (opening at the front, back, or sides) or sleeved like a poncho. The plates overlapped, and each plate had rivets only along one edge so that it could work flexibly over the plates below it. Originally simple and tubular in outline, shortly after the middle of the century the coat-of-plates developed a tailored, narrow waist that mirrored civilian fashions.

Over time, the coat-of-plates evolved in two different directions. On some armors the plates became smaller and more numerous, allowing greater flexibility but sacrificing a degree of protection. References to "brigandine" appear as early as 1368, and it is likely that then, as later, the term referred to this sort of armor. The name came from its popularity among mercenary footsoldiers known as "brigands," although knights also wore this type of protection.

Knights wearing coats-of-plates. Flemish, 1338–1344
(RA). Vernier.

Other coats-of-plates developed in the opposite direction. A large
plate spreads the force of a blow better than several small ones and is
less likely to catch the point of a weapon. By the middle of the century
some coats-of-plates included a large oval plate directly over the chest.
By the 1370s this plate commonly covered the entire front of the ribcage:
with the head, chest, and limbs now protected by solid plates, the suit of
full plate armor had come into being.

The breastplate could be either an integral part of the coat-of-plates or a
separate reinforcement. Once it became large enough to protect the entire ribcage it was often worn as a separate defense in its own right, over the habergeon, supported by crossed straps in back. By the 1370s the separate steel
breastplate was increasingly common. It might have v-shaped stop-ribs to
deflect lance points from the neck, or a medial ridge to add strength and help
deflect blows. Many were fitted with a hook near the right armpit known as a
lance-rest or arrest, so named from the French *arrest de lance* (lance-stop). The
rest helped control the lance, but most importantly it spread the impact from
the lance through the wearer's breastplate, allowing more power to be delivered at the tip of the weapon, and reducing the risk of injury to the wielder.

The breastplate only covered the front of the ribs. Some men-at-arms
considered this sufficient supplement to the mail shirt, but by the 1370s
it was often worn with a short apron of overlapping plates or horizontal hoops that protected the abdomen, which would eventually become a
skirt of plates reaching to the hips. Around the same time additional plates
began to carry the breastplate's protection partway around the back. Evidence for complete backplates appears around 1400.

By this time much of the habergeon's protection was duplicated by plate armor worn over it. Eventually it began to be replaced by separate mail defenses that protected those areas not covered by plate: breeches of mail or a skirt (called a pauncer) to protect the belly and groin. With pisan, pauncer, and plate armor, the only place where a habergeon offered additional coverage was at the armpit and inside the elbow; and by the early 1400s gussets or sleeves of mail were being attached to the doublet at these points to make the habergeon unnecessary.

A breastplate, with V-shaped stop-rib just below the neckline to deflect lance points, and two holes next to the right armpit for attaching a lance-rest. Vernier.

Arm Harness

The next step was to put on the arm harness. At the top was the rerebrace, which covered the upper arm. Like the cuisses, it often had a leather strip riveted to the top edge, with holes for laces to secure it to the doublet. The rerebrace did not always extend all the way around: some examples covered only the back or side of the arm. Full rerebraces enclosed the entire upper arm, with a hinge to allow them to be opened and straps and buckles to fasten them shut.

Below the rerebrace was the elbow piece called a couter. The couter was small and conical, often shaped to a point, with a wing on the outer side as on the poleine, and with buckled straps to secure the arm harness snugly to the arm. At the bottom of the arm was the vambrace, which protected the forearm and was hinged and buckled like a rerebrace.

The best rerebraces and vambraces were made of plate; but as with the leg harness, splint was a common alternative. In fact, many men-at-arms wore only mail on their arms almost to the end of the century. The rerebrace, couter, and vambrace might all be attached to each other by articulated joints, with extra lames in between to allow more flexibility; or they might all be separate pieces, lacing to each other or to the doublet.

The shoulder was the most difficult joint to protect. It is a ball-and-socket joint with greater range of motion than any other major joint, and its mobility was crucial in combat. Plate shoulder armor was by no means universal even by the end of the century. The earliest and virtually the only surviving specimens from the fourteenth century are from graves from the Battle of Wisby (1361). They are simple spade-shaped or oval plates lightly hollowed, hinged to the shoulders of the coat-of-plates. A more developed sort of protection appeared in the 1340s: eventually coming to be known as a pauldron, it consisted of a shoulder cap with several narrow overlapping lames descending below it over the edge of the shoulder,

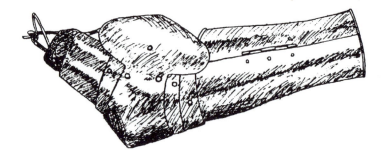

Arm harness consisting of couter and vambrace. Vernier.

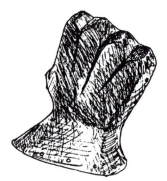

An Italian gauntlet of c. 1370. Vernier.

held together by leather strips underneath for flexibility. The pauldron either connected directly to the rerebrace or, later in the century, was strapped down over it.

In many cases the torso armor was covered by a decorative cloth over-garment, often padded for extra protection. The garment was known as a gambeson, jupon, or coat armor—the last referring to the heraldic device with which it was decorated, using embroidery, paint, or even gold leaf. During the reign of Edward III the garments were typically tight-fitting and sleeveless, but by the end of the century a variety of forms were popular following the line of civilian gowns, often with banana, bagpipe, angel-wing or elbow-length sleeves. Loosely fitted A-line body shapes were worn alongside more tailored versions, particularly for coat armors. In some instances the garment was worn under the breastplate. Some common soldiers relied on a long multilayered quilted coat as their sole body protection.

Gauntlets

Finally, the man-at-arms donned gauntlets and a helmet. Steel gauntlets in this period had a distinctive hourglass shape, with a narrow wrist and flaring cuff to protect the wrist while allowing it to move freely. The knuckles were sometimes equipped with metal spikes known as gadlings; on the Black Prince's gauntlets the gadlings were cast in the shape of small lions. Usually the finger lames were attached to a leather strip running down the finger; the entire gauntlet assembly was stitched to a glove of leather or fabric. Less expensive gauntlets were made of leather or fabric reinforced with baleen or iron plates.

Helmets

The most characteristic style of helmet in the fourteenth century was the basinet. It resembled a kind of steel hood, with a point somewhere above the crown of the head, a profile that helped deflect attacks from above. The basinet covered the entire head above the neck, except for the face. The basinet evolved from a hemispherical skull cap worn in the thirteenth century and was already well developed by the 1320s. Towards the end of the century the point became more pronounced. Typically a light crest ran up

A French jupon of c. 1380. Vernier.

the front to the point, continuing about one-third of the way down the back; as with crested breastplates, this design helped deflect incoming weapons.

For extra protection, the face opening could be fitted with a visor. The most characteristic form of visor was the so-called "hounskull," which featured a pointed snout that helped to deflect weapons, as well as giving the wearer an intimidating, bestial look; other visors had a rounded face.

In addition to its distinctive snout, the hounskull visor had eye slits and an angular mouth slit. In the later part of the century, the mouth was cut in vertical slits suggesting teeth, adding to the fierce look of the helmet. Breathing holes were often pierced on the right side only, as the left side was the typical target for incoming lances. There might also be additional holes around the mouth opening to improve ventilation.

Even with additional holes, a man-at-arms wearing a helmet with a closed visor had poor airflow and a severely limited field of vision. The visor was designed to be opened easily to allow the wearer to catch a breath, look around, and presumably to take water. Many contemporary illustrations show soldiers fighting with the visor open, or with no visor at all. Most visors pivoted on bolts at the temples, although some had a single hinge at the forehead. The side pivots generally had a hinge-and-pin arrangement that allowed the visor to be removed.

To protect the neck, the basinet was fitted with a mail skirt, or aventail. This was stitched to a leather strap pierced with holes. The holes fitted over eyes, or vervelles, protruding around the lower edge of the basinet. The aventail was held in place by a heavy cord passing through the vervelles. The basinet also had a row of closely spaced holes around the edge to which a lining was stitched. The lining was stuffed with wool or hair to provide extra protection for the head; surviving linings are cut into scallops at the top, through which a cord is drawn to adjust for size. The aventail might also be equipped with a padded lining. Basinets with

A late fourteenth-century basinet with hounskull
visor and aventail. Higgins Armory Museum 938.a.

A great helm placed over a basinet, after an Italian manuscript of
c. 1380. Vernier.

aventails do not appear to have been fitted with chin straps. Helmets were often
equipped with a strap hanging down the
back that buckled to the wearer's back-
armor between the shoulder blades.

In the early part of the century the
basinet was often worn under a great
helm, a less fitted form of helmet that
had evolved from the barrel-shaped
helms of the thirteenth century. As the
century progressed, the great helm was
less used on the battlefield but gave rise
to a specialized jousting helmet, the frog-
mouth helm. This form of helm was fully
developed by the end of the century.

Light helmets were also common in
the late fourteenth century, especially for
the ordinary footsoldier. One style was

the kettle hat, so called from its vague resemblance to a medieval pot turned upside-down. In the fourteenth century it was typically pointed like the basinet, with a brim generally not too broad and often pointed at the front. The brim helped to deflect descending weapons without impairing vision or ventilation. This highly practical helmet was worn by knights and even by kings, although it was particularly popular among footsoldiers. Such helmets might be equipped with chin straps.

The barbuta was also common during this period, particularly in Italy. It was pointed like the basinet, though the point was more or less centered on the top of the head. This style was distinguished by its narrow face opening and long sides, which were deep enough to protect the neck without an aventail.

The simplest helmets were rounded, covered little more than the top of the skull, and were apparently known as pallets. Light helmets were often worn over a mail hood.

Decoration

Most surviving armor of the fourteenth century is fairly plain and utilitarian, but armor was a status symbol as well as a tool and was often embellished for display and delight. Brass borders, sometimes engraved, were one of the more common sorts of adornment. The surface of the armor might be finished in one of several ways. Often it was covered with cloth—almost every part of the armor might be treated in this way except the knees, elbows, and visor. Alternatively, the plates might be painted. Towards the end of the century it was becoming fashionable to leave the armor uncovered and highly polished, a style known as "white" armor that was to dominate the fifteenth century.

Surcoats, tabards, and coat-armors were decorative as well as practical. Indeed, exaggerated sleeves and dagging sometimes diminished the garment's practicality. Sir John Chandos, one of the great captains of the Hundred Years' War, came to an untimely end in 1370 when he tripped over his long robe and pitched forward onto a French spear. Such garments might be decorated with a single large representation of the wearer's arms, or a small badge or device might be repeated over the entire garment. On top of the armor or surcoat the aristocratic warrior often wore the distinctive plaque belt that was fashionable in civilian use.

Protection

Full armor of this era could be highly protective, but there was considerable variation. Men-at-arms made individual choices in how completely to armor themselves, and many chose to sacrifice protection for the sake of better mobility and vision. The metal itself ranged from expensive medium-carbon steel heat-treated for extra hardness to cheaper wrought iron. The typical profile for documented pieces of the period is low- to medium-carbon steel, sometimes heat treated, but still somewhat inferior to modern mild steel because of slag impurities left over from the refining process.

The level of protection also depended on the nature of the attack. Edge blows with a sword might be effective against unarmored or lightly armored targets, or they might damage armor straps and laces, but they had little impact against the main defenses of a man-at-arms in full plate harness. Combat manuals from Chaucer's lifetime and shortly afterwards teach the man-at-arms to thrust against armored opponents, holding the sword like a short spear, with the main hand on the hilt and the secondary hand on the blade. This gave the combatant the point control he needed in order to target gaps between the plates. The openings at the neck, armpits, elbows, groin, and back of the legs normally had secondary protection of mail, but this could be broken through by a powerful piercing attack. Other gaps such as the eyeslot and inside the palm and the cuff of the gauntlet had no backup protection.

Axe blades had a better chance of damaging plate armor and injuring its wearer, particularly when a long weapon was wielded with two hands. Powerful piercing weapons, such as crossbow bolts and the beaks on pol-laxes and halberds, were capable of penetrating plate steel, and generally had heavy cross-sections to make this possible. However, this required a forceful impact at something near a 90-degree angle to the surface, so plate armor was generally designed with glancing surfaces to offer the minimum opportunity for a square hit. Even when an attack penetrated, armor reduced its effectiveness because the weapon expended much of its force in breaking through the metal.

Recent tests have attempted to quantify the protectiveness of armor, par-ticularly against missile weapons. Results suggest that even the thinner plates of the best harness could probably defeat a heavy 140-pound bow at close range. This is in keeping with the evidence of sources like Frois-sart, who attributes the French victory at Cocherel in part to the quality of the French armor: "The archers . . . began to exert themselves handsomely in shooting, but the French were so strongly armed and shielded against their arrows, they were but little hurt by them, if at all."[1] With an inferior iron harness, a breastplate worn over mail and the helmet front could also defeat such a bow at short range, but the thinner limbs and the sides of the helmet would be vulnerable to a 100-pound bow out to 180 yards if the arrow hit squarely.

Crushing weapons like maces and hammers might injure or stun a man-at-arms through the armor. Padding was worn under the harness to reduce this risk, although this padding was less substantial for the limbs than for the head and torso. Such weapons could also crack the plates, particularly since slag impurities in the metal constituted points of weak-ness that could lead to fracture. Even if the armor did not crack, it could be deformed from the impact, which could impede the normal motion of the joints, putting the wearer at considerable disadvantage.

Maintenance and Encumbrance

Armor demanded a good deal of maintenance. Unlike modern stainless steel, medieval iron was very susceptible to rust. Because armor was often exposed to sweat, rain, and mud, it had to be cleaned and polished frequently. This was especially difficult with mail—mail components were typically rolled in a special rotating barrel, probably with bran and sand, to scour them free of rust. A man-at-arms needed at least one servant in order to maintain his expensive equipment while on campaign.

Full armor was somewhat less encumbering than is commonly supposed. Surviving fighting harnesses from before 1600 weigh between 45 and 70 pounds for a complete suit, less than a modern infantryman is expected to be able to carry, and the weight was well distributed. Modern stories about unsaddled knights being unable to lift themselves from the ground are not to be trusted. In fact, an ordinary man in full armor can lie down, get up, and do squat thrusts.

THE COUNT D'ARMAGNAC OVERHEATS
IN HIS ARMOR AND DIES, 1391

This was an unfortunate day for the count, who was so overcome by the heat, and near fainting, that he withdrew from the battle, without friend or foe knowing whither he was gone. He had retreated to a small grove of alders, through which ran a little brook; and he no sooner felt his feet in the water, than he thought he was in paradise; and seated himself by the side of the stream. He, with some difficulty, took off his helmet, and remained covered only by the linen skull-cap, and then plunged his face in the water, at the same time, unfortunately, drinking large draughts; for he was thirsty from the heat, and could not quench it. He drank so much that his blood was chilled, and a numbness of limbs seized him, with a strong inclination to faint. He could not move, and lost the use of his speech . . .

A short time after this, a squire belonging to the duke of Milan perceived the count d'Armagnac, . . . he called out, 'Who are you ? Surrender; for you are my prisoner.'—The count heard him, but could not make any answer, as he was unable to articulate, but held out his hand, and made signs that he surrendered. He then endeavored to raise him, but, finding his attempts vain, seated himself beside him . . .

The squire . . . called to some of his companions to assist in carrying him to the town . . . where the count was disarmed, undressed and put to bed . . .

He died, however, that same night.

From Jean Froissart, *Chronicles of England, France Spain, and The adjoining Countries,* transl. Thomas Johnes (London: George Routledge and Sons 1868), 2. 492–94.

Nonetheless, fighting in armor was physically challenging. Armor is hot and stuffy, particularly with the visor down. Heat stroke was a real danger for the medieval knight, as was dehydration. The extra weight was fatiguing, particularly when on foot, where the weight of the leg armor burdened every step. The armored man-at-arms depended on his horse to get him to the battlefield in fighting condition; marching infantry did not generally wear leg armor. Even if a man-at-arms was able to rise from a fall without help, things could be different in battle conditions, where he might be stunned from the fall, surrounded by enemies, and lying on a wet battlefield with the ground churned into a sea of mud by the horses' hooves and strewn with bodies and debris.

All of these factors required the man-at-arms to be in excellent physical condition. Knights trained in a variety of athletic activities that including footraces, jumping, and horseback acrobatics—the origin of the modern sport of vaulting, and the reason it is practiced on a vaulting horse. The biography of Jean le Maingre, known as Boucicault, one of the most famous knights of Chaucer's day, describes an exemplary training regime:

He practiced leaping on his warhorse fully armed; sometimes he ran or walked long distances on foot to develop length of breathing and endurance; sometimes he wielded a heavy and long axe or hammer to strengthen himself for his harness and to build up his arms and hands for striking for long periods, and to adapt himself to lifting his arms with agility. . . . He would do somersaults in full armor (leaving off the basinet), and dance wearing a coat of mail. He would also leap in full armor onto a warhorse without putting his foot in the stirrup. He would also leap from the ground onto a large man mounted on a large horse to ride on his shoulders, only grabbing him by the sleeve to help himself up. . . . And he would scale the underside of a large ladder leaned against a wall, up to the top, without using his feet, but only jumping with both hands together from one rung to the next, wearing a steel coat; and without the coat he would scale many rungs with just one hand.[2]

Shields

Shields were still carried in Chaucer's day, though with the increased protection afforded by armor, they were becoming less important for the man-at-arms. The typical fourteenth-century shield was made of wood; this was covered with canvas, leather, or both. A knightly shield would also be covered with a gypsum-based sealant called gesso and painted with his personal emblem or arms. The man-at-arms used a fairly small shield, about two feet long, often curved and shaped like the base of a clothes-iron (whence its modern name, a heater). It was equipped with a complicated arrangement of straps so he could keep it in position and still use his hands to control the reins of his horse. When he dismounted, his armor gave him enough protection that he could put the shield aside to use a weapon with both hands.

Ordinary infantry shields were larger. They were either circular, oval, or rectangular, and equipped with a simple pair of straps, or strap and handle, for the arm. Small round shields called bucklers had a single handle in the center behind a protruding iron boss or spike. One surviving example has a hook in front allowing it to be hung from a belt with the grip outwards, ready for a "quick draw." Because the buckler could be carried conveniently when not in use, it was particularly popular with archers and civilians. It was also used in the medieval precursor to fencing, which was practiced unarmored with a sword and buckler.

WEAPONS

During the fourteenth century, weapons evolved to meet the advances in armor. As plate armor improved, the thrust became more important. Cutting weapons were of limited use against plate steel, but a thrust could find the weak points in a harness. For this reason the spear was highly popular and effective throughout the period, wielded either from horseback or on foot. When wielded by a rider moving at speed (probably around 25 miles per hour), the lance could deliver immense force, and under favorable conditions it could penetrate steel plate. A horseman's lance had a steel head on an ash shaft; the overall length was probably around 9–12 feet in the middle part of the century, but with the introduction of solid breastplates and lance rests it was beginning to extend to the 14 feet that would become common in the following century. Spears for footsoldiers might reach 15 feet in length, though such long weapons required a fair bit of training to handle effectively in formation, and those carried by militia levies were almost certainly much shorter. Men-at-arms on foot seem to have preferred a shorter spear about eight feet long for single combat, and before going into battle on foot French men-at-arms would sometimes cut down their lances as short as five feet in length.

Sword design also changed to emphasize the thrust. The older, parallel-sided, blunt-pointed blades were replaced by stiffer, more pointed blades. The new type of sword generally had a diamond cross-section, sometimes with a pronounced central ridge near

Foot combat, c. 1400. Staff weapons include spears, axes, and war-hammers. McLean, after BL Royal 20 C. VII.

the hilt for stiffness. The edges were straight and converged at the tip, making a point narrow enough to punch through mail. The traditional single-handed sword, generally weighing from two to three pounds, with a blade around 30 inches long, continued in use as a sidearm, especially for footsoldiers and for civilian self-defense.

For men-at-arms on the battlefield, it was increasingly common to carry a longsword, also known as a bastard sword or hand-and-a-half sword. The blade of a longsword was about three feet long, and the weapon might weigh between three and five pounds. A longer grip allowed the weapon to be wielded with either one or two hands, and the long blade facilitated the spear-like use favored between armored combatants. Some swords, called estocs, were designed purely for thrusting: these had square, diamond, or triangular cross-sections, an almost straight taper from hilt to point, and no edge to speak of.

Sword pommels, which made the grip more secure and helped balance the weight of the blade, were also an opportunity for decoration. Some were round or oval, but the fig or scent-stopper shape, sometimes faceted, became increasingly common, being easier to grip with a second hand. The crossbar of the hilt, later called quillons, which protected the hand, was of square, rectangular or octagonal section. The arms of the cross were typically either straight or turned slightly away from the hand towards the tips, the better to catch an opponent's weapon. The grip was of wood wrapped with cord or fine wire; sometimes the cord was covered with a layer of thin leather or parchment. The grip of a single-handed sword was short enough that the pommel rested snugly against the hand, affording better control.

Scabbards were made of very thin wood covered with leather, following the contours of the sword. Eelskin was a popular leather for covering scabbards, being available in convenient dimensions. Scabbards often had metal mounts, sometimes cast from copper alloys for decorative effect: a chape protected the bottom end of the scabbard, a throat reinforced the opening, and there was sometimes an intermediate mount in between. The throat might have rings on either side for attaching belt straps, and the intermediate mount might have a single ring for a strap to hold the scabbard angled back. The scabbard could fasten to the belt or directly to the body armor, using laces, short straps and buckles, or ring and hook arrangements. In all cases the scabbard was mounted on the opposite side from the dominant arm, allowing the sword to be drawn across the body. Longswords were often mounted directly to a saddle, sparing the man-at-arms some encumbrance. Some swords also had guard chains that attached to the breastplate, preventing them being lost in the heat of battle.

In addition to the knightly styles of straight, double-edged swords, there were also curved, single-edged types often favored by lower-status swordsmen. These included the falchion, which had a grip like a normal single-handed sword and a short, heavy, single-edged blade like a machete. Earlier examples, dating up to the first quarter of the fourteenth

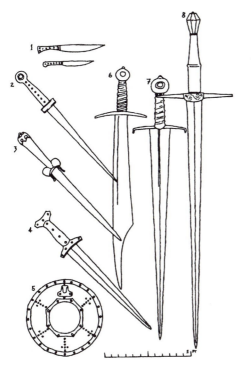

1. Common knives.
2. Rondel dagger.
3. Ballock knife.
4. Baselard.
5. Buckler.
6. Falchion.
7. Single-handed thrusting sword.
8. "Bastard" or "hand-and-a-half" sword. Vernier.

century, have a broad, single-curved tip, but later examples have a point like an exaggerated Bowie knife, designed for thrusting.

The sword was associated with knightly status, and was versatile and relatively easily carried at the side, but in warfare many combatants chose more specialized weapons that delivered greater reach and power. Many of these fell into the family of hafted weapons, consisting of a metallic head mounted on a wooden shaft. A variety of clubs, axes and hammers were in use, both in one-handed and two-handed versions. Single-handed variants included the mace, a club with a flanged head capable of dealing damaging blows to an armored opponent. The most complex hafted weapon was the pollaxe. This was a two-handed weapon used chiefly for armored combat, consisting of a heavy head on the end of a shaft five feet or longer. The head might include an axe-blade, useful for chopping at unarmored or lightly armored opponents, and a hammer-head for smashing plate armor; or in place of the axe or hammer there might be a spike or fluke designed to pierce steel. At the tip of the pollaxe was a heavy spear-point, while the bottom of the shaft could be reinforced with a spiked cap also used for thrusting.

Swords and other large weapons were not commonly carried in civilian use; they were mostly worn by soldiers or by travelers on robber-infested roads. Daggers, on the other hand, were a common feature of male attire.

They were worn by men of all classes, either with civilian clothes as the only weapon, or with armor, mounted on the opposite hip from the sword. Daggers for military use might have hilts that matched the sword they accompanied. Military daggers were often fitted with a guard-chain to prevent loss of the weapon in battle. The dagger was also the most typical weapon for self-defense, although it was equally an emblem of the bearer's masculinity.

The most common dagger for civilians was the baselard, which had a wooden handle, cross, and pommel forming an H-shape. The blade was usually double-edged, of diamond section, and varied in length from a few inches to two feet. Ballock daggers also were popular in the later fourteenth century. These were distinguished by their kidney-shaped lobes in the place of the cross. The lobes gave the dagger a phallic appearance, a characteristic deliberately emphasized by the fashion for wearing this style of dagger at the front of the belt. Some ballock daggers had conical-shaped handles that widened towards the pommel. The blades were usually of heavy triangular section, intended to be inflexible for thrusting. Rondel daggers, with a round hand-guard in the place of the cross, were also popular, especially for military use; these too had heavy thrusting blades. The rondel guard in the fourteenth century was usually small; often the pommel was a second rondel.

Daggers were weapons, not tools. Smaller, thinner knives were used for everyday cutting and for eating; their forms and dimensions were similar to modern steak knives. Several knives might be mounted in a single scabbard made with several pockets: there was usually a large knife with a smaller knife or two and a skewer for making holes—the equivalent of the modern Swiss army knife.

Missile Weapons

One of the most significant weapons on the fourteenth-century battlefield was the English bow, later known as the longbow, which consisted of a bowstaff made of elm, ash, or (ideally) yew, as long as the height of the man that drew it, with a bowstring of wax-coated linen. The arrows were half the length of the bow, or a yard long for a tall man. For war they were equipped with a small pointed tip that could penetrate mail or even—at close range with a solid, well-placed hit—plate armor. An experienced archer might wield a bow of 80 pounds draw or more, even as much as 150 pounds. The maximum range of the weapon might exceed 350 yards, although effective range was considerably less. In theory, a trained archer might loose upwards of 10 shots a minute, although some modern estimates suggest that 10 would be a stretch in practice. Nonetheless, longbows were outstandingly effective for those armies able to field them in substantial numbers. However, longbowmen had to be nurtured from childhood rather than simply hired as needed. To draw an 80-pound bow repeatedly and with control required

Men-at-arms disembarking. Detail after the tapestry of Jourdain de Blaye, Museo Civico, Padua, c. 1385. Vernier.

enormous strength in the right muscles, and was only possible for an archer who had practiced intensely for a long time. England's success in fielding longbowmen owed something to government efforts to encourage archery as a sport—in part by promulgating laws against other recreations, such as football. Perhaps even more important was a growing popular enthusiasm for archery: the earliest clear reference to the Robin Hood legend appears in *Piers Plowman* in about 1378.

Other armies relied on the crossbow instead. Early in the century it typically had a bowstaff made of wood reinforced with horn and sinew, but by mid-century it was largely replaced by a more powerful steel staff. The crossbow had a far lower rate of fire than the English bow, since it was harder to load, although the lower rate of fire also meant that the crossbowman would be slower to run out of ammunition. Lighter crossbows had a foot stirrup in front: the bowman attached the string to a hook on his belt, crouched down to place his foot in the stirrup, and used the strength of his legs to string the bow. Other crossbows had to be strung with a lever or a small winch. The heaviest crossbows had much more power than a longbow, but the principal advantage of the crossbow was that it required much less training to use effectively.

During the course of the fourteenth century a new form of missile weapon made its appearance in battle—the cannon, or gun. Large versions were used on board ships and to assail fortifications, but there were also hand-guns resembling a small cannon barrel mounted on a staff. Such weapons were as yet not a major factor on the battlefield, but they would eventually give rise to the firearms that rendered the armored knight of the Middle Ages obsolete.

NOTES

1. Sir John Froissart, *Chronicles of England, France, and Spain,* transl. Thomas Johnes (London: William Smith, 1842), 1.320.

2. D. Lalande, ed., *Le Livre des fais du bon messire Jehan le Maingre, dit Bouciquaut, mareschal de France et gouverneur de Jennes* (Geneva: Droz, 1985), 25–26.

8

FOOD AND DRINK

Daily Diet

As with other aspects of medieval life, people's social and economic status determined the food they ate. Ironically, the diet of working commoners may actually have been healthier than that of the aristocracy, at least in terms of nutritional balance. The wealthy were able to indulge a taste for fine and rich foods with higher proportions of red meat, sugar, and fat, while the common people consumed more fiber and vegetables.

Bread was a staple food for all people, but aristocratic taste favored the whitest wheat bread possible (although it was less white than modern white bread—Wonder Bread might well have been considered the ultimate treat on the table of Edward III). The aristocratic diet also included a great deal of meat, principally beef, followed by pork and mutton, with game and poultry as the smallest component. Dairy and egg products were found in the aristocratic diet, but not particularly favored. Neither were vegetables, which mostly appeared as flavorings in the form of leeks, onions, garlic, or herbs. Sweets, including conserves and sugar candy, were also a feature of the aristocratic diet. The daily ration for a person living in an aristocratic household typically included from two to three pounds of wheat bread, two to three pounds of meat or fish, and a gallon of ale.

A prosperous peasant might consume from two to three pounds of bread, eight ounces of meat or fish, and from two to three pints of ale per day. The bread was likely to be a coarser wheat bread, possibly mixed with flour from rye, oats, barley, or even beans and peas. Those who could afford it

---

**FOOD EXPENSES OF THE HOUSEHOLD OF JOHN DE
MULTON OF LINCOLNSHIRE, 1347**

Expenses of the household of John de Multon from the day after Michael-
   mas in the 21st year of the reign of King Edward III
Sunday, the day after Michaelmas, for beef, pork, and mutton: 4s. 6d.
Monday, for eggs: 3d.
Tuesday, for herring: 3d.
Wednesday: from the stores
Thursday, for fresh fish: 2d.
Friday, for salt and fresh fish: 11d.
Sunday, for beer purchased because of problems with the brewing: 5s. 9d.

Translated by J. L. Forgeng from the Latin in C. M. Woolgar, *Household Accounts from
Medieval England* (Oxford and New York: Oxford University Press, 1992–1993), 241 ff.

---

ate the same sorts of meats as the aristocracy, although perhaps somewhat
less beef and somewhat more pork and mutton. For most people, protein came less from meat than from eggs, butter, and cheese; seafood and
legumes were also inexpensive sources of protein. Beans and bacon were
the proverbial foods of the peasant. Vegetables figured more prominently
in the diet of commoners than in that of the aristocrat.

At the bottom of the economic scale, people were more likely to drink
water or whey than ale, and to consume their grains boiled whole in pottages, puddings, or gruel rather than in the form of bread, which was
more expensive than an equivalent serving of whole grains (and in fact,
grinding the grains into flour actually wastes some of their caloric content). Nonetheless, the diet of the lower classes seems to have improved
during this period, as a part of the general rise in the standard of living of
the poor following the Black Death. Wage earners during this period were
able to negotiate improved rations for their work: one contract from 1397
stipulates a daily ration of two pounds of beef or mutton, four pints of ale,
and two pounds of wheat bread.[1]

Cuisine

There is a popular misconception that medieval food had less variety than
modern food, possibly due to the number of new ingredients introduced
to the cuisine after the discovery of the New World. Yet the fourteenth-
century aristocracy ate a much greater range of meats than is common today.
Not only did they consume domestic livestock such as cows, sheep, pigs,
chicken, geese, and ducks, but they also hunted game such as deer, boars,
rabbits, and wildfowl. Commoners were generally not supposed to hunt,
but they often poached rabbits and wildfowl in defiance of the laws. Moreover, fourteenth-century cooks used the animals more completely than we
do today (with the possible exception of the production of hot dogs).

An aristocratic feast. French, 1378–1380 (Grands Chroniques de France, Bibliothèque Nationale MS Français 2813, f. 394). McLean.

People also ate a variety of seafood, especially herring and cod; eels, mussels, and oysters were common as well. Dairy products were consumed in various forms. Plain milk could be curdled, and the curds either eaten as is or used to make cheese. Cheese was an extremely important staple, as it essentially served as a means for preserving milk. Pure milk was normally not consumed by adults. It might be given to children, but most milk was reserved for dairying. Instead, people (and especially children) might drink whey, the watery by-product of cheesemaking which is strained out of the curds.

The range of vegetables was probably less diverse than it is today, especially because of the difficulties of preservation. Onions, leeks, cabbage, garlic, turnips, parsnips, peas, and beans were all staples. Among fruits, plums, cherries, pears, grapes, strawberries, figs, and apples all grew in England. Nuts, particularly walnuts and hazelnuts, were also to be found domestically. Other vegetable foods were imported, such as almonds and dates.

A major factor in shaping medieval cuisine was the issue of food seasonality and preservation. There was no technology to transport or preserve fresh produce. This meant that fresh fruits and vegetables were only available when that produce happened to be in season locally; eggs were only available when hens were laying; milk was only available when cows were nursing calves.

Foods could be made available out of season through various modes of preservation. Fruits and some vegetables might be preserved by drying (as with raisins) or cold storage (apples and root vegetables could be stored for some time in cool cellars). Peas and beans were important staples precisely because they dried well. Meats and fish could be preserved

An al fresco meal with white wine, pears, and cherries.
The table is mounted on three-legged trestles. Italian,
c. 1395 (TS Vienna, 86). McLean.

by drying, salting, or pickling. Salted meats were essential during the
winter months in commoners' households; they had to be soaked several
times before cooking to remove the excess salt. Of course, the best way
to preserve meat was to keep it alive. Those who could afford the cost of
winter fodder had fresh meat all year round, and in general livestock were
not slaughtered until the last possible moment. After all, not only did this
preserve the meat longer, but beef was easier to transport when it could
still walk on its own four legs!

Most spices used in fourteenth-century cooking are still familiar today.
It is often suggested that huge amounts of spice were used either to mask
spoiled meat or to ostentatiously display wealth, but modern research
suggests that this was not really the case. In fact, household accounts
of the period suggest that no more spices were used per person than
today, and in some cases even less. Spices were much more expensive in
the fourteenth century than they are now, and smaller amounts would
have been required to display wealth. Moreover, evidence suggests that
imported spices were saved for special occasions. For daily use, people
relied on ordinary seasonings such as salt, vinegar, mustard, onions, and
garlic. Other domestic herbs included parsley, scallions, cress, and chervil.
Another important flavoring agent was verjuice, the juice of sour apples
or grapes.

Among imported spices, the most common were pepper, ginger, cinnamon, cloves, and nutmeg; of these, pepper and ginger were the cheapest.
Sugar, a fairly expensive commodity, was also used as a spice rather than

as a basic ingredient as we use it today. Candies and sweet dishes did exist, but desserts as we know them were not a feature of the fourteenth-century table. Honey was available domestically but was a relative luxury. For most people, the principal source of sugars was fruit; baked apples would be as close as one would get to what we might call a dessert.

Spices were often used in ways quite different from modern European cooking: medieval flavorings had more in common with modern Near Eastern and Indian cuisine. Some spices were used primarily or entirely for their coloring effects: saunders (ground red sandalwood) and the root of the plant alkanet gave a red coloring, and turnsole (a Mediterranean plant) yielded blue, for example. Part of the appeal of saffron, which features in many recipes, is the rich golden color it imparts.[2] Nonetheless, fourteenth-century recipes suggest that the high cuisine of the period was less elaborate than it was to become in the fifteenth century.

Bread

One item invariably present at meals was bread. Loaves of bread were always placed on the table to be eaten, in addition to sliced bread used as plates, called trenchers (described below in the section on "The Table"). The type of bread served and its freshness depended on the status of the host and guest. The finest breads were known as pain-demain, wastel, cocket, and simnel; these were made with highly refined wheat flour (although even the finest was not as white as modern white flour). Such flour was finely sifted to extract bran and husk. Less expensive wheat breads were made with flour that had been sifted less finely and consequently had a higher proportion of bran and husk. This made the flour darker and coarser but added bulk and nutritional value. The bread was not baked in pans, and the loaves were generally round.

Less expensive breads were made from rye, barley, oats, or a mixture of grains. Poor people also ate oat cakes. Biscuits, which had a low water content and therefore preserved well, were useful for long journeys and sea voyages. In times of scarcity, people sometimes had to eat bread made from peas or beans.

Meals

The simplest meal was breakfast, which was not normally reckoned as a meal at all: it appears to have been an informal, catch-as-catch-can affair, consisting perhaps of leftovers from the previous day or of a sop, a popular snack consisting of bread dipped in wine, ale, milk, or water—Chaucer's Franklin "well loved . . . by the morning a sop in wine" (*CT* A.334). As in England today, fish were sometimes eaten at breakfast. The principal meals of the day were dinner, served around midday, and supper, which took place in the evening. Practice varied as to which was the larger meal of the two. Some people also had a mid-afternoon snack of bread and ale called a noon-shenche, or nuncheon, ultimately the source of the modern word luncheon or lunch. The truly decadent ate an extra meal late at night called a rear-supper.

In upper-class households, the diners were typically seated in "messes" of two-to-four people, each mess receiving their food out of the same serving vessels. After the family and their guests had finished their meal, there might be a second seating to feed the servants.

Ordinary people ate their food all at once, but those of social pretensions had it served in a number of courses—usually three, but often more on a special occasion. Many menus survive for a variety of the more formal sorts of meals, ranging from the dinner and supper of a townsman to the coronation feasts of a monarch. Such menus generally consisted of three to six courses, each being made up of a number of dishes. More elaborate meals might include special dishes between courses (called an entremess or subtlety), sometimes artfully designed to delight the eye as well as the palate. One moderately fancy menu suggests the following:

> At the First Course: Boar's Heads Larded, Broth of Almain as Pottage, Baked Capons and Chevettes [small pies], and therewith Pheasants and Bitterns.
>
> The Second Course: Swans, Curlews, Pigs, Roast Veal, and Tarts, therewith Blandesire [white pottage] and Murrey [a dish colored with mulberries].
>
> Third Course: Coney, Partridge, and Woodcock, Roast Plovers and Larks, and therewith Fritters, Pot-wise, Sack-wise [minced meat molded in pots and sacks], and Urchins [sausages made to look like hedgehogs], and therewith Egredoun [a sweet-and-sour dish].[3]

The Goodman of Paris (*Le Ménagier de Paris*), a French text of the same period, offers this slightly less elaborate menu for a Parisian supper:

Another Meat Supper

> First Platter: Capons with herbs, a cominy, "daguenet" peas, loach in yellow sauce, venison in soup.
>
> Second Service: The best roast you can get, meat-jelly, blancmangier "parti" [see Recipes, "Blanc Manger"], little cream tarts well sugared.
>
> Third Service: Capon pies, cold sage soup, stuffed shoulders of mutton, pike in broth, venison with boar's tail, crayfish.[4]

The sequence of a medieval menu contrasts markedly from a modern one. Today we proceed from salad or soup to main course and dessert. Fancy medieval meals were more likely to proceed from the heavier dishes to the more delicate ones. There was no dessert as such, and sweet dishes were mingled among the rest. The diners' status might determine how many of the courses they received. Everyone present was served the first course, but sometimes only the most privileged tables received the last one.

Fish Days

An important feature of the medieval menu related to "fish days." The church designated certain days as occasions for religious penance. On these days people were forbidden to eat meat, which in strictest usage included eggs and dairy products but did not include fish or shellfish. Sea-mammals such as porpoises were considered fish for these purposes, as were barnacle geese (the name derives from the medieval belief that these birds hatched from barnacles), but such foods were not often found on the tables of ordinary people.

Fish days occurred every Friday and Saturday; they might also be observed on Wednesdays and on the evenings before major feast days. Not everyone observed the Wednesday and Saturday fasts, but they were especially called upon to do so on the Ember Days: these were the Wednesday, Friday, and Saturday after the first Sunday in Lent (six weeks before Easter), after Whitsunday (six weeks after Easter), after Holy Cross Day (September 14), and after St. Lucy's Day (December 13). Fish days were also in force throughout all weekdays of Lent, and, for the pious, during Advent. Exceptions were made for pregnant or nursing women, the very young, the very old, the sick and the poor, and in some cases laborers. It was even possible to purchase an exemption. Nevertheless, the vast majority of the populace apparently followed the strictures to at least some degree. As a result, people consumed a great deal more fish than is common today.

One fourteenth-century menu for a fish day suggests the following:

> The First Course: Oysters in Gravy, Pike and Smoked Herring, Fried Stock-fish and Whiting.

> The Second Course: Porpoise in Galantine, and therewith Conger and Fresh Salmon Gilded and Roasted and Gurnard, therewith Tarts and Flampoints [an egg and cheese pastry].

> The Third Course: Rosee [a rose-colored dish] as Potage and Cream of Almonds, therewith Sturgeon and Whelks, Great Eels and Lampreys, Dariol [custard tart], Lechefres of Fruit [fruit tarts], and therewith Nirsebeke [a kind of fritter].[5]

Drinks

Ale, unhopped beer, was the staple drink of medieval England. It provided a significant portion of people's nutritional intake, women

CHAUCER'S LIFETIME ALLOWANCE OF WINE, 1374

Edward, by the grace of God king of England and France and lord of Ireland to our dear and loyal chancellor John Knyvet, greetings. As by our special grace we have granted to our dear squire Geoffrey Chaucer a pitcher of wine to take each day at the port of our city of London by the hands of our butler from ourselves and our heirs . . . for his entire life, we order that you have made letters to this effect under our seal in due form.

Translated by J. L. Forgeng from the French in Martin M. Crow and Clair C. Olson, *Chaucer Life-Records* (Austin: University of Texas Press, 1966), 112.

and children included. It was most often brewed from barley malt, but wheat and oats were also used. Ale was flavored with herbs. Because it had no hops, it lacked the bitter edge of modern beer but also lacked the preservative properties of the hops, so it did not keep very well.

Daily intake appears to have been substantial, with allowances of a gallon per person being common in the households of the aristocracy, and from two to four pints among peasants and laborers. However, medieval ale was not necessarily very strong. Making ale involved soaking the grains and allowing them to germinate (which converted the grain's starches into sugars), then roasting them in a kiln. This malt was then ground, and boiling water was mixed in with it. The liquid wort was poured off and mixed with herbs and yeast to make ale, which could be consumed after only a day of fermentation, although it could be left longer to increase the alcoholic content. After pouring off the initial wort, water was poured through the mash several more times. Ale brewed from the wort from each successive draining was progressively weaker. The different strengths of ale were consequently known as ale of the first, second, or third water; ale made from the last washing of the malt was called small ale.

By the 1370s, beer, the hopped version of ale, was being imported from the Low Countries into the coastal towns of southern and eastern England. At first the main consumers of beer were the large number of foreigners living in these ports, but during Chaucer's lifetime the drink was gaining popularity in the towns.

There were alehouses in the country, but these were less likely to be a permanent establishment than a temporary arrangement whereby one of the local women who had just finished brewing a batch of ale would put out the ale-stake (a bush or broom that hung outside the house—very possibly the same one which had just been used to scoop the scum off the new batch of ale). Anyone who wished might come and purchase a drink—ale did not keep well, and any given batch was likely to be more than the household could consume.

Wine was especially favored among those who could afford it. Wine had to be imported, and even a knight might find it expensive and rely on

The figure on the left is drinking from a goblet of pale green glass. From a manuscript of before 1349 (Psalter of Bonne de Luxembourg). McLean.

ale for daily consumption. France was probably the principal source, but wines were also imported from the Rhine valley, from Spain and Portugal, and even from as far away as Greece. Wines in this period were most often drunk young—vintage wines were just becoming fashionable at the end of the century. Wine was often watered or sweetened; sometimes it was spiced to make the drink known as hippocras.

Other drinks included cider (made from apples), perry (made from pears), and mead (made from honey). Distilled liquors were relatively rare and were generally consumed only for medicinal purposes. People at the lowest end of the economic scale had to rely on water, a drink less flavorful, less nutritive, and less healthy than the alcoholic alternatives—particularly in towns, where overcrowding made water pollution a problem. Milk was not much favored by adults, although whey was sometimes consumed in poor households.[6]

The Table

It was uncommon to have a room permanently set aside as a dining room; a single room generally served for all public activities. For this reason, the medieval dining table was characteristically a temporary structure—a long board set up on trestles, which could be taken down after the meal to avoid cluttering the hall. The table was laid first with a boardcloth

THE PUNISHMENT OF A DECEITFUL
WINE-VENDOR, 1364

Pleas held before Adam de Bury, Mayor, and Aldermen, and an immense Commonalty, in the Guildhall, on Tuesday the morrow of St. Martin . . .

John Rightwise and John Penrose, taverners, were attached to make answer . . . in a plea of contempt and trespass. As to the which, John de Brikelesworth, who prosecuted for the king and the Commonalty of the City of London, said that John Rightwise and John Penrose . . . in the Parish of St. Leonard Eastcheap, in the tavern of Walter Doget there, sold red wine to all who came there, unsound and unwholesome for man, in deceit of the common people, and in contempt of our lord the king, and to the shameful disgrace of the officers of the City . . . And the four supervisors of the sale of wines in the City claimed to have cognizance of all defaults therein; and John Rightwyse and John Penrose were committed to Newgate . . .

And on the Saturday following the said four supervisors appeared . . . and they said that John Rightwise was in no way guilty of the sale of the wine. Therefore he was to be acquitted thereof. And they said that John Penrose was guilty of the sale of such wine, and they wished him to be imprisoned for a year and a day. Afterwards on the 22nd day of November . . . the four supervisors came and gave another judgment, in form as follows: that the said John Penrose shall drink a draught of the same wine which he sold to the common people, and the remainder of such wine shall then be poured on the head of the same John, and he shall forswear the calling of a vintner in the City of London forever, unless he can obtain the favor of our lord the kind as to the same.

Henry Thomas Riley, *Memorials of London and London Life* (London: Longmans, Green, and Co., 1868), 318.

(tablecloth) and with towels and napkins. In poorer households these might be coarse cloths of hempen canvas. Those who could afford it used white linen, while the wealthy used silk. Diners sat on wooden stools or benches, which could be made more comfortable with cushions. Salt was set out in salt-cellars, which might be quite ornate in aristocratic households. Drinks were served in pitchers made of pottery or of a metal such as pewter.[7]

The place settings for the guests were organized differently than modern formal settings. Rather than each diner getting an individual portion on a plate in front of him, each serving portion would go on a serving plate to a "mess" of two to four people who would share it. The number of people in a mess depended on circumstances and social status; only kings and similar dignitaries got a plate all to themselves. Each individual would have their own trencher, drinking vessel and spoon if needed. Drinking vessels could be goblets, beakers or bowls. The individual might get their own napkin, or share one with their messmates.

The trencher was a piece of old bread that could serve as a plate. Since the shared plate was usually within easy reach, the trencher could also function like a napkin for hors d'oeuvres at a modern party: a temporary parking place for morsels the diner wasn't going to swallow in one gulp. The bread used for trenchers was less fresh than bread served as part of the meal—perhaps four days old, to ensure a good crust. The original round loaf was sliced in two to make two disks, and the edges were then squared off: a typical trencher would probably have been a rectangle six inches across and four inches deep. The trencher soaked up the juices from the meal and might afterwards be given to the dogs or the poor. During a fancy meal the trenchers might be replaced with fresh ones at some point—often a new one was presented at the start of each course.[8] Illustrations also show tables furnished with what looks like pieces of bread cut into a convenient size for manipulating food in the absence of forks or for dipping into sauces.

Tableware varied with the means of the owner. Rich households made extensive use of silver; glass was also a relative luxury. Pewter was a cheaper alternative, so those of lesser means used it instead. The poorest relied heavily on wood and ceramics; drinking vessels were sometimes made of waxed leather. Drinking vessels included glasses, cups, beakers, and even bowls.

A surprising feature of medieval table settings is the absence of knives. People generally carried their own knives and used these at the table. Note that knives were *not* the same as daggers: they were smaller, single edged, and lacked the protective hand-guard of a dagger—besides, medieval people would probably not have been enthusiastic about eating with a tool used for killing people. The knives used at table were invariably pointed, since they had to serve for spearing as well as cutting. The fork was a cooking rather than an eating implement in fourteenth-century England, and it remained so until the seventeenth century.

Spoons were made of wood (such as boxwood, juniper, poplar, or fruit woods), bone, horn, pewter, latten (a copper alloy containing zinc), silver, or gold.[9] Their bowls were generally round, fig-shaped, or—rarely—leaf shaped. The stem was a slender stick with a cross-section either round, square, hexagonal, or diamond-shaped. Sometimes the stem ended in a sharp point, or was cut at right angles, or cut at a diagonal (called a slip knop). Otherwise there might be a fancy knop, a decorative knob on the end of the stem. The knop might be in the shape of a simple diamond point, a simple round ball, a ball with spirals (called a wrythen knop), an acorn, a castle tower, or a figurehead or bust (called a maidenhead). Sometimes the spoon was quite fanciful: the entire stem and knop might be in the shape of a horse's leg, ending in a hoof for a knop. The typical length of the spoon was from six to seven inches overall.

There were several other popular styles of spoons. One was the fist-spoon, which had a shallow, round bowl and a very short, thick stem. There were also folding spoons, which had a hinged stem and were easy to carry—such spoons were particularly useful for travelers.

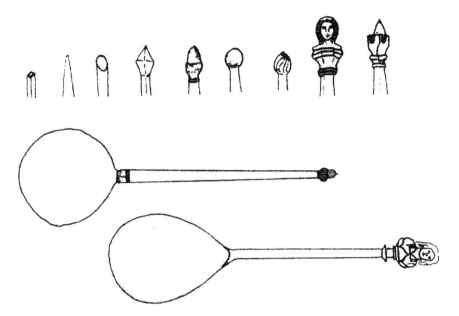

From top to bottom: Knop Shapes (Cut, Point, Slip, Diamond, Acorn, Ball, Wry-then Knop, Maiden-head, Finial), Fourteenth Century French Acorn Spoon and English Maidenhead Spoon. Reames.

Serving the Meal

In a wealthy household, numerous servants might be involved in bringing the food and drink from the kitchen to the tables. One of the most skilled among these was the carver, who had the task of carving the various roasts according to an elaborate etiquette. The panter was responsible for the bread, both the trenchers and the table loaves. It was he who trimmed the loaves and made sure that the appropriate types of bread went to the correct recipients. The role of the butler was very different from that associated with the butlers of today. His title was originally bottler: he was responsible for the wine and ale, which included watering and spicing the wine as appropriate. The ewerer was responsible for the laving-water and towels with which the diners washed their hands.

Other dining staff included the sewer, charged with arranging dishes before and after they reached the table; the almoner, guardian of the alms dish in which leftovers were gathered for distribution to the poor, and the surveyor, who oversaw the surveying board to which the cook sent the individual serving platters; and the ordinary servants who carried the food to the diners.

The servants might be ordinary hired help, but in the most important households the major serving positions were actually held by aristocrats. These could be sons, fosterlings, or squires living in the household. At important royal feasts the king might be waited on by leading noblemen.

Aristocratic feasters sharing a napkin. French,
c. 1350 (Bibliothèque Nationale MS Français 1586,
f. 55). McLean.

Manners

Grace was customarily said both before and after a meal. It was also customary to wash one's hands before and after the meal. In the better households, a servant would come around with a jug of laving-water, sometimes scented with herbs such as sage or rosemary, a basin, and a towel. He would pour the water over the diner's hands into the basin, and the diner would dry them with the towel.

Medieval table manners were largely shaped by the sharing of food. Diners were supposed to use their knives rather than their fingers to obtain salt from the communal salt cellars. Dishes were commonly shared among two to four people, and two people often shared a cup. In the absence of forks, it was acceptable to dip fingers into common dishes; in fact, many rules of courtesy at the table centered around this. It was considered unmannerly to reach in with dirty fingers, and it was similarly rude to take all the best pieces for oneself. Likewise, when sharing a cup, it was polite to wipe one's mouth before drinking.[10] When children were learning their manners they were taught not to slurp, fidget at the table, speak with food in their mouths, or pick their teeth with their knives. When finished with their food, they were to remove their spoons from their dishes.

The Medieval Picnic

Not all meals were eaten indoors. Outdoor workers often brought food for a midday meal, or had it brought by their wives: handy foods like bread, cheese, and meats could be carried in cloths or baskets for this purpose. Among the aristocracy, outdoor meals were especially common during a hunt. A glimpse of this sort of meal comes to us from the *Book of the Hunt* by Gaston Phebus, a French contemporary of Chaucer whose work was translated into English early in the fifteenth century by the Duke of York:

The assembly that men call gathering should be made in this manner: . . . The place where the gathering should be made should be in a fair meadow, quite green, where fair trees grow all about, the one far from the other, and a clear well or some running brook besides. . . . The officers . . . should lay the towels and boardcloths all about on the green grass, and set diverse foods upon a great platter according to the lord's status, and some should eat sitting and some standing, some leaning upon their elbows, some drink and some laugh, some jangle, some joke, some play, and in short do all manner of disports of gladness.[11]

The Kitchen

A modern cook working in a medieval kitchen might very well give up in despair. All cooking involved the careful manipulation of fire, a skill that every girl had to learn from her mother during the years of her child-hood. Meats were roasted on a spit—requiring the attention of someone to turn the spit, to ensure that the meat would be evenly cooked. The meat was roast *beside* the fire rather than over it; this not only prevented flaring but allowed the fat to be caught in a dripping pan for later use. Frying and boiling took place above a fire or hot coals. Baking was the most involved process of all. A fire was lit inside a clay-lined oven, and allowed to burn until the oven was sufficiently heated. Then the coals were raked out, the interior was quickly wiped with a damp cloth, and the item to be baked was placed inside. Those who didn't own an oven could bake in a metal or ceramic vessel placed in the fire and covered with hot coals.

One early fifteenth-century chef offered the following suggestions for a lavishly appointed kitchen:

There should be a provision of good big cauldrons to boil large cuts of meat, and a great number of moderate sized ones for making pottages . . . and for other cooking operations, and great suspended pans for cooking fish and other things, and a great number of large and ordinary-sized boilers for pottages and other things, and a dozen good big mortars. Decide on the place where sauces will be prepared. And you will need some twenty large frying pans, a dozen great kettles, fifty pots, sixty two-handled pots, a hundred hampers, a dozen grills, six large graters, a hundred wooden spoons, twenty-five holed spoons, both large and small, six pot hooks, twenty oven-shovels, twenty roasters, both those with turntable spits and those with spits mounted on andirons. You should not put your trust in wooden skewers or spits, because you could spoil all your meat, or even lose it; rather you should have six score iron spits which are strong and thirteen feet long; and you need three dozen other spits which are just as long but not as thick, in order to roast poultry, piglets and water birds. . . . And besides this . . . four dozen slender skewers for doing glazing and for fastening things.[12]

Kettles (the pots used to heat water) were often three legged and made of brass. Brass does not rust and it heats more rapidly than iron; however, it is hard to clean and is therefore less suited to cooking food. Cast iron was being produced in parts of Europe by this time, but the technology was not well developed, and had not yet reached England. Instead, cookware was typically made of wrought iron or clay. Kitchen utensils might be made of iron or copper. Spices were often stored in pouches, and kitchens generally had various ceramic vessels for storage. There would also be basins and cloths for washing dirty dishes.

RECIPES

Quite a number of recipes survive from Chaucer's day. The following all derive from late fourteenth-century sources: the *Diversa Servicia*, the *Forme of Cury,* and British Library Manuscript Royal 17 A iii, a collection of medical recipes. In each case, the original recipe is given in italics (the language is somewhat modernized to aid the modern reader), followed by an interpretation for the modern cook.

Ground Beans

Take beans and dry them in an oast or in an oven. And hull them well, and winnow out the hulls, and wash them clean; and make them to seethe in good broth, and eat them with bacon.[13]

Place **1 lb. kidney beans** in a saucepan. Add **1/3 cup chopped onion** and **2 cups beef or chicken stock.** Add enough water to cover the beans, and simmer until tender (about 1 1/2 hours). Chop up **1/4 lb. thick-sliced bacon,** mix in with the cooked beans, salt to taste, and serve.

This is one of the simplest recipes surviving from the period. It probably gives a good idea of the ordinary fare of most Englishmen of the period.

Cabbages in Pottage

Take cabbages and quarter them, and seethe them in good broth with minced onions and the white of leeks slit and chopped small. And add thereto saffron and salt, and season it with powder douce.[14]

Take **1 head of cabbage,** quarter it, and boil it for at least 30 minutes in **beef or chicken broth** with **1 diced onion** and **1 diced leek.** Season with **3 threads pounded saffron, salt** to taste, and **1/8 teaspoon cardamom** and **1/8 teaspoon coriander** and **1 teaspoon sugar.**

This is slightly finer recipe; the cabbages, onions, and leeks would have been found in an ordinary peasant's garden, but the saffron, cardamom, coriander, and sugar all indicate that this simple fare has been made more appealing to a richer diner's palate. A poor family might have eaten the same thing, seasoned only with salt.

Turnips in Broth

Take turnips and make them clean and wash them clean; quarter them; parboil them; take them up, cast them in a good broth and seethe them. Mince onions and cast thereto saffron and salt and serve it forth with powder douce. In the same wise make of carrots and parsnips.[15]

Peel and quarter **4 small to medium turnips,** and parboil them in salted water for about 5 minutes. Drain, and add to **2 cups meat broth.** Add **2 minced onions,** pinch of **saffron** and **salt,** and **1/8 teaspoon cardamom** and **1/8 teaspoon coriander** and **1 teaspoon sugar.** Simmer until tender. Carrots and parsnips may be cooked in the same way.

As with the cabbages above, this is a simple dish made somewhat more fancy for a wealthy table.

Fried Spinaches

Take spinaches; parboil them in seething water. Take them up and press out the water and hew them in two. Fry them in oil and add thereto powder douce, and serve forth.[16]

Parboil and drain **1 bunch spinach.** Fry in **2 tablespoons oil or grease,** season with **1 teaspoon sugar, 1/8 teaspoon cardamom** and **1/8 teaspoon coriander.**

Again, this is simple fare spiced for a rich family's table.

Salad

Take parsley, sage, green garlic, scallions, onions [one manuscript replaces this with "lettuce"], *leek* [three manuscripts add "spinach" here], *borage, mints, leeks, fennel, garden cress, rue, rosemary, purslane; rinse and wash them clean. Pick them clean. Pluck them small with thine hand, and mix them well with raw oil; lay on vinegar and salt, and serve it forth.*[17]

Wash and tear up **salad greens** (lettuce, *not iceberg lettuce,* spinach, borage). Drain well. Wash and finely slice **2 leeks, 1 bunch green garlic** (if available—these are the green shoots of garlic) and **1 bunch green onions.** Add to the salad greens. Next add at least 1 tablespoon each (fresh) or 1 teaspoon each (dried): **parsley, sage, mint, rosemary** (rue and purslane, if available). Add **2 cloves minced garlic** and **1/2 cup olive oil.** Mix well. Add **3 tablespoons vinegar** and **1 1/2 teaspoon salt** just before serving (as the vinegar causes the greens to wilt).

Egurdouce of Fish

Take loaches or roches or tenches or soles; break them in pieces. Fry them in oil. Take half wine, half vinegar, and sugar, and make a syrup; add thereto chopped onions, dried currants, and great raisins. Add thereto whole spices, good powders, and salt; serve up the fish, and lay the sauce above and serve forth.[18]

Break up **2 filets of sole.** Fry in **2 tablespoons oil.** Mix **1/2 cup wine** with **1/2 cup vinegar** and **1 tablespoon sugar.** Add **1/4 cup chopped onions, 1/2 cup dried currants,** and **1/4 cup raisins.** Season with **1/2 teaspoon cinnamon, 1/2 teaspoon cloves, 1/2 teaspoon nutmeg, 1 teaspoon pepper,** and **salt** to taste. Pour the sauce over the fish and serve.

Fish would have been a regular part of most people's diet, although the fresh fish in this recipe would have been for a wealthy table; ordinary people were more likely to eat dried or pickled cod or herring.

Blanc Manger

Put rice in water all night, and in the morning wash them clean. Afterward put them to the fire until they burst, and not too much. Then take meat of capons, or of hens, boiled, and draw it small. After take milk of almonds and put into the rice and boil it. And when it is boiled, put in the meat and mix it therewith until it be thick, and mix it finely well so that it stick not to the pot. And when it is enough and thick add thereto a good part of sugar, and put therein almonds fried in white grease, and serve it forth.[19]

Soak **1 cup rice** overnight in water. Drain. Chop finely **1 lb. chicken breast.** To make almond milk, pound in a mortar **1/2 lb. blanched almonds.** Slowly add **3 cups water,** allow to soak, then strain through a cloth to get the almond milk. Add the almond milk to the rice and boil for 20 minutes. Add the chicken and stir. Add **1 1/2 tablespoons sugar.** Fry **1/2 cup blanched almonds** in **2 tablespoons butter,** and mix into the rice and serve.

This is the ancestor of the modern blancmange, which is now a dessert dish.

Mustard (for a Roast)

If you wish to provide for keeping mustard a long time do it at wine-harvest in sweet must. And some say that the must should be boiled. Item, if you want to make mustard hastily in a village, grind some mustard-seed in a mortar and soak in vinegar, and strain; and if you want to make it ready the sooner, put it in a pot in front of the fire. Item, and if you wish to make it properly and at leisure, put the mustard-seed to soak overnight in good vinegar, then have it ground fine in a mill, and then little by little moisten it with good vinegar: and if you have some spices left over from making jelly, broth, hippocras, or sauces, they may be ground up with it, and then leave it until it is ready.[20]

Add **4 teaspoons mustard seed** to **5 tablespoons vinegar.** Soak overnight. Mix in **1/4 cup vinegar,** a pinch of **ginger, cardamom, nutmeg, galingale** (if possible—it can sometimes be had from a specialty shop under the name "galangal" or "laos"), and a pinch and a half of **cinnamon.** Grind (a coffee mill can be used for this purpose).

This mustard would have been used to flavor a roast meat; it was also commonly used on herring. No roasting recipes survive from this period, but you may wish to follow a recipe from *The Joy of Cooking* or another modern cookbook.

Tarts of Flesh (Pork Dumplings)

Take boiled pork and grind it small with saffron; mix it with eggs, and dried currants, and powder fort and salt, and make a foil of dough and close the stuffing therein. Cast the tartlets in a pan with fair water boiling and salt; take of the clean flesh without eggs and boil it in good broth. Cast there powder douce and salt, and serve the tarts in dishes, and pour the juices thereon.[21]

Parboil **1/2 lb. ground pork** (about 1 cup). Drain and add **6 threads pounded saffron, 2 beaten eggs, 1 cup dried currants, 1 teaspoon pepper, 2 teaspoons ginger, 1 teaspoon mace, 1/2 teaspoon cloves,** and **salt** to taste.

For the shells, mix **2 cups flour, 2/3 cup water, 1/2 teaspoon salt.** Knead and roll to a thin sheet, about 1/16". Cut circles or squares of at least 3" diameter, and moisten the edges with water. Place filling into centers, fold in half, and seal the edges by pressing them firmly.

Boil about 3" of water in a pot. Set the dumplings carefully into the water, and simmer them for 10 minutes. Add to the water **1/8 teaspoon ground cardamom, 1/8 teaspoon coriander, 1 teaspoon sugar,** and **salt** to taste. Serve the dumplings forth, and pour the liquid over them.

Tart in Ember Day

Take and parboil onions and herbs and press out the water and hew them small. Take green cheese and bray it in a mortar, and temper it up with eggs. Add thereto butter, saffron, and salt, and dried currants, and a little sugar with powder douce, and bake it in a trap, and serve it forth.[22]

Pastry

Mix **1 1/2 cups whole wheat pastry flour, 1/2 cup butter, 1 tablespoon sugar, 1/8 teaspoon salt, 1 thread saffron, 3 tablespoons water.** Knead to a stiff dough, refrigerate, roll out to 1/8" thickness, cut circles to make tarts fitting mini-muffin shells. Makes 12 tarts.

Filling

Parboil, drain, and chop **1 medium onion.** Add **1/4 cup chopped parsley** and **1/4 cup chopped dill.** Add **6 oz. grated farmer's cheese, 2 beaten eggs, 2 tablespoons butter, 4 threads saffron,** and mix well. Mix in **1/2 cup dried currants.** Fill the pastry shells, and bake for 20 minutes at 375°F, or until golden brown.

The Ember Days were the Wednesday, Friday, and Saturday after the first Sunday in Lent, Whitsunday, Holy Cross Day, and St. Lucia's Day, which were supposed to be days for fasting and prayer. Accordingly, these tarts are made without meat.

Tart de Bry

Take a crust an inch deep in a trap. Take yolks of eggs raw and "rewen" [semi-soft] cheese and mix it and the yolks together. Add thereto ground ginger, sugar, saffron, and salt. Put it in a trap; bake it and serve it forth.[23]

For pastry recipe, see Tart in Ember Day, above.

For the filling, grate **8 oz. semisoft cheese** (e.g., Pont l'Eveque). Add **6 egg yolks, 1 teaspoon ground ginger, 1 teaspoon sugar, 4 threads pounded saffron, salt** to taste. Fill pastry shells and bake for 20 minutes at 375°F, or until golden brown. Makes twelve 1 1/2" tarts

This tart was another likely candidate for meals during periods of fasting.

Apple Tarts

Take good apples and good spices and figs and raisins and pears, and when they are well pounded in a mortar, color with saffron well and put it in a covered shell and set it forth to bake well.[24]

For the pastry recipe, see Tart in Ember Day, above.

Pare and core **3 apples, 2 pears,** and **3 figs.** Chop, and add **1 cup raisins, 1 teaspoon cloves, 1/8 teaspoon pepper, 1 teaspoon mace, 1 teaspoon cinnamon, 1/4 teaspoon salt, 4 threads saffron,** and crush. Fill pastry shells and bake for 20 minutes at 375°F, or until golden brown. You can add **1/4 teaspoon saunders (ground red sandalwood)** to the spices, if it is available to you.

Hippocras

Take a half lb. of choice cinnamon, of choice ginger a half lb., of grains of paradise [cardamom] *3 ounces, of long pepper 3 ounces, of cloves 2 ounces, of nutmegs*

2 ounces and a half, of caraway 2 ounces, of spikenard [valerian] *a half ounce, of galingale 2 ounces, of sugar 2 lb. If sugar is lacking, take a pottle* [half-gallon] *of honey.*[25]

Add the following to **1 bottle red wine: 1 1/2 tablespoons sugar** or **3 tablespoons honey, 1 teaspoon cinnamon, 1 1/2 teaspoon ginger, 1/2 teaspoon cardamom, 1/2 teaspoon pepper, 1/4 teaspoon cloves, 1/4 teaspoon nutmeg, 1/4 teaspoon caraway.** Allow to sit at least overnight before drinking. You may want to filter it through a coffee filter to remove the dregs.

Hippocras was a spiced wine, reputed to be very good for the health—the name derives from Hippocrates, the Greek physician known today as the originator of the Hippocratic Oath. Galingale is similar to ginger.

Mead

Take honeycombs and put them into a great vessel and lay therein great sticks, and lay the weight thereon till it be run out as much as it will; and this is called live honey. And then take that forsaid combs and seethe them in clean water, & boil them well. After press out thereof as much as thou may and cast it into another vessel into hot water, & seethe it well and scum it well, and add thereto a quart of live honey. And then let it stand a few days well stopped, and this is good drink.[26]

Boil **1 cup honey** in **9 cups water** for 30 minutes, scumming the froth as it rises. Allow the liquid to cool, and pour it into a sealed container; a plastic milk jug or the like is a good choice, as it will expand to accommodate the carbon dioxide emitted by fermentation. Try to leave as little air as possible at the top. Allow to stand 4 days in the dark at room temperature. Keep an eye on the fermenting liquid, letting off excess pressure if necessary (it is wise to store it in a place that will be easy to clean if it bursts). If you like you can flavor it by adding **1 sliced and boiled apple, 1/2 teaspoon ground pepper,** and **1 teaspoon ground cloves** to the liquid before bottling it (all these additives are suggested in another mead recipe from the same manuscript).

This is a very quick and lightly fermented mead—it may sparkle slightly but has very little alcohol content. Finer meads are made to be kept for years before drinking.

Bread

Bread was a crucial part of any medieval meal, but, regrettably, no bread recipes survive from the period. The following recipe for a fairly ordinary sort of bread is based on early seventeenth-century sources:

Sift **3 cups unbleached whole wheat flour.** Dissolve **1 teaspoon active dry yeast** in **1 cup lukewarm water or beer** and stir in **1 teaspoon salt.** Make a well in the flour and pour the yeast mixture into it. Mix and knead for 5 minutes. Since the wheat can vary in initial moisture you might have to add water or flour to ensure that it is moist to the touch but not sticky.

Let the dough rise in a warm place for about an hour. Form into a flat round loaf, and prick it on top with a knife. Let the loaf rise again until it has doubled in volume, which should be about 45 minutes to an hour.

Preheat the oven to about 500°F. When the dough has risen, place it in the oven, and reduce the heat to 350°F. After about 20 minutes the bread should be golden and ready to remove from the oven.

NOTES

1. On diet, see Christopher Dyer, *Standards of Living in the Later Middle Ages* (Cambridge: Cambridge University Press, 1989), 60, 63–64, 156–57; Christopher Dyer, "English Diet in the Later Middle Ages," in *Social Relations and Ideas*, ed. T. H. Aston, P. R. Coss, et al. (Cambridge: Cambridge University Press, 1983), 193, 196, 202, 206, 209–10, 214.

2. On seasonings, see Dyer, *Standards of Living*, 63; C. Anne Wilson, *Food and Drink in Britain from the Stone Age to Recent Times* (London: Constable, 1973), 285; Bruno Laurioux, "Spices in the Medieval Diet: A New Approach," *Food and Foodways* 1 (1985), 43–76.

3. Constance B. Hieatt and Sharon Butler, *Curye on Inglisch* (London: Oxford University Press, 1985), 41.

4. *Le Ménagier de Paris* (Paris: Crapelet, 1846), 2.100.

5. Hieatt and Butler, *Curye*, 40–41.

6. On drinks, see Dyer, *Standards of Living*, 62; Wilson, *Food and Drink*, 375; G. G. Coulton, *Medieval Panorama* (New York: Macmillan, 1938), 314.

7. On the table, see John Russell, *The Boke of Nurture*, in *The Babees Book*, ed. F. J. Furnivall (London: Trübner, 1868), ll. 62, 185 ff.; Michael R. McCarthy and Catherine M. Brooks, *Medieval Pottery in Britain A.D. 900–1600* (Leicester: Leicester University Press, 1988).

8. On trenchers, see John Russell, *Boke of Nurture*, l.56.

9. On spoons, see Peter Hornsby, Rosemary Weinstein, and Ronald Homer, *Pewter: A Celebration of the Craft 1200–1700* (London: Museum of London, 1990); Arthur MacGregor, *Bone, Antler, Ivory and Horn* (London: Croom Helm, 1985).

10. On etiquette, see John Lydgate, "Stans Puer ad Mensam," in *The Minor Poems of John Lydgate*, ed. H. N. MacCracken (London: Trübner, 1934), 2.739–44.

11. *The Master of Game by Edward, Second Duke of York*, ed. William A. and F. Baillie-Grohman (London: Chatto and Windus, 1909), 163.

12. Terence Scully, ed. and trans., *Chiquart's "On Cookery"* (New York: P. Lang, 1986), 12–13.

13. Hieatt and Butler, *Curye*, 4.3.

14. Hieatt and Butler, *Curye*, 4.6.

15. Hieatt and Butler, *Curye*, 4.7; Constance B. Hieatt and Sharon Butler, *Pleyn Delit* (Toronto: University of Toronto Press, 1979), recipe 16.

16. Hieatt and Butler, *Curye*, 4.188.

17. Hieatt and Butler, *Curye*, 4.78, adapted by David Tallan.

18. Hieatt and Butler, *Curye*, 4.137.

19. Hieatt and Butler, *Curye*, 4.200.

20. *Ménagier de Paris*, p. M-36, in David Friedman and Betty Cook, *A Miscelleny* [sic], 5th ed. (private printing, 1990), 75, adapted by David Tallan.

21. Hieatt and Butler, *Curye*, 4.51.

22. Hieatt and Butler, *Curye*, 4.173.

23. Hieatt and Butler, *Curye*, 4.174.

24. Hieatt and Butler, *Curye*, 2.82.

25. Hieatt and Butler, *Curye*, 5.148–49.

26. Hieatt and Butler, *Curye*, 5.151.

9

ENTERTAINMENTS

LEISURE AND RECREATION

Leisure time for most people in the Middle Ages was more limited than now, yet entertainment remained an important part of their lives—perhaps even more so because of the limited opportunities to enjoy it. For the aristocracy, play was almost a characteristic way of life. In addition to their designated role as rulers and warriors, the culture of the aristocracy was in many respects defined by their recreations: hunting, hawking, tourneying, and courtly literature were among the pastimes that identified the aristocrat. Even the working commoner had at least some eight weeks of Sundays and holy days in the course of a year, so there was plenty of time to indulge a taste for entertainment.

Recreational activities were especially important because they gave order and meaning to the rest of people's lives. The cycle of Sundays and holy days shaped the ritual year: it is sometimes said that the medieval peasant lived in memory of the last festival and in anticipation of the next. Through their games, amusements, and festivities, they expressed their values, their aspirations, and their sense of identity. As we shall see, the games people played have much to tell us about the way they saw their world.

The Settings of Play

Entertainment had more of a ritual dimension than is true today. This was partly because for most people the heavy schedule of work forced entertainment into specific, often ritualized, settings. For the medieval commoner, entertainment activities were concentrated on festival occasions, especially Sundays and holy days after church. As can be seen from the calendar in Chapter 4, the various festivals of the year often had special entertainments associated with them.

People might socialize in their homes, or repair to an alehouse. Outdoors play might happen in a churchyard, which was one of the principal public spaces in a village—although some people felt this was a violation of the sacred space of the church. The common lands of a village were also places for play, as were the streets of a village or town.

For the aristocracy, opportunities for entertainment were less restricted: they did not have to conform to strict work schedules, and they had plenty of spaces for entertainment in their halls and on their lands.

Although people's opportunity for entertainment depended on their social status, the entertainments themselves tended to cross class boundaries. A few entertainments belonged especially to one class or another— hawking, for example, was an aristocratic pastime, whereas football was more popular among common folk. Yet for the most part, entertainments seem to have been less class-specific than other activities. The courtly poetry of the aristocracy may have been more refined than the folk verse of the commons, but both lord and peasant enjoyed many of the same stories; the dice used by the peasantry may have been made of simple bone or wood, but commoners played many of the same sorts of games as the nobility played with their dice of ivory.

**PARLIAMENTARY STATUTE ON WEAPONS,
ARCHERY, AND GAMES, 1388**

It is accorded and assented that no Servant of Husbandry, or Laborer, nor Servant or Artificer, nor of Victualler, shall from henceforth bear any Baselard, Sword nor Dagger, upon forfeiture of the same, but in the time of war for defence of the realm of England, and that by the surveying of the Arrayors for the time being, or travailing by the country with their Master, or in their Master's message; But such Servants and Laborers shall have Bows and Arrows, and use the same the Sundays and Holydays, and leave all playing at tennis or foot-ball, and other games called coits, dice, casting of the stone, kailes, and other such importune games. And that the Sheriffs, Mayors, Bailiffs and Constables, shall have power to arrest, and shall arrest, all doers against this Statute, and seize the said Baselards, Swords and Daggers, and keep them till the Sessions of the Justices of Peace, and the same present before the same Justices in their Sessions, together with the names of them that did bear the same. And it is not the King's mind that any prejudice be done to the franchises of Lords, touching the forfeitures due to them.

Cited in John Hewitt, *Ancient Armour and Weapons in Europe* (London: Henry and Parker, 1860), Vol II 23–24.

Although games may have been enjoyed across the social classes, there were important distinctions between the sexes. Both boys and girls played the same games freely, but adult women were more restricted in the games they could play. As a rule, women do not appear to have engaged much in physically demanding sports, although they were often present as spectators. However, they very commonly played table games and were especially likely to take part in dancing.

Professional Entertainment

On the whole, entertainment in the Middle Ages involved people interacting directly with each other in a way that is less true today. There was no mass media and no means of mass production. Even reading was more personal, in a sense—since there were no printing presses, every text had to be written out by hand, and every book was a unique creation. There were professional entertainers, but such people generally had to do their entertaining in person. Medieval England was rich in such people: musicians, acrobats, animal trainers, and even puppeteers, who traveled from town to town, and among the residences of the wealthy, in search of patrons and audiences. Yet they were only a tiny fraction of the population, and most of the time people often had to create their own fun.

Theatrical performances were also popular. Some of these were simple folk-plays or minor entertainments performed by strolling players, but the custom of major productions sponsored with church funds or public money was developing. It peaked in the fifteenth century, when a number of English towns staged major play-cycles telling the story of the Bible from the Creation to the Last Judgment. In Chaucer's day, plays were less ambitious and were more likely to tell a story of miracles performed by God, a saint, or the Virgin Mary.[1]

A puppet show, strongly suggestive of Punch and Judy. Flemish, 1338–1344 (RA, f. 54v). McLean.

Literature

One of the most important forms of entertainment across society was literature, in its broadest sense. Poetry in particular was a common part of people's lives and was composed on very diverse topics. There were courtly lyric verses about love. There were devotional poems about God, the saints, or the Virgin Mary. There were social satires and political prophesies. There were epics and romances about the heroes of legend—King Arthur and his knights, the Siege of Troy, King Richard the Lion-Hearted, Robin Hood, and many others were the subjects of lengthy narrative poems. People delighted in lengthy versifications of the Bible or of English history. Chaucer's own major poetical work, *The Canterbury Tales,* is an excellent example. The poem is constructed as the account of a pilgrimage by a diverse cross-section of characters to the shrine of St. Thomas à Becket at Canterbury. Chaucer has the pilgrims tell an enormous variety of stories: chivalric epics, animal fables, bawdy farces, saints' lives, and more. *The Canterbury Tales* were an enormous hit in their own day and had many imitators in following centuries, testament to the popularity of narrative verse.

In addition to verse tales, there was prose storytelling, although fewer texts have survived—apparently people didn't find it as important to record the exact words of a prose narrative. It would seem that many of the same sorts of stories were told as were popular in poetic form. Of course, the single most important source of prose narratives was the Bible. People heard Bible stories every Sunday in church, and they saw them illustrated in paintings, carvings, and stained glass windows. Biblical tales were taken seriously, but they were a form of entertainment too.

With more rapid cursive hands and less expensive paper supplanting expensive parchment, books were coming down in price, though they were still not cheap. An inexpensive romance might cost 2s., a primer 16d., and a calendar 8d. Thomas Walynton, a clothier, left two volumes in his will in 1402. By 1420 even a tailor like John Brinchley could leave two copies of Boethius' *The Consolation of Philosophy,* one in English and one in Latin, and a copy of *The Canterbury Tales.* Large libraries were rare, but this somewhat understates the number of books read. Books could be borrowed, or they could be purchased, read and then resold.

Because every book was written individually by hand, many volumes were personal anthologies containing a collection of texts of interest to the compiler. One example, probably collected by a Berkshire lawyer in the 1260s, contained formularies (model legal documents), a treatise on accounting and on the laws of England, the *Romance of Horn,* Robert Grosseteste's *Le Chasteau de Amor* (a religious text), the *Fables* of Marie de France, and a bestiary (a moralized description of animals). Additional legal material was added by a later owner in the fourteenth century. Another popular genre was the collection of moral tales, stories with edifying lessons derived from the Bible, the lives of saints, fables, and classical sources. Medieval readers of such works might be familiar with the characters of Æneas and Helen of Troy even if they never read Virgil or Homer. A well-to-do French townsman of Chaucer's day known as the Ménagier de Paris composed an instructional treatise for his daughters in which he cited the Bible, the lives of the saints, and the works of St. Augustine, St. Gregory, St. Jerome, the classical historians Josephus and Livy, and Cicero, as well as such medieval works as *Romance of the Rose* and Petrarch's tale of Patient Griselda—many of which he probably knew only in excerpted form.

Music

Music was another universal form of entertainment. Some of it was provided by professional musicians, who were often hired by the aristocracy and rich townsfolk. Ordinary people could scarcely afford such a luxury; although they might occasionally have the opportunity to hear traveling musicians, they had to create most of their music themselves. It was common for people to sing for their own entertainment, sometimes as part of holiday revelry, sometimes during work to make the labor go more easily. The subjects of songs were diverse: there were love songs, drinking songs, and religious songs, songs about historical events and current politics, satirical songs about money or sex, and even nonsense songs. Froissart relates how the leading men in England entertained themselves with music while waiting to encounter the Spanish fleet at the battle of Winchelsea in 1350: "The king . . . ordered his minstrels to play before him a German dance which Sir John Chandos had lately introduced. For his amusement, he made the same knight sing with his minstrels, which delighted him greatly."[2]

People also enjoyed instrumental music, and some ability to play an instrument was common among the aristocracy: household accounts record the purchase of a recorder for Henry Bolingbroke and harp strings for his wife Mary Bohun in 1387–1388, and later for their son—the future Henry V—in 1397. Bagpipes were one of the most popular instruments, especially among commoners: they were easy to hear at an outdoor festival, and their driving sound made them excellent for dancing. The pipe and tabor were also popular: the pipe was a three-hole recorder played with the left hand while beating a drum (the tabor) with the right. This provided both melody and rhythm at once, and was especially favored among common folk. Simple flutes and recorders were also in use, as was the shawm, an extremely loud double-reeded ancestor of the oboe.

There were several sorts of bowed instruments. The most familiar is the fiddle, which was about the size of a modern viola, more plain in construction, and held against the chest rather than under the chin. The rebec was a smaller cousin, small enough to lie on the musician's forearm, and having a rounded back. Other stringed instruments included the harp and the citole or gittern, a plucked instrument vaguely comparable to a mandolin. The psaltery was a triangular box with strings running across it, comparable in appearance to a modern zither; the medieval psaltery was plucked with a plectrum. Percussion was provided by drums, especially for dance music. Somewhere between percussion and wind instruments was the instrument then called a trump but known today as a Jew's harp, an inexpensive and common instrument in medieval England.

The sounds of all these instruments were generally coarser and harsher than is favored today, and many medieval instruments were quite loud. All this helped to ensure that the instrument would be audible. There were no amplifying systems, and one couldn't always count on good acoustics. The rhythms of fourteenth-century music were often complex, and in many respects European music of the period has affinities with the music of the Islamic world today.

One common way of enjoying music was through dancing, which was widely popular throughout society and seems to have been fairly consistent at all social levels. People of Chaucer's day generally danced in a circle or chain, as is still common in some folk traditions of modern Europe. Courtly dancers liked to alternate men and women in the chain, but among ordinary people there seems to have been less concern about gender. It was especially common for women to dance together at all levels of society, while male-only dances seem to have been most popular among common folk. The music for the dance might be provided by musicians, but often the only music was the singing of the dancers themselves, a custom that also survives in a few parts of Europe.

Animal Sports

A number of pastimes at various levels of society involved animals. One of these was hunting, which was a distinctive feature of aristocratic culture. In fact, it was generally illegal for commoners to hunt, as the rights to use land for hunting were generally reserved for the aristocratic holders. The favorite targets of the aristocratic hunt were deer and boar—most of the other large game had become extinct in England. Smaller game included rabbits and foxes, although these were considered less interesting prey. The medieval hunt was highly ritualized: a skilled huntsman needed to know all about the habits of the quarry, know the special vocabulary of the hunt, recognize the various horn calls used as signals, be able to manage the hunting dogs, and have mastered the art of carving up the quarry when it was killed. Hunting was considered excellent training for warfare, but it was also treated as something of an art form, in which the process of the hunt was as important as the actual killing of the prey.

Women did not generally hunt, but they did take part in the related sport of falconry. This sport was physically less demanding, but it had its own challenges. There were complex protocols as to what sorts of falcons should be sent after what quarry, and falcons were much more difficult to manage than hunting dogs. Hunting falcons were trained to bring down birds on the wing, especially waterfowl—falconry was generally practiced near rivers, and the favored game were cranes, storks, and herons.

Hunting and hawking required trained hunting animals, who were to be found in any major aristocratic household. Privileged households also kept animals as pets: Chaucer's Prioress Eglentyne has some small dogs "that she fed/With roasted flesh, or milk and fine white bread," and others like her kept cats or birds. Ordinary homes would have cats and dogs as well, but these were mostly for practical purposes: cats for catching mice and rats, dogs for security and herding.

Several popular games involved some sort of violence between or against animals. Bulls and bears were baited, which involved setting dogs against them and betting on the outcome of the fight. Cockfighting was also popular: two cocks were set to fight each other, and the onlookers bet on which would win. Cocks could also be the objects of violent sports. Not only were they used in cockfighting and as archery targets, but there was a sport called cockthrashing, in which a blindfolded person would attempt to hit one with a stick.

Combat at the barriers during a siege, 1410–1411.
McLean, after L'Epitre d'Othea (BL Harley 4431).

Combat Sports

Among the most characteristic pastimes of the aristocrat was the tournament and related martial sports, generally called deeds of arms. The oldest form was the tournament proper, which involved a mass of armored
horsemen fighting as two teams. By Chaucer's day, this riotous sport had
evolved a number of rules to minimize casualties. Combat would take
place within a limited area, typically about the size of a modern football
field, often surrounded by heavy barriers. Judges regulated the combat,
allocating the different retinues to create two approximately equal teams
and taking their oath to follow the customary rules. The two sides could
initially charge each other with lances, but the main combat was fought
with blunt tourneying swords; daggers and pointed swords were prohibited. Tourneyers tried to unhorse their opponents and capture their horses.
The tournament was falling out of favor: the last recorded fourteenth-
century tournament in England was fought in 1342.

The joust was less chaotic, and gained favor as the tournament lost it.
The joust pitted armored horsemen against each other one by one, charg-
ing with sharp or, more often, blunted lances. At any given occasion a
number of horsemen would challenge each other, divided into two teams
of holders and comers. In some jousts the jousters could win an opponent's horse by dismounting him as in a tournament.

The behourd was a less formal version of the mounted tournament,
fought with less rules and ceremony, and with lighter weapons and armor,
or without armor at all.

Weapons included spears and wooden wands wielded like swords.
Some of the informality of the behourd is suggested by thirteenth- and
fourteenth-century ordinances that prohibit those taking part from attacking bystanders on foot and requiring participants to wear bells—presumably
to give innocent bystanders fair warning.

Tournaments and jousts were sometimes officially organized by the
king as a means of displaying his magnificence and political power. They
were occasions for rich display, costumes, and even play-acting, and often
attracted large crowds of all classes. The event would often begin with
a ceremonial procession to the tournament field. The defenders would
often be all dressed in one livery, or fantastically costumed—some of the
most fanciful costumes included Tartars, the pope and his cardinals, and
the seven deadly sins. Masks were frequently worn in such processions,
and sometimes each knight was accompanied by a lady, perhaps dressed
in the same livery, leading him by a gold or silver chain. Awarding prizes
was a consensus decision in the hands of judges, often consisting of a
panel of ladies.

Beginning with the famous "Combat of the Thirty" in 1351, challenges
to formal combat under agreed conditions, often on foot, became a popular alternative to the tournament or festive joust. These combats were

THE ANNOUNCEMENT OF A JOUST WITH STAGING MANAGED BY CHAUCER AS CLERK OF THE WORKS, 1389 OR 1390

Hear ye, Lords, Knights, and squires. We make known to you a very great deed of arms and very noble Joust that will be performed by a Knight, who will carry a red shield, with on it a white hart having a crown around its neck with a hanging chain of gold, on a green bank; and the said Knight to be accompanied by twenty knights all dressed in one color. And Sunday, the ninth day of October next they will come to the new Abbey near the Tower of London.

And from that place these same knights will be led by twenty ladies dressed in one livery, of the same color and suit as the said knights, all around the outside of the noble city called New Troy, otherwise known as London. And just outside the same gate the said knights will hold the field called Smithfield by the Hostel of Saint John called Clerkenwell. And there they will dance, and sing, and conduct themselves in joy.

And the following Monday the said twenty knights, in one livery as aforesaid, will be within the said field of Smithfield, armed and mounted within the lists, before the hour of High Prime, to satisfy all manner of Knights who wish to come and Joust . . . And the following Wednesday the same twenty knights aforesaid will come to the said field to satisfy all knights and squires whatever with as many lances as it pleases them to joust with . . . And the lady or damsel who dances best or conducts herself with the greatest joy those three days aforesaid, that is to say Sunday, Monday, and Tuesday, will be given a golden brooch by the knights.

Translated by Will McLean from the French in F. H. Cripps-Day, *The History of the Tournament* (London: Quaritch, 1918), Appendix, pp. xli–xlii.

always between national enemies using the weapons of war. The Combat of the Thirty was fought between 30 French men-at-arms and 30 men from an English garrison: the encounter vented local animosities and left fifteen men dead on the field. Such group combats were comparatively rare, and particularly dangerous. Each combatant expected to fight until he was captured or killed, and the best way to win was to eliminate one or more members of the opposing team early so the rest could be overpowered in a succession of unequal contests.

Yet some degree of control was never absent from these challenges. Even the Combat of the Thirty was fought on agreed terms. The sides were to be equal, with no interference from others. The fight was interrupted by a pause for refreshment, and reportedly concluded by the award of a prize of valor to the best warrior on each side.

By the 1380s, challenges to single combat became popular. These challenges could be fought on foot, mounted, or both, and multiple combats might be arranged for the same day. Although the weapons were still designed for war, these combats were easier to control than group encounters. Each fight was for an agreed number of blows, often spread among a variety of weapons, such as five blows with spear, axe, sword, and dagger.

The encounter with that weapon would end when one or the other champion had struck or attempted that number of blows. Judges could end the fight earlier if a combatant was in danger or clearly outmatched, and it was possible to complete these encounters without either side being considered the loser, and with honor on both sides.

All of these combat sports involved substantial risk, and even the carefully controlled joust could result in fatalities. The less dangerous practice of tilting at the quintain was popular both as training for the joust and as a sport in its own right. The quintain was a post, or shield either fixed rigidly to a post or designed to pivot against a counterweight. The pivoting quintain provided a more realistic target, since it gave way under the impact of the encounter. The quintain was a primarily a target for horsemen, but fourteenth-century illuminations also show youths jousting at the quintain on foot, or jousting at the quintain while riding a sort of wheeled sawhorse pulled by two others.

Commoners practiced martial sports too, although they were less elaborate. Their favorite weapons included short staves, quarterstaves, and sword-and-buckler (the buckler being a small round shield). As with aristocratic combat, such pastimes could be very dangerous—or even more so, since commoners did not wear armor.

Wrestling was a form of combat sport that was enjoyed by all classes. For men-at-arms, it was an essential battlefield skill, since armored combat could easily devolve to wrestling techniques. Among commoners it was a popular form of public entertainment. Play could be full-contact or could allow grasping an opponent's clothes or a cloth baldric worn over one shoulder. The aim could be either to give the opponent a fall or to

Young gentlemen fencing with sword and buckler.
Italian, c. 1395 (TS Vienna, f. 96v). McLean.

force him outside a circle. Commoners also engaged in what is now called chickenfighting, with two wrestlers mounted on the shoulders of two supporters, each trying to throw his opponent off.[3]

Athletics and Sports

Some entertainments were pure demonstrations of athleticism. Men and boys showed their speed in foot races, or exhibited their strength by casting bars or heavy stones. For villagers, such contests were often a chance to impress the opposite sex: in the words of a contemporary song, "At stone-casting my lover I chose, and at the wrestling I did him lose." For aristocrats, these sports served as physical training to develop the strength and stamina needed for armored combat. During the winter, people skated on frozen rivers and lakes on skates made of bone.

Ball games existed in a number of variations. An edict of 1363, attempting to promote English archery, forbade other sports including handball, football, stickball, and cambok. Medieval football was similar to its modern European namesake, known in North America as soccer. The game was invariably rowdy and sometimes extremely dangerous. In 1373 a group of tailors and skinners in London were arrested for playing football in Cheapside, a broad London street crowded with market stalls—the players had been wearing daggers at the time.

Similar in structure was the game of Cambok, a sort of field hockey, named for the cambok or cammock, a curved stick similar to a modern field hockey stick, carried by shepherds to help manage their sheep. Variants (or other names) included Goff and Bandy. A rather more dangerous ball game was Camp-Ball, comparable to rugby and American football. There were two goals, which might be miles apart; each team would score by bringing the ball to the other team's goal. The ball could be conveyed by any means chosen: some versions of this game even included horsemen, and serious injury was common.

ROBERT BRAYBROKE, BISHOP OF LONDON, COMPLAINS OF BOYS PLAYING AROUND LONDON CATHEDRAL, 1385

Certain boys, also, good for nothing in their insolence and idleness, instigated by evil minds and busying themselves rather in doing harm than good, throw and shoot stones, arrows, and different kinds of missiles at the rooks, pigeons, and other birds nesting and perching in the walls and porches of the church. Also they play ball inside and outside the church and engage in other destructive games there, breaking and greatly damaging the glass windows and the stone images of the church, which having been made with the greatest skill, are a pleasure to the eyes of all beholders.

From Edith Rickert, *Chaucer's World* (New York: Columbia University Press, 1948), 48.

One family of ball games was related to tennis. Commoners played a simple game called Handball, and aristocrats played an early version of tennis in which the ball was struck with the hand. Closely related was the game of Shuttlecock, the medieval equivalent of badminton, played with wooden paddles. Other ball games involved sticks or bats, and were related to baseball and cricket. A fifteenth-century text mentions Stoolball, which in later centuries involved one player pitching a ball at a stool and another attempting to ward it off, either with his hand or with a bat.

Another type of ball game was Bowls, in which the players would try to cast their balls as close as possible to a target. In the game of Quoits the players cast flat round stones at a target. Somewhere between medieval Bowls and modern ten-pin bowling was the game of Kailes or Loggats, in which a number of wooden or bone pins would be set up and the players would attempt to knock them over by casting a stick at them.

Archery

Many of the games played by commoners were the object of official disapproval, since they encouraged idleness, rowdyism, and gambling. The one major exception was archery, which was strongly encouraged as a means of bolstering England's military might: the Statute of Winchester in 1285 had decreed that every man whose property was worth less than £6 13s. 4d. was required to own a bow. In fact, archery was genuinely popular at all levels of society.

There were at least two different ways of shooting bows for recreation or practice in fourteenth-century England. The first was shooting at the butts. The target to be shot at was set in front of a bank of earth or turf. Butts were shot at distances from 30 to 120 yards.

The second was known as shooting at pricks—the term meant "points, marks," and implied a small target. The mark was at a fixed and known distance from the shooter, far enough that significant elevation and strength was required. A twelvescore prick could be 240 yards from the shooter, and some marks were even further. Recorded marks of London's Finsbury archers during the 1500s ranged from 180 to 380 yards. Butts and pricks often used a pair of marks, so the archers could shoot from one mark to the other and then back again, to reduce the time spent walking.

Other formats were recorded in the 1400s, and may have been used earlier. In shooting at rovers, archers would shoot from mark to mark, choosing the second mark when they reached the first, selecting some feature within range to shoot at like a tree or bush or one of several marks positioned in advance for the purpose. Because the distance varied at each shoot, rovers was seen as better training for combat or hunting.

The mark itself could take a number of forms. The early fourteenth-century Luttrell Psalter shows a garland or circlet set against the butt about chest-high, and garlands are also the mark in the fifteenth-century

Gest of Robin Hood. Other early marks were small circular pieces of paper or pasteboard, fixed to the butt or a post in front of it by a wooden pin or wand. And alternative target was the "clout" (cloth), a piece of white fabric large enough to be seen from the shooting distance, fastened to a sharpened stick driven upright into the ground so that the bottom of the clout almost reached the ground. The modern archery target of concentric circles seems to have been a seventeenth-century innovation.

For most marks the winner was simply the closest arrow to the mark, and at longer ranges, the mark itself would rarely be hit. The garland was probably scored similarly to eighteenth-century "shooting within the inches": each shot that hit within a 12-inch diameter circle counted at 30 yards. At 60 yards the circle was twenty inches. Typically, each archer shot two arrows at the mark, the arrows were collected and scored, and then the bowmen would shoot at the next mark. The heads of arrows for shooting at marks had a specialized shape that differed from heads used for hunting or war: barbless and streamlined with a swelling shoulder so the archer could consistently draw to full length by feel. When shooting at rovers, archers might carry more than one pair of arrows so they could have arrows suited for different ranges.

Not all contests involved shooting at marks. In shooting at the popinjay, archers took turns attempting to knock an artificial bird off the top of a church steeple or tall pole. Alternatively, arrows could be purely for distance, either with lightweight flight arrows or the heavier standard arrow.[4]

Children's Games

Some games seem to have been particularly the pastimes of children. Such was Prisoner's Base, known as Bars, Base, or Post and Pillar: in 1332 an injunction was issued forbidding children from playing this game in the precincts of Westminster Palace when Parliament was in session—one can imagine the noise being a distraction from the business of government. Another characteristic children's pastime was the whip-top, a form of top beaten with a scourge to make it turn.

Quite a few children's games were based on the giving and receiving of blows. In the game later known as Hot Cockles one player sat and took the head of the player who was "it" in his lap, to keep him from peeking; the other players took turns slapping the victim's rear, and if he correctly guessed who had struck the blow, that person became "it." Closely related was Hoodman's Blind, or Bobet, the ancestor of Blind-Man's Buff (also called Bear-Baiting after its more bloodthirsty cousin). In this game, one player had a hood pulled over his eyes and tried to catch one of the other players in order to change places with him or her. This was complicated by the fact that at the same time the other players were hitting him with their own hoods tied in a knot, or even with sticks—it is from these buffets that the game received its modern name. As in Hot Cockles, the object may sometimes have been to identify who had given the last blow. A similar game was Frog in the Middle, in which the player who was "it" crouched on the floor: the rest would try to touch, pinch, or slap him—anyone he caught would be "it." All these games were popular among both boys and girls.

Table Games

In addition to these physical pastimes, there were a number of popular table games. Chess occupied a prestigious position and was particularly favored among the aristocracy. The form of chess played in fourteenth-century England was similar to the modern game, but there were a few substantial differences—notably in the moves of the Queen and the Bishop, which were much more restricted.[5]

After chess, perhaps the most popular class of board game was Tables, a family of games of which Backgammon is the only surviving descendant. The board and pieces were essentially the same as in modern Backgammon. Backgammon itself was not invented until the seventeenth century—in the fourteenth century there existed a variety of games at Tables, each with different initial set-ups and conditions for victory, though the procedure for moving was largely the same.

Another familiar game was that of Draughts or Jeu-de-Dame (called Checkers in North America today), which had originated by placing Tables pieces on the board for Chess. Even simpler was the game of Merels, usually known today as Nine-Man Morris. Often a Tables set was built as a box, with two square halves folding together. The Tables board would be on the inside; on the back of one half would be a chessboard, on the back of the other a board for Merels.

One of the most simple, popular, and morally suspect forms of play was dicing, a practice that required almost no space and only the simplest equipment—two or three dice (bone was an inexpensive and popular material; ivory was used by the wealthy) and stakes to play for. The spots on the dice had special names borrowed from French: ace, deuce, trey, cater, sink, and sise. Dice games were generally very simple, involving pure chance and almost no strategy, so their interest lay in the gambling.

Cross and Pile was another simple pastime, exactly the same as modern Heads or Tails—one side of the medieval coin had a cross on it, the other a face, or pile. Somewhat comparable was the practice of drawing cuts (the same as drawing straws today, and indeed done with actual pieces of straw)—this is how the pilgrims decide who should tell the first story in the *Canterbury Tales*.

Cards

Most of the games played in late medieval Europe had been around for centuries, but a major change was happening during Chaucer's lifetime with the introduction of playing cards to Europe. These arrived from the Near East, perhaps through Venetian trade with the Mameluk Turks. The first clear written evidence for playing cards in Europe occurs in 1377, from which date onward there survive numerous references from France, Italy, Spain, Switzerland, Germany, and the Low Countries.[6] Many of these are laws banning card playing on holidays, or for tradesmen, or both, suggesting the broad popularity of the pastime from its very first arrival.

The more isolated parts of Western Europe took to cards more slowly. England appears to have been backward in this respect. The earliest English references to playing cards date to the early fifteenth century. Nonetheless, the close cultural contacts between England and the Continent in this period suggest that at least some Englishmen must have been exposed to the practice.[7]

Old playing cards have not generally survived, and no European examples are known from before the fifteenth century. Most surviving examples from before 1500 are cards that were never meant for ordinary use—collectors' items displaying the wealth of the owner. They were hand painted and illuminated by master painters, and were very expensive. Of the millions of playing cards produced for common use, scarcely a single example remains.

Playing cards are easily worn, torn, spoiled, or lost. This characteristic, combined with the evidence of widespread popularity, indicates that a large number of decks were being produced. For the tradesmen of Paris to afford the cards that they were forbidden in 1377, cards must have been cheap and plentiful enough for them to acquire the habit. The likeliest means of production is block-printing. An alternative would be the stenciling technique that was commonly used to color block-printed playing cards in the fifteenth century.

The modern deck of cards is almost always divided into suits of Hearts, Spades, Clubs, and Diamonds. This suit system is only one of many and did not appear until about 1480, in France, for which reason it is called the French suit system. Several other suit systems survived for hundreds of years in Europe.

Visual evidence suggests that the first playing cards in Europe were of the Italian suit system of Coins, Cups, Swords, and Batons, similar to the suits found on modern Tarot decks. This conclusion is supported by the close resemblance between this system and the Mameluk suits of Coins, Cups, Swords, and Polo-Sticks. In the Italian deck, the Swords are stylized and curved scimitars, and they are interlaced so as to cross each other at the hilts and near the points of the swords. The Batons are long straight staves that are also stylized and interlaced at the center of the card. Coins are large round disks, often with designs on their faces, and Cups are stylized basins with ornate tops. The Spanish suit system, probably slightly later in date, had more naturalistic swords and batons, not interlaced but arranged like modern suit signs.

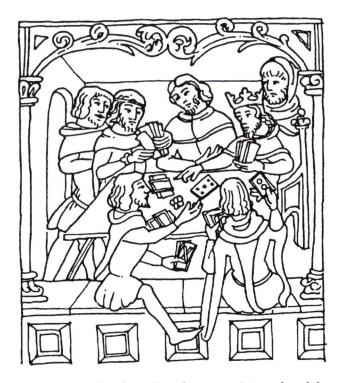

A game at cards, after a French manuscript produced for
Louis II, King of Naples c. 1352. It appears to show the Italian suits of Coins and Batons (British Library MS Add. 12228,
f. 313v). McLean.

One of the first references in Europe is the *Tractatus de moribus et disciplina
humanae conversationis,* written by a Dominican friar from Basel in 1377.
The text describes the deck as having four suits, three court cards in each
suit, and ten number cards in each suit. The number cards, as now, bear
a number of pips of the suit sign equal to their value (i.e., twos have two
pips, fives have five, and so on).[8] This description exactly parallels modern
decks. The earliest surviving decks have the same pip cards as in a modern
deck (i.e., 1 to 10), but the face cards might include a Knight as well as the
Knave (the modern Jack), Queen, and King. This is again reminiscent of
the modern Tarot deck. German decks sometimes replaced the Queen and
Knave with an Over and an Under, two figures holding the suit sign high
and low respectively. The Joker was not a feature of medieval decks.

Gambling and the Element of Risk

An important difference between medieval and modern games is the role
of betting. Physically demanding sports might be played for the pleasure
of exercise, and chess for the intellectual challenge, but most other games

were likely to involve some form of wager. Moralists railed against the vice of gambling, and social reformers saw it as a destructive vice (particularly among commoners, who were supposed to be working for their living), but the excitement provided by a stake was regarded as an integral part of play. Even relatively poor people gambled, and for the aristocracy it was practically a way of life. Most table games involved some degree of gambling, and wagers were a common feature of all types of games. Some, like animal-fights, were gambling sports by definition, and many other classes of games might be enlivened by the addition of a wager.

The penchant for gambling may well be related to the interest in sports that were inherently dangerous, such as jousting or swordplay, or in sports that could get perilously rough, like football. In general, medieval people seem to have been quite willing to risk serious personal injury in the pursuit of entertainment. This could reflect a lower value placed on security of life and limb, but it could also be attributed to the greater importance of games in medieval culture. Games gave meaning and interest to people's lives. Perhaps because medieval society was comparatively structured and static, people vented a desire for excitement and challenge by deliberately choosing risky forms of play. The importance of play to medieval people is reflected in its ongoing part in their lives as they aged. In the modern world, people tend to abandon game-playing as they mature. For medieval people, games remained an important activity even in adulthood, even if only the aristocracy had the leisure to pursue them on a daily basis.

RULES FOR GAMES

In reconstructing fourteenth-century games, we are obliged to supplement contemporary and nearly contemporary sources with additional information from later centuries. A few compilations of rules for board games and dice games survive from the thirteenth to fifteenth centuries, but for card games and physical games the rules must be inferred from later sources. Fortunately, the conservatism of games has meant that many of the games whose rules were first written down in the seventeenth century had changed little, if at all, since the Middle Ages. In fact, medieval games—especially physical games—were much less formalized and rules-oriented than their modern counterparts and were probably subject to regional and local variation; in this respect they resembled modern playground games more than the games now played as professional sports. It is therefore potentially misleading to speak of "correct" reconstructions of medieval games, and they may be regarded as valid as long as they preserve the basic dynamic of the game.

Dice Games

Most of the excitement in these games comes from the betting. They are particularly amusing if you can provide yourself with a supply of medieval coins (see Appendix C). Details of medieval betting practices are sparse, but the modern conventions of similar games such as Craps are both workable and consistent with what we know of the medieval games. In all dice games, order of play can be determined by the roll of one die. The highest roll goes first, and ties roll again.

Hazard

This was by far the most popular and enduring game at dice. Any number can play, forming a ring around the table or patch of ground where the dice are rolled and the bets are placed. The first player to cast the dice puts up the amount he is willing to bet, and any of the other players can wager against all or any part of the caster's bet, or against any remaining portion of it, at even odds. If two speak at once, the most recent loser takes precedence. The caster may at any time remove any part of his bet that has not been wagered against. As in modern Craps, there could be side bets between any two players at any time on any outcome at mutually agreed odds. In an honest game, judging the correct odds to offer or accept on these side bets is the only element of skill in this kind of contest. Once a bet has been made and accepted, it can only be canceled by mutual consent. If the caster wins, he may retain the dice and declare a new center bet; if he loses, the dice pass to the next player on his left. New players should enter the game to the caster's right if possible and convenient.

There appear to have been two forms of this game, one played with three dice, the other with two. The three-dice version is found in a thirteenth-century Spanish treatise on games compiled for the Spanish king Alfonso X of Castile:

- The first player casts the dice. If the first cast is 15 or above or 5 or less, he wins and starts again.
- If the player casts a number from 6 to 14, that number becomes the opponent's "Chance." The player then rolls again.
- If the second cast is 15 or above or 5 or less, the player loses and passes the dice.
- If the second cast is between 6 and 14, that number becomes the player's Chance.
- The player then continues to cast until he either rolls the opponent's Chance and loses, or rolls his own Chance and wins.

The two-die version is described in a seventeenth-century treatise:

- The first player rolls two dice until he gets a Main, which can be any number from 5 through 9. He then rolls again:
- On a 2 or 3, he loses (the former roll was known ames-ace).
- If the Main is 5 or 9 and the player again rolls the Main, he wins. If he rolls an 11 or 12, he loses.

- If the Main is 6 or 8 and the player rolls the Main or a 12, he wins. If he rolls an 11, he loses.
- If the Main is 7 and the player rolls the Main or an 11, he wins. If he rolls a 12, he loses.
- Any other roll is called the Mark, and the player continues to roll until he gets the Mark and wins, or gets the Main and loses.[9]

Raffle

This game is mentioned by Chaucer and described in Alfonso's treatise. Seventeenth-century sources imply a multi-player game with all players putting in an equal stake. The caster throws until he gets doublets (two dice the same). He then throws the third die again and reckons the total of the three. The other players roll in turn in the same manner, and the highest score wins. If the score is tied, the game begins again with the pot carried over.[10]

Passage

This game is attested from the early fifteenth century and described in the seventeenth. The caster throws three dice until he gets doublets (two dice the same). If the total of the three dice is under 10, he is out and loses; if over 10, he passes and wins. If the roll is 10, the dice pass to the other player but the pot is not collected.[11]

Board Games

Chess

Medieval chess was somewhat different from the modern form. The form Chaucer probably played was Anglo-French Long Assize.[12] The moves of several pieces are different from those in the modern form.

King. Starts to right of Queen. On the King's first move (if not in check) he can move to any square he could reach in two moves, or QKn1 or QKn2, provided he does not move through a space occupied by an opposing piece. This move cannot be used to capture a piece.

Queen. May only move one square diagonally. On her first move she too can go to any square she could reach in two moves, even if the intervening square is occupied; this move cannot be used to capture a piece.

Bishop. May move no more or less than two squares diagonally, but may jump over intervening pieces.

Pawn. As in the modern game, the pawn can capture *en passant*. It may only convert to a Queen upon reaching the final rank. On the pawn's first move as a Queen, the Queen's first move rules apply.

If one King has lost all his pieces, the game is over unless the opposing King also loses his last man on the next turn. A stalemate is considered a draw. This is a slower game than the modern version—more recent innovations were introduced specifically with the aim of speeding up play.

Fourteenth-century chess pieces were also somewhat different from their modern counterparts. Chess sets came in two forms, figurative and conventional. In figurative sets the Kings looked like kings, the Queens like queens, and so on. Surviving fourteenth-century French chessmen of this type are rather elegant in proportion but still well designed to stand up to rough handling, with a minimum of fragile projections. In conventional sets the pieces are stylized, as in most modern sets, although some of the conventions are different. For example, Bishops have a pair of upright horns, and Rooks a pair that curve downward. Other pieces are more like their modern form, although there are differences of detail and proportion.

Tables

Backgammon as such had not yet been developed, but several forms of Tables are actually described in a fourteenth-century English manuscript.[13] The basic outlines of these games are similar to Backgammon. They typically involve two players, one sitting on side **a-l** of the board and moving towards point **x**; **a-f** is called his entering table, **s-x** his bearing table. The other player sits on side **m-x** and moves towards point **a**; **s-x** is his entering table, **a-f** his bearing table. At the beginning of the game, the pieces are set on certain points of the board. The players take turns rolling two or three dice, depending on the game. The roll of each die is assigned to a piece: on a roll of 6 and 5, one piece may be moved forward 6 points and another 5, or a single piece may be moved 6 and then 5. If a piece is left alone on a point and the opponent is able to move a man onto that point, the first piece is removed and must be played in again onto the player's entering table. A point with more than one piece on it cannot be landed on by the opponent and is said to be doubled. A player may not move any of his men until he has entered any that are waiting off the board. No man may be borne from the board until all are in the bearing table.

Many of the games differ only in initial set-up, as suggested by these three examples:

Imperial.   Player 1 starts with 5 men on **f**, 5 on **g**, and 5 on **j**; his opponent has 5 on **s**, 5 on **r**, and 5 on **o**. This game uses 3 dice.

Provincial.   As Imperial, but Player 1 starts with 8 men on **f** and 7 on **g**, Player 2 with 8 on **s** and 7 on **r**.

The English Game.   (*Ludus Anglicorum*): This was said to be the most common form of Tables in England. Player 1 starts with all 15 pieces on point **x**, and Player 2 has all his 15 on point **a**. This game uses 3 dice. A

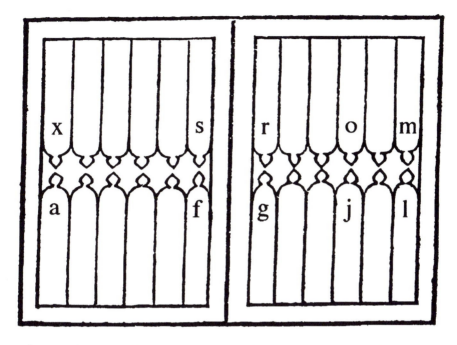

A fourteenth-century backgammon board (the letters have been added to help explain the games). Fiske.

player's pieces cannot be doubled as long as they are on his own side, so that a man cannot re-enter the board onto a point already occupied by one of his men. In addition to the usual means of winning, victory can be achieved by doubling the first 5 points on the far side of the board while the opponent has one man in each of the 6 points in his table of entry, 8 on the last point of his bearing table, and 1 in his hand (this win is called limpolding). Another victory is called lurching, and occurs under the same circumstances, save that the opponent has fewer than 8 men on the last point of his bearing table.

Merels

This was a very popular game; Merels boards were often placed on the reverse side of chessboards or on the outside of Tables boards. The game existed in several versions, including two that correspond to modern Nine Men's Morris and Three Men's Morris. In Nine-Man Merels, each player has nine pieces, each called a merel. Players draw lots to start and then take turns placing their merels on the board, one merel on each corner or intersection. After all merels are placed, the players take turns moving them. A merel can be moved to any adjacent corner or intersection, provided it is

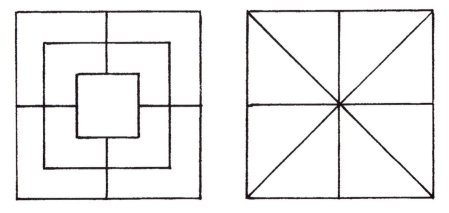

Merels Boards: Nine Men's (left) and Six-Man (right) versions. McLean.

connected with the merel's current location by a line. A player who manages to place or move such that three of his merels come to be in a row removes one of his opponent's merels; and a player whose merels are so hedged in that they cannot move also has a merel removed by his opponent. To be in a row, the three merels must be connected by a single line. The last player on the board wins.

A simpler version of the game is Three-Man Merels, which amounts to a moving game of Tic-Tac-Toe. In this version, each player begins with three merels. Pieces are positioned and moved as in Nine-Man Merels, and the first player to get his three merels into a row wins.[14]

Cards

Although we know that playing cards appeared on the Continent in the last quarter of the fourteenth century, we have almost no idea of what games were played or what the rules were. The names of games do not appear until the fifteenth century, and rules were rarely written down prior to the late seventeenth century. The games included here are those mentioned in fifteenth-century sources.

All these games can be played with an ordinary modern deck. If you want something a bit more like a medieval deck, a Tarot deck is a good choice (leaving out the cards of the Major Arcana). In fact, it is even possible to buy Tarot decks that reproduce the appearance of surviving fifteenth-century decks.

One and Thirty

Players: 2 to 8. This is perhaps the simplest of traditional card games, and widely popular: games called Thirty-One appear frequently in literature from 1440 onwards in all of Western Europe. It is also the ancestor of modern Blackjack.

Players ante into the pot. The cards are cut for the deal, and the lowest card deals; the deal rotates clockwise among the players thereafter. Each player is dealt three cards. Next, each player in turn may ask the dealer to deal him cards, attempting to come as close as possible to 31 without going over—face cards count 10, and all others according to the number of their pips. Once all players are finished, the cards are turned up and reckoned. A player who has exactly 31 wins double the pot. If no player hits 31 exactly, the highest hand under 31 wins the pot. The eldest hand (i.e. the hand closest to the dealer's left) wins all ties.[15]

Karnoeffel

Players: 4 (partners). The German game of Karnoeffel is the oldest documented card game, attested as early as 1426.[16] In the description below, the court cards in each suit are the King (K), Over (O), and Under (U). Depending on the deck, the Knight or Queen can serve as Over (the other being discarded), the Knave (Jack) as Under. Aces are discarded.

Players ante into the pot, and five cards are dealt to each. Opposite players are partners, and each side tries to win the most tricks. Each player's first card is dealt face up, and the lowest ranking of them (using the normal order: K O U 10 9 8 7 6 5 4 3 2) establishes a quasi-trump suit. If there are ties, use the suit dealt first for trump.

The eldest player (i.e., on the dealer's left) leads by playing a card, and each player does likewise in turn, proceeding clockwise. Players need not follow suit (i.e., play a card of the suit led by the first player), and partners may discuss between them what card to play. When each has played, the trick is taken by the highest card of the suit led, or by the highest trump if any are played. In plain suits the ranking of cards is normal, from King down to deuce. In the quasi-trump suit, the following cards are able to trump:

Card	Name	Rank
trump Under	Karnoeffel	beats any other cards
7 of trumps	the Devil	beats any cards except the Karnoeffel, but only if led
6 of trumps	the Pope	beats all plain suit cards
2 of trumps	the Emperor	beats all plain suit cards
3 of trumps	the Over-taker	beats all plain suit cards except Kings
4 of trumps	the Under-taker	beats all plain suit cards except Kings and Overs
5 of trumps	the Suit-taker	beats all plain suit cards except face cards

The other cards in the quasi-trump suit (i.e., the K, O, 10, 9, 8) do not trump—they act as a normal suit. The seven of trumps (the Devil) beats all other cards (except the Karnoeffel) only if it is the first card led to a trick, and it may not be led to the first trick. It will not beat any card in any other circumstance—it is thus second highest if led, and lowest otherwise. This gives the following order in the trump suit: U, (7), 6, 2, K, 3, O, 4, 5, 10, 9, 8, (7).

Play continues until either side has taken three tricks, at which point they collect the pot, and a new deal begins.

Glic, Pochspiel

Players: 3 or more. Pochspiel, or Bockspiel, appears in the records as early as 1441 in Strasburg, Alsace, and regularly thereafter in other German-speaking areas. Glic appears first in 1454 in France and seems to be virtually the same game. Other names used for the same game are Boeckels, Poque, Bocken, and Bogel; the name is the ultimate source of modern Poker. Even without surviving rules, the names can be recognized as belonging to the same game by their playing boards—a number of brightly painted boards survive from the sixteenth century.[17]

Pochspiel is played with a board, usually with eight compartments or spaces, labeled Ace, King, Queen, Knave, Ten, Marriage, Sequence, and Poch (a board can be improvised by writing with chalk on a piece of wood). Some of the earliest boards omitted the Marriage and Sequence spaces, or substituted Over and Under for Queen and Knave. First the players place stakes in each compartment except Poch. This can be done starting at the dealer, with each player in sequence putting a single coin into a compartment until one coin has been put in each. Five cards are then dealt to each player, and the top remaining card is turned up for trump.

There are three separate phases to a round of Pochspiel. The first phase is a sweepstakes. Anyone who holds the Ace of trump wins the stakes in the Ace compartment, and likewise for the King, Queen, Knave, and Ten compartments. Marriage is won by the player holding the King and Queen of trump (who also wins the stakes in the King and Queen compartments). The Sequence compartment is won by the player who holds the 7-8-9 of trump. If any compartment is not claimed, the stakes in it remain for subsequent hands.

The second phase is a betting phase, like Poker, and focuses on the Poch compartment (so called from the German word *pochen*, to brag). The winning hand is that with the best combination. Four of a kind beats three of a kind, three of a kind beats a pair, and a pair beats a hand without a pair. Higher valued cards beat lower ones in the same class (i.e., a pair of Kings would beat a pair of sixes but would be beaten by three Knaves). Each player in turn may put a stake into the Poch compartment. Other players may see it, raise it, pass, or fold. When the betting returns to the first player, he may bet again. You may want to set a limit on the total bet—say, 12 pence on a 1 penny stake. Betting stops only when every player has passed or folded. When betting stops, if only one player remains he wins the stakes in the Poch compartment. If two or more players remain (having all bet the same amount), the winner is the one with the best hand.

The third phase involves playing cards in a sequence, building up to 31. This is similar to modern Cribbage: each player in turn lays down a card so that the total of the cards laid does not exceed 31. When no one can play a card and remain under 31, each player must pay one penny to the person who laid the last card. Then the person who laid the last card plays the first card of the next sequence. As soon as one player runs out of cards, all the players who have cards remaining must pay him one penny for each card they still have remaining in their hands, and the game begins again.

Physical Games

Base

The rules for this game are first recorded in the seventeenth century. A number of players are divided into two sides. Each side has a designated Base and a designated Prison. One player on each side touches the Base, a second player touches him, a third touches the second, and so on. One of the outermost players "leads out" by leaving contact with his chain. The outermost player on the other side may chase him; if he does, the new outermost player on the first side may chase him, and so on. A player caught by his pursuer is taken to his pursuer's Prison, where he begins a chain as before. A player who can reach any of his imprisoned teammates without being caught releases them, and they may walk untroubled back to their Base. A player who reaches his own Base cannot be caught.[18]

Football

Equipment

- 1 Football (this would have been round, probably a bit smaller than a soccer ball, and made of an inflated bladder encased in a leather covering)
- 2 Goals (e.g., two pairs of stakes set up at opposite sides of the field)

The rules for this game are first recorded in the seventeenth century. Two sides are chosen, and separate to their respective sides of the field. A third party throws the ball out into the center, and each side tries to kick it through the opponent's goal. After each goal, the ball can be thrown out again, or given to the side scored against.

The game Cambok was similar in outline, except that the ball was smaller and harder and was driven with sticks comparable to modern field hockey sticks. The ball might be made of leather or sturdy canvas stuffed with cloth (the cloth might be wrapped in twine for extra hardness).[19]

Bowls/Quoits

Equipment

- 2 Wooden Balls for each player, about the size of an apple (each pair of balls should be color-coded to distinguish them from other pairs)
- 1 Mistress (a wooden cone, a stake, or some other object that can be set upright in the ground) or 1 'Jack' (a ball smaller than the others, preferably of a bright and contrasting color)

The rules for this game are first recorded in the seventeenth century. A point is designated as the casting spot, and the Mistress is set up on the pitch some distance away (two Mistresses can be set up, each serving as the other's casting spot, which will save walking back and forth); if using a Jack, the first player casts it out onto the pitch. Each player in turn casts one ball onto the pitch, trying to get it as close to the Jack or Mistress as possible; then each in turn casts the second ball. The player whose ball is closest at the end scores 1 point, 2 points if he has the two closest balls. A ball touching the target counts double. Balls can be knocked about by other balls, and the Jack can also be repositioned in this way. Play is normally until one player reaches 5 or 7.

Quoits is played in the same manner, save that the bowls are replaced by quoits, large flat stones or pieces of metal, and the Mistress by an iron stake, or Hob, driven into the ground (or the Jack by a small quoit).[20]

Kailes

Equipment

- 6–8 Pins (wooden cones or other objects that can be made to stand upright without fixing them into the ground). One of these should be taller than the others; it is called the King Pin.
- 1 Casting Stick

No rules for this game survive, but some help is afforded by seventeenth-century rules for the game of Nine-Pins, a close relative played with a ball rather than a casting stick. A casting spot is marked, and the players set up the pins some distance away in a row, a square, or a circle, with the King Pin in the middle. One player then throws the casting stick at the pins and scores as many points as he can knock over pins. The King Pin is worth 10 if it can be knocked over by itself, but only 1 if any other pins are knocked over. The pins are then set up again for the second player. The first player to reach 31 wins; a player who goes over 31 goes back to 15 but gets another cast.

SONGS

Very little popular music has survived from Chaucer's lifetime; the songs that follow include some from fifteenth-century manuscripts.

ANGELUS AD VIRGINEM

Text and music: Fourteenth-century [Furnivall (1902), 687-88].

An- ge- lus ad vir- gi- nem sub- in- trans in----- con-
Vir- gi- nis for- mi- di- nem de- mul-cens in----- quit
Ga- bri- el from hea-ven's king sent to the mai---- den
Brought her bliss- ful ti-------- dings and fair he did---- her

cla- ve A- ve re- gi na vir------ gi- num
"A- ve!
sweet---- "Hail be thou, full of grace---- a- right,
greet----

Cœ- li ter- ræ que do----- mi- num con------
For God's own son, this hea- ven- ly light, for------

ci- pi- es et pa- ri- es------- in- tac---------- ta sa-
love of man will man be- come--- and take------------- flesh

lu- tem ho------ mi- num tu-------- por- ta cœ------- li
of the mai----- den bright, man--- kind free for------ to

fac---------- ta me- de- la cri------- mi- num."
make------------- of sin and de------ vil's might."

"Quomodo conciperem quae virum non cognovi?
Qualiter infringerem quod firma mente vovi?"
"Spiritus sancti gratia perficiet haec omnia,
Ne timeas sed gaudeas, secura quod castimonia
Manebit in te pura Dei potentia."

Ad haec virgo nobilis respondens inquit ei,
"Ancilla sum humilis omnipotentis Dei;
Tibi cœlesti nuntio tanti secreti conscio,
Consentiens et cupiens videre factum quod audio
Parata sum parere Dei consilio."

Eia mater Domini quæ pacem reddidisti
Angelis et homini cum Christum genuisti;
Tuum exora filium ut se nobis propitium
Exhibeat et deleat peccata, præstans auxilium
Vita frui beata post hoc exilium.

Mildly to him answered then the maiden ever mild,
"How should I, untouched by men, be now to bear a child?"
The angel said, "Now dread thee nought,
Through Holy Ghost shall it be wrought,
This very thing, whereof tidings I bring,
Mankind shall be rebought
Through thy most sweet childing
And out of pain be brought."

When the maiden understood and had the angel heard,
Mildly then and mild of mood the angel she answered,
"Our Lord's handmaiden I am in this,
His that in heaven eternal is,
By way of me, fulfilled be what you say,
That I, since it His will is,
A maid contrary to way
Of motherhood have such bliss."

Maiden, mother without peer, with mercy sweet and kind,
Pray to Him that chose thee here, with Whom thou grace did find,
That He forgive us sin and mistake
and clean of every guilt us make
And heaven's bliss, when our time is to perish
Us give, for thy sweet sake,
That we Him here may cherish
and He us to Him take.

This religious song was extremely popular in the fourteenth century—
the merry scholar Nicholas in Chaucer's *The Miller's Tale* sings it. It is a rare
example of surviving popular music of the period. It commemorates the

Annunciation, the occasion on which the Archangel Gabriel announced to the Virgin Mary that she was to bear Jesus. The English version is modernized from a translation found in a manuscript of around 1300.

The Latin would have been pronounced with more or less the same sounds as in Spanish. The letters *c* and *g* are hard (as in *cat, get*) before consonants and before *a, o,* and *u*, soft (as in *cedar, general*) before *i, e, æ,* and *œ. Æ* and *œ* would be pronounced as *e*. Otherwise each vowel in a combination is pronounced; *tuum* is pronounced *tu-um; eia* is pronounced *ey-a*. The combinations *-tium, -tia* and *-tio* would be pronounced as *-ci-um, -ci-a, -ci-o*.

Si Quis Amat
Text and Music Probably Before 1395–1401 (Cambridge University Library Add'l. Ms. 5943 f. 163r, Reproduced in Richard Rastall, Two Fifteenth-Century Song Books [Aberystwyth: Boethius Press, 1990])

The statutes of Winchester College, in an effort to avoid idle gossip, required that everybody leave immediately after the meal was over, with an exception for feast days in winter, when the scholars and fellows were allows to stay and "amuse themselves decently for the purposes of recreation with songs and other honest pastimes." This is particularly relevant to the three-part Latin round "Si quis amat," whose lyrics translate as "If anyone enjoys slandering the lives of the absent, let him know that this table is not fitting for him."

Danger Me Hath
Text and Music Probably Before 1395–1401 (Cambridge University Library Add'l. Ms. 5943 f. 166r, Reproduced in Rastall, *Fifteenth-Century Song Books***)**

"Danger me hath" is a two-part song of slighted love. The lyrics mean: "Adversity holds me in its power, I can do nothing but let it pass, and live both glad and merrily, but things are not as they were."

DOLL THY ALE

Text: Fifteenth-century [Greene # 423]; Music: Traditional.

Ale makes many a man to stick upon a briar,
Ale makes many a man to slumber by the fire,
Ale makes many a man to wallow in the mire.
[Chorus] *So doll, doll, doll thy ale, doll, doll thy ale.*

Ale makes many a man to stumble on a stone,
Ale makes many a man to stagger drunken home,
Ale makes many a man to break his bone.

Ale makes many a man to brandish forth his knife,
Ale makes many a man to make great strife,
Ale makes many a man to beat his wife.

Ale makes many a man shed tears upon his cheeks,
Ale makes many a man to lie in the streets,
Ale makes many a man to wet his sheets.

Ale makes many a man to stumble at the blocks,
Ale makes many a man to break his head with knocks,
Ale makes many a man to languish in the stocks.

Ale makes many a man to run across the fallows,
Ale makes many a man swear by God and All Hallows,
Ale makes many a man to swing upon the gallows.

All Hallows: All Saints

BRING US IN GOOD ALE

Text: Fifteenth-century [Greene #422];
Music: Fifteenth-century [Chappell 42].

Bring us in no beef, for that is full of bones, but

bring in ale e- nough, for that--- goes down at once! *And*

bring us in good ale, good ale, and bring us in good ale!

and for our dear La- dy's love, bring--- us in good ale!

Bring us in no bacon, for that is passing fat,
But bring us in good ale, and bring us enough of that.
Bring us in no mutton, for that is tough and lean,
Nor bring us in no tripes, for they be seldom clean.
Bring us in no eggs, for there are many shells,
But bring us in good ale, and give us nothing else.
Bring us in no capons, for that is often dear,
Nor bring us in no ducks, for they wallow in the mere.

This song offers a good survey of some of the staples of the medieval diet, including ale itself, the unhopped form of beer that was the standard form of liquid refreshment.

DANCE

There survive no detailed descriptions of dance before the fifteenth century, so any reconstruction of fourteenth-century dance must rely on visual evidence in comparison with later treatises on dancing and with more recent folk-dancing traditions. The reconstructions offered here cannot be a precise re-creation of fourteenth-century dances, but they appear to preserve the general shape and feel these dances would have had.[21]

Music and Dance (*Sonare et balare*), c. 1395. TS Codex
s.n.2644, f. 104. Vienna. Photo Credit: Alinari/Art Resource, NY.

The Forms

The typical fourteenth-century dance was a circle or chain dance, which
we can call a carole. This term was used in the Middle Ages to describe
dances of this sort, especially if the music was sung. The reconstructed carole may be done in two forms, here called the single bransle (pronounced
brawl) and the farandole.

Single Bransle

The single bransle is a style of dance described in a sixteenth-
century treatise. It is one of the most archaic dance forms in Europe—
versions are still danced in places from the Faeroe Islands to the Balkans.
The dancers form a circle or a chain. They may be all men, all women,
or a mixed group, not necessarily of even numbers. There are a number
of possible grips: the dancers may link hands, link hands and elbows, or
hold onto kerchiefs or garlands. The dance is very simple: it consists of
two steps to the left and one to the right in time with the music, repeated

Saint Cecilia and musicians. Fourteenth cen-
tury. Manuscript VA 14F, fol 47r. Location:
Biblioteca Nazionale, Naples, Italy. Photo
Credit: Scala/Art Resource, NY.

throughout the dance. Alternatively, it can be done with two steps to the
left and two back to the right; the steps to the right should be slightly
smaller, so that the dancers slowly process toward the left.

This type of carole has no figures and relies for its interest on the song
or music, the elegance or spirit of the dancers, and the interaction among
them.

Farandole

In the farandole type of carole, the dancers form a chain, linking up as
in the single bransle. The dance consists of a simple walking step, moving to the left. The dancers follow the leader, who decides at will to begin
any of the following figures:

The Snail. The leader leads the chain around into a circle, then spirals
inward towards the center. Once there, he may turn back and spiral out
again, or he and the second dancer may lift their joined hands to make an

arch under which the rest of the dancers pass (without anyone dropping hands) until they are all out of the spiral.

Threading the Needle. The leader turns to face the second dancer, who drops hands with the third, and the two make an arch perpendicular to the direction of the chain. The third dancer passes under the arch. He may choose to become the leader and lead the entire chain under the arch. In this case the previous leader takes the free hand of the last dancer with his left as he passes underneath the arch, and passes under himself, so that the second dancer becomes last. Otherwise, the third dancer may form an arch with the fourth, the rest following suit. In this case, the leader takes the last dancer's hand as before, and the other odd-numbered dancers follow suit.

The Arches. The leader doubles back to the space between the second and third dancers. They raise their joined hands, as do all the other dancers. The leader passes under the arch, then backwards under the arch between the third and fourth dancers, then forward under the arch between the fourth and fifth, and so on, pulling the rest of the dancers through behind him.

The Hey. The leader turns to face the second dancer, dropping hands, and the rest of the dancers drop hands too. The leader and the second dancer take right hands and pass each other, then the leader and the third dancer pass each other taking left hands. Then the leader passes the fourth dancer taking right hands, while the second dancer turns around and passes the third taking left hands, and so on. When any dancer comes to the end of the line, he turns around and gives hands with the dancer coming towards him, and the chain continues until the original order is restored.

Music

Although it's not known exactly what music was used for the carole, it can be danced to any music with a strong and lively beat, whether vocal or instrumental. Pictures from the fourteenth century show a woman singing and accompanying herself on the tambourine while her fellows dance in a line or a circle. There are dozens of surviving thirteenth- and fourteenth-century pieces with names such as "estampie," "istampitta," "saltarello," "ductia," or "dance," which indicated their use for dancing and hint at the stamping, jumping nature of such dances. Timothy McGee's *Medieval Instrumental Dances* presents most of them in modern musical notation, and numerous recordings of them are available, for example, the Dufay Collective's "A Dance in the Garden of Mirth," The New York Ensemble's for Early Music's "Istanpitta" and "Istanpitta II," and Ensemble Unicorn's "Chominciamento di gioia." In addition, the *Llibre Vermell*, written down in Spain around 1400, includes a number of songs intended for dancing; recordings include Alla Francesca's "Llibre Vermell de Montserrat" and

Ladies dancing—the music is provided by a singer who accompanies herself on the drum. Italian, c. 1365 (Andrea Buonatuti da Firenze, fresco from the Spanish Chapel [detail], Santa Maria Novella, Florence). McLean.

the New London Consort's "Llibre Vermell: Pilgrim Songs & Dances." Although the English songs in this book are not known to have been used for dancing, they might serve the purpose, too.

NOTES

1. On theater, see E. K. Chambers, *The Medieval Stage* (Oxford: Clarendon Press, 1903).

2. John Froissart, *Chronicles of England, France, Spain, and the Adjoining Countries* (London: Smith, 1842), 1.196.

3. On deeds of arms, see Barber, Richard and Juliet Barker, *Tournaments: Jousts, Chivalry and Pageants in the Middle Ages* (New York: Weidenfeld and Nicolson 1998). Barker, Juliet R. V., *The Tournament in England, 1100–1400* (Woodbridge: Boydell Press, 1986). Cripps-Day, F. H., *The History of the Tournament* (London: BernardQuaritch, 1918). Muhlberger, Steven, *Deeds of Arms: Formal Combats in the Late Fourteenth Century* (Highland Village: Chivalry Bookshelf, 2004). Muhlberger, Steven, *Jousts and Tournaments: Charny and the Rules for Chivalric Sport in Fourteenth Century France* (Union City: Chivalry Bookshelf, 2002).

4. On archery as a sport, see: Ascham, Roger, *Toxophilus, the Schole of Shooting Conteyned in Two Bookes* (London: Edward Whytchurch, 1545). Partridge, James, *Ayme for Finsburie Archers* (London: J. J. and E. B., 1628; reprinted Royal Leamington Spa: W. C. Books, 1998). Roberts, T., *The English Bowman or: Tracts on Archery, to which is added the second part of The Bowmans Glory* (London: for the author, 1801) "Old Toxophilite," *The Archer's Guide* (London: T. Hurst, 1833).

5. On chess, see H.J.R. Murray, *A History of Chess* (Oxford: Clarendon Press, 1913).

6. Dummett, David, *The Game of Tarot* (London: Duckworth, 1980), 10. On cards, see: Beal, George, *Playing-Cards and Their Story* (Newton Abbot: David and Charles, 1975). Dummett, David, *The Game of Tarot* (London: Duckworth, 1980). Dummett, Michael, "The Earliest Spanish Playing Cards," *Journal of the International Playing Card Society* 18:1 (Aug. 1989). Hoffmann, Detlef, *The Playing Card: An Illustrated History* (Greenwich, CT: New York Graphic Society, 1973). Parlett, David, *The Oxford*

Guide to Card Games (Oxford: Oxford University Press, 1990). Varekamp, T., "A Fifteenth-Century French Pack of Painted Playing Cards with a Hunting Theme (Part 1)," *Journal of the International Playing Card Society* 14:2 (Nov. 1985). Varekamp, T., "A Fifteenth-Century French Pack of Painted Playing Cards with a Hunting Theme (Part 2)," *Journal of the International Playing Card Society* 14:3 (Feb. 1986). Wintle, Simon, "A 'Moorish' Sheet of Playing Cards," *Journal of the International Playing Card Society* 15:4 (May 1987). Willughby, Francis, *Francis Willughby's Book of Games: A Seventeenth-Century Treatise on Sports, Games and Pastimes,* ed. David Cram, Dorothy Johnston, and Jeffrey L. Forgeng (Aldershot: Ashgate, 2003).

7. *MED* s.v. **carde** n. (2) and **carder** n. (2). See also Joseph Strutt, *Sports and Pastimes of the English People* (London: Methuen, 1903), 261.

8. Dummett, *Game of Tarot,* 11.

9. The three-die version is from Alfonso X, *Das spanische Schachzabelbuch des Königs Alfons des Weisen vom Jahre 1283* (Leipzig: Hiersemann, 1913); the two-die version is from Charles Cotton, *The Compleat Gamester* [1674], in *Games and Gamesters of the Restoration* (London: Routledge, 1930).

10. Rules from Alfonso, *Das spanische Schachzabelbuch.*

11. Rules from Cotton, *Compleat Gamester,* 81.

12. Murray, *Chess,* 464 ff.

13. Described in H.J.R. Murray, "The Medieval Games of Tables," *Medium Ævum* 10 (1941), 57–69; edited in W. Fiske, *Chess in Iceland* (Florence: Florentine Typographical Society, 1905).

14. Rules from Willughby, *Book of Games,* 215–17.

15. Parlett, *Card Games,* 80–81; rules from Willughby, *Book of Games,* 136.

16. Parlett, *Card Games,* 165.

17. Thierry Depaulis, "Pochspiel: An 'International' Card Game of the Fifteenth Century," *Journal of the International Playing Card Society* 19:2–4 (Nov. 1990, Feb. 1991, May 1991), 2; cf. also Parlett, *Card Games;* Dummett, *Tarot.*

18. Rules from Willughby, *Book of Games,* 166.

19. Rules from Willughby, *Book of Games,* 167.

20. Rules from Willughby, *Book of Games,* 203–7.

21. The earliest European dance treatises are from early fifteenth-century Italy. The earliest treatise from north of the Alps is a mid-fifteenth-century French collection of basse dances, an English translation of which was printed in 1521. The earliest English dance treatise, referred to as the Gresley manuscript, is dated to the late fifteenth or early sixteenth century.

10

CHAUCER'S WORLD

Modern readers of the *Canterbury Tales* are sometimes struck by the familiarity of the human world Chaucer describes: a world of professional rivalries and personal ambitions; a world of complex relationships between spouses, parents and children, friends and neighbors; a world of very believable people with very human strengths and shortcomings. Alternatively, the reader may be struck by the alienness of Chaucer's world, with its rigid class hierarchies, all-pervasive church, and sharply delineated gender roles.

Both reactions accurately reflect the real similarities and differences between Chaucer's world and our own. The past is always a foreign country, and Chaucer's medieval society is in many ways more unlike the world we live in than was the classical world of the Romans. Yet Chaucer was living at a time of major cultural transformation, and many of the features that define our world today were becoming distinctly visible during the poet's lifetime.

TRAVEL

At the heart of Chaucer's most famous work is the story of a pilgrimage in which a few dozen travelers from all walks of life share a journey from Southwark, at the southern end of London Bridge, to the shrine of St. Thomas à Becket in Canterbury. The story may be fictional, but the scenario is very real. Despite the challenges facing travelers in the fourteenth century, many Englishmen of Chaucer's day journeyed often and extensively. Chaucer describes the Wife of Bath as a wide traveler on pilgrimages:

CHAUCER'S TRAVELS TO ITALY, 1378

Account of Geoffrey Chaucer, squire, of his receipts, payments, and expenses traveling as an emissary of the king to Lombardy . . . to Bernabò lord of Milan . . .

Item, he renders account for £66 13s. 4d. . . . paid to the aforesaid Geoffrey as emissary of the king to the aforesaid parts of Lombardy to the lord of Milan and to John Hawkwood for certain business touching the prosecution of the war . . .

Expenses: Item, he reckons in his wages traveling on this embassy . . . from the 28th day of May in the first year [of Richard II], on which day he began his journey from the city of London to those parts, to the 19th day of September following on which day he returned to that city, namely going, staying, and returning 115 days, reckoning in total £76 13s. 4d., taking for each day 13s. 4d. . . . plus £4 for his passage and return overseas for men and horses. . . .

Sum of expenses, £80 13s. 4d., leaving an excess of £14, for which he is to have reimbursement.

Translated by J. L. Forgeng from the Latin in Martin M. Crow and Clair C. Olson, *Chaucer Life-Records* (Austin: University of Texas Press, 1966), 58–59.

> Thrice had she been at Jerusalem;
> She had passed many a distant stream.
> At Rome she had been, and at Boulogne,
> In Galicia at Saint James, and at Cologne;
> She knew much about wandering by the way. (*CT* A.463–67)

The Wife of Bath's wanderings are not mere fictions. During his exile from England in the 1390s, Henry Bolingbroke, the future Henry IV, traveled through the Baltic, eastern Europe, Vienna, Venice, Rhodes, Jerusalem, Cyprus, Italy, and France before returning to England. Such experiences were not limited to men. Not long after Chaucer's death, the Norfolk mystic Margery Kempe began a series of pilgrimages that took her to the Baltic, Germany, Spain, Italy, and the Holy Land. Even peasants and the poor traveled regularly within England, visiting nearby markets and fairs, searching for work, or seeking out local or national shrines as do Chaucer's pilgrims.

Pilgrimage

Pilgrimage in particular brought ordinary people into contact with the wider world, whether traveling in person or through contact with those who had traveled. Those of limited means might simply visit a nearby saint's shrine, which were to be found across the map of England. Those who had the money might travel to a major national shrine such as that of St. Thomas à Becket at Canterbury. The most prestigious destinations were the overseas sites of universal significance to the Christian community: Santiago de Compostela in Spain, believed to be the burial site of

Buying sour milk from a vendor. Italian, c. 1395 (TS Vienna, f. 59v). McLean.

the apostle St. James; Rome, where St. Peter and St. Paul were martyred; and of course the numerous sites in the Holy Land, especially at Jerusalem.

The theoretical purpose of pilgrimage was the spiritual enrichment gained by physical proximity to the places and physical relics associated with the holy people of Christianity. Yet many aspects of medieval pilgrimage are strongly reminiscent of modern tourism. It involved curiosity to see places deemed to be of cultural importance; many people were avid travelers, visiting multiple sites during their lifetimes; and visitors to the shrines could even purchase cheap trinkets, typically of cast pewter, to bring home with them as "souvenirs" of their journey.

Modes of Travel

The simplest means of travel was on foot, which, as contemporaries reckoned, would be about a mile in 20 minutes during the summer or 30 minutes in winter. A person traveling on foot could expect to cover 10 to 20 miles in a day, a merchant train 15 to 18, and a household or army on the move, with carts and pack animals, about 10 to 12. The typical round-trip journey between a village and the nearest market town could be made in a single day, with enough time to do the necessary buying and selling in between. Travel to a fair might take a full day each way.

The journey made by Chaucer's pilgrims between Southwark and Canterbury might take them a few days on foot, but the story suggests that they cut this time by riding. Travel on horseback was used by both men and women across a wide social spectrum. Horses were plentiful: even a peasant might own some for agricultural work. Horses could even be rented, much as people rent cars today. A rider might typically cover 40 miles in a day, and a mounted courier could cover some 60 miles on a good road, half as much over rough country. A rider traveling by post (that is, with prearranged changes of horses) might cover as much as 100 or 120 miles in a day.

Horses came in a variety of breeds for different purposes: a man-at-arms had a heavy warhorse, or destrer, for battle, but rode a lighter horse for travel, usually called a palfrey. There were a variety of other lesser riding horses know n as runcies, hobbies, nags, and hackneys, as well as specialized carthorses and packhorses (the latter usually known as sumpters). Mules and donkeys might also be used as riding or pack animals.

Packhorses were excellent for carrying goods over rough terrain, but if there was a decent road, a wheeled vehicle was more efficient. Two-wheeled carts and four-wheeled wagons were both used for transporting goods, and there were special covered wagons and enclosed coaches for people. Noblewomen were particularly likely to use these, although the ride was far from comfortable, since these vehicles had only rudimentary systems for shock absorption.

In practice, rates of travel varied enormously. English roads in Chaucer's day could be difficult and even dangerous to travel. Apart from the remains of the Roman road system, few roads in medieval England had any foundations, and none were paved, so they became pools of mud in bad weather. As if this were not enough, the traveler had to face the ever-present threat of ambush by robbers. Poor communications made law enforcement difficult, so the traveler was always at risk. Chaucer describes his 29 pilgrims as setting out together for company on the route, but security would have been as great a consideration. Robbers haunted the well-traveled road from London to Canterbury, and there were many lonely stretches that could be dangerous to the solo traveler. In 1390, Chaucer himself was robbed on this road, at a spot near the border between Surrey and Kent known as "the Foul Oak": "felons and malefactors . . . by force and arms did insult to him, and struck, wounded, and maltreated him, robbing him of a horse worth £10, goods and chattels worth 100s., and £20 6s. 8d. of his own money."[1]

Water was an important factor in travel, whether as a hindrance or a medium. The routes of overland travel were governed by the availability of bridges, fords, and ferries. For long-distance journeys and carrying bulk goods, water transport was considerably easier and cheaper than overland travel. Small boats and barges plied England's inland waterways, while larger ships carried people and goods around the coastline and across the seas to destinations on the Continent. A ship of 60 to 80 tons burden with a crew of 15 sailors was considered a substantial seagoing vessel, and one of 300 tons suitable for a royal flagship. By comparison, the Mayflower that carried the Pilgrims to Plymouth, a modest ship for her day, was 180 tons burden. A ship could sail at about five to six knots under favorable conditions, or some 75 to 100 miles a day, but the actual rate of travel varied enormously with the weather. The voyage from London to Bordeaux in southwestern France could take as little as 10 to 12 days or as much as a month.

In most of the country, travelers had to make arrangements to lodge in private homes. Upper-class households regularly took in travelers as guests, and peasant householders might also be willing to lodge a guest overnight. Only in the towns were there regular commercial establishments catering to the needs of travelers, like the Tabard Inn in Southwark where Chaucer's pilgrims begin their journey. The workings of a fourteenth-century inn are illustrated by the testimony in a case regarding the theft of two small chests containing 40 marks and miscellaneous documents from a Southwark inn in 1381:

The said John [the innkeeper] . . . says that on the said Monday about the second hour after noon the said William [the Sheriff of Somerset and Dorset] entered his inn to be lodged there, and at once when he entered, the same John assigned to the said William a certain chamber being in that inn, fitting for his rank, with a door and a lock affixed to the same door with sufficient nails, so that he should lie there and put and keep his things there, and delivered to the said William the key to the door of the said chamber. . . .

William says that . . . when the said John had delivered to him the said chamber and key as above, the same William, being occupied about divers businesses to be done in the city of London, went out from the said inn into the city to expedite the said businesses and handed over the key of the door to a certain servant of the said William to take care of it meantime, ordering the servant to remain in the inn meanwhile and to take care of his horses there; and afterwards, when night was falling, the same William being in the city and the key still in the keeping of the said servant, the wife of the said John called unto her into her hall the said servant who had the key, giving him food and drink with a merry countenance and asking him divers questions and occupying him thus for a long time, until the staple of the lock of the door aforesaid was thrust on one side out of its right place and the door of the chamber was thereby opened, and his goods, being in the inn of the said John, were taken and carried off by the said malefactors. . . .

The said John says . . . [that] the said servant came into the said hall and asked his wife for bread and ale and other necessaries to be brought into the said chamber of his master.[2]

Some travelers brought their own accommodations: tradesmen at a fair might have simple tents made of wood and canvas, while aristocrats in an army or a tournament might erect pavilions made of the same materials but brightly painted—the ordinary soldier billeted where best he could.

GEOGRAPHY AND COSMOLOGY

Even if the roads were dry, the weather was good and there were no bandits on the way, travelers might find it a challenge to reach their destination. There were no road signs, and although maps did exist, these were merely schematic diagrams of no real use for wayfinding, although more accurate charts did exist to assist in maritime navigation. People traveling on land either had to know the route already, or ask someone who did. Travelers commonly hired guides to assist them, and the innkeeper of the Tabard in the *Canterbury Tales* generously offers to serve as a guide for the pilgrims. Directions were based on geographical features, since the

CONVERSATIONS FOR TRAVELERS IN FRANCE, ABOUT 1400

"Sir, God give you good day"...
"Sir, you are most welcome"...
"What time of the day is it, prime or tierce, midday or none?—What hour
    is it?"
"Between six and seven."
"How far is it from here to Paris?"
"Twelve leagues or thereabouts."
"Is the road good?"
"Yes, so God help me."...
"And in which direction should I go?"
"Stay to the right hand, and then turn to the left hand, then right to the
    end."...
"Tell me, is there any danger of robbers, and where can I pass safely?"
"Sir, it is safe enough by day, but at night it is dangerous."

"Say, porter, where is the lady of the house?"
"Sir, in the hall or in her chamber."
"Go take my message to her... Madam, God give you good day."
"Sir, good day to you."
"Madam, do you have lodging for us three fellows?"
"Sir, how long do you wish to stay?"
"Madam, we don't know."
"Then what would you pay for your board by the day?"
"Madam, what would you wish to take for each of us?"
"Sir, nothing less than six pence a day."
"Madam, we will gladly give you that."
"Sir, by God, you are welcome."
"Then, madam, we will send our things here.... Have them put
    upstairs."
"Sir, they will be kept safe."

Translated by J. L. Forgeng from the French in Edmund Stengel, "Die ältesten Anlei-
tungsschriften zur Erlernung der französischen Sprache," *Zeitschrift für neufranzösische
Sprache und Literatur* 1 (1879), 11–12.

modern bird's-eye ability to conceptualize geography from above only
became possible with the rise of cartography.

The further one went from home, the vaguer the sense of geography
became. By Chaucer's day, European missionaries and merchants had
traveled overland as far east as Mongolia and China. On the seas, Por-
tuguese sailors were looking to circumvent the Islamic control of the Silk
Road trade routes, and by 1400 they were beginning to venture south-
wards along the coast of Africa. But the more distant reaches of the Afro-
Eurasian landmass were still semi-legendary to most western Europeans,
for whom Asia and sub-Saharan Africa were the stuff of science fiction.
One of the most popular books in Chaucer's day was the *Travels of John*

Tents. *Roman du Roy Meliadus de Leonnoys* BL Add. 12228, f.150. Italian, c. 1360. McLean.

Mandeville, a fictional account of an Englishman who journeys across Eurasia. The text reflects the same sort of geographical knowledge one finds in Chaucer's own works, and a curiosity about the world mingled with a dimension of fantasy:

Since many men desire to hear of diverse lands, and of the Holy Land and of the Promised Land, and of other diverse realms beyond the sea in diverse parts of the world, I John Mandeville, knight, passed the sea upon the day of St. Michael the Archangel in the year of our Lord Jesus Christ 1322. I was beyond the sea a long time, saw and passed through many diverse regions, lands, and realms, and isles, that is to say the realm of Turkey, Armenia, . . . Tartary, Persia, Syria, Arabia, Egypt, Libya, Chaldea, . . . Ethiopia, Amazonia, India.[3]

For regions as far away as the eastern Mediterranean, *Mandeville* contains a significant amount of real geographical and cultural information: it speaks of the church of Haya Sofia in Constantinople, and describes the religion of the Muslims "as it is recorded and written in the book of their law that is called Alkoran; Mohamed, who made their law, gave them this book of their law."[4] Deeper into Asia the landscape becomes increasingly fantastic, with islands inhabited by "men of great stature as if they were giants, horrible and foul to the sight, for they have but one eye, and that is in the midst of their forehead. . . . In another island of that country are found men formed without heads. They have one eye in each shoulder, and their mouth is as round as a horseshoe and stands in the middle of their chest."[5]

The blessing of the Fair of Lendit on the road to Saint-Denis by the
bishop of Paris, showing booths set up by the merchants. Pontifi-
cal. French (Paris), fourteenth century. Paris, Bibliothèque Nationale
Ms.lat. 962, fol. 264r., Paris. Photo Credit: Snark/Art Resource, NY.

Yet even at the further reaches of Eurasia *Mandeville* includes snippets of
first-hand information brought back by merchants and missionaries over the
previous century, offering glimpses of the lands of Giboth (Tibet) and Cathan
(China), both ruled by the descendants of the "great Can" (Jengiz Khan).

Contrary to modern popular mythology, Chaucer's contemporaries did
not believe in a flat earth. Anyone who had any education knew that Earth
was round, in keeping with the shape of the heavenly cosmos above. However, it was generally thought that the ocean encompassing the known
continents of Europe, Africa, and Asia was too broad to be crossed, and
that the heat of the equatorial regions made them impassable. The three
known continents, believed to comprise only a quarter of the actual earth,
were all that humans would ever be able to see. Most medieval maps offer
a schematized view of this known portion of the world—they are intended
as diagrams rather than as maps in the modern sense. Yet already in Chaucer's day some people were thinking seriously about the possibility of
expanding the horizons of this known world: as one version of *Mandeville*
observes: "The land and the sea are of round shape and form . . . and men

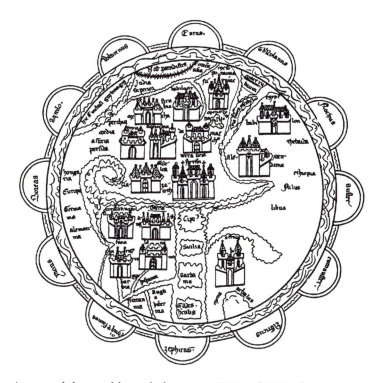

A map of the world, made between 1364 and 1372; the text is in Latin. East is at the top, as is usual with medieval maps. The lobes around the edges represent the winds—each had its own name depending on the direction from which it came. Within these is the encircling ring of the ocean. The upper portion of the map represents Asia, with Paradise at the top, and Jerusalem at the center. Africa is on the right, separated from Asia by the Nile. At the lower left is Europe, separated from Africa by the Mediterranean Sea and from Asia by the Black Sea; the cities of Constantinople, Athens, Rome, and Paris are shown. England is at the bottom and slightly to the left, marked "Anglia." Santarem.

may well prove by experience and subtle reflection of wit that if a man were to voyage in ships that could go to explore the world, men might go by ship all about the world, both above and beneath."[6]

The Heavens

Chaucer's round earth was at the center of a universe imagined as a nested series of spheres. The sphere of the earth lay at the physical center, and was itself divided into four concentric spheres, one for each of the four basic elements of matter: Earth, Water, Air, and Fire. Above the sphere of

Fire were the spheres of the moving planets: the Moon, Mercury, Venus, the Sun, Mars, Jupiter, and Saturn. After Saturn came the sphere in which the fixed stars were lodged. Beyond was the *primum mobile*, the first mobile sphere. The *primum mobile* was turned by God and imparted its motion to the spheres within.

Beyond the *primum mobile* was Heaven. According to medieval thought, God at once lay at the center of the created universe and encompassed it—the dual arrangement is described powerfully by Dante earlier in the century, where the poet first ascends through the heavenly spheres, then as he crosses into Heaven itself, finds himself at the outermost sphere of an ethereal cosmos where God is at the center.

SYSTEMS OF BELIEF

The medieval model of the cosmos is just one aspect of the Church's unique influence over the broadest and deepest questions that shaped a medieval person's world. Society, family, and even personal identity were deeply permeated by religion. The Church was never fully able to control people's systems of belief, but it did exert a pervasive influence, and Chaucer's contemporaries could not envision being functional as individuals or as a society without the mediation of the Church.

Being a part of society in medieval England was equated with being part of the Church: a person entered both the Church and society through the ceremony of baptism. All Christians in Western Europe were subject to the spiritual authority of the Pope—the Catholic Church was the only officially accepted church in Western Europe, although there were other Christian churches in Eastern Europe and elsewhere. Papal politics in the fourteenth century were at an unprecedented low point. When Chaucer was born, the papacy was politically dominated by the French king, and had actually been resident at Avignon in southern France since 1305. An attempt to move the Pope back to Rome in 1378 resulted in a split in the church, with two rival popes in Rome and Avignon; the schism would not be solved until 1417. Nonetheless, the ideal of religious unity remained essential to medieval thought. Only the Pope could maintain unity in the Church, and in a world that made very little distinction between church and state, religious disunity was seen as the road to social anarchy.

The only organized alternative to church orthodoxy in Chaucer's England was the movement known as Lollardy. The Lollards had arisen in part as a result of general anti-clerical feeling in England. The obvious shortcomings of priests, monks, and friars in the official church made many doubt whether such men had any power to bring people closer to God, and the sorry spectacle of two rival popes did little to enhance the prestige of the papacy. At the same time, the Lollards espoused a new set of doctrines. They minimized the importance of traditional church rituals, offices, and customs, and emphasized the personal relationship of the individual with God, especially as achieved by reading the Bible. To promote this goal they undertook the first full translation of the Bible from Latin into English, a project completed in the 1380s. The leader of the Lollard movement was an Oxford scholar and priest named John Wycliffe. The movement was only a tiny minority, vigorously opposed by the Church and apparently mistrusted by most people, but it had some powerful supporters and was not finally forced underground until the beginning of the fifteenth century.

There was no significant Jewish presence in fourteenth-century England because the Jews had been expelled from the country in 1290. However, a few may have trickled into the country from time to time, since additional measures were taken to remove them in 1358 and 1376. The culture of medieval England, as of the rest of Christian Europe at the time, was intensely anti-Semitic, although few Englishmen of Chaucer's day had actually met a Jew or had any real understanding of Judaism aside from what they knew of the Old Testament. Medieval society in general did not tolerate religious diversity, and in the eyes of medieval Christians, Jews bore the guilt for the crucifixion of Christ, so Jews were regarded at best with suspicion, at worst with the most brutal hostility. Modern scholars often try to mitigate the unpleasant implications of Chaucer's anti-Semitic *Prioress's Tale,* in which a Christian child is murdered by Jews, but Chaucer's contemporaries would have found nothing objectionable in this story of the evils that could be perpetrated by people who were different from themselves.

The prejudice against Jews reflects a broader pattern in which medieval people saw society as an organic whole where individuals existed to fulfill a predetermined part in the structures of society. Modern western society is pervasively organized on a free-market principle in which people are assumed to negotiate their social, economic, and spiritual places. Medieval society assumed that these places were determined at birth by the roles into which the individual was born based on their sex, social class, and family relationships. A person was expected to play the part into which they were born, and a successful life was one in which that part was played in accordance with accepted expectations and norms.

The pressures to conform to external expectations were reinforced by a general lack of privacy. At every level, the activities and even thoughts of the individual were subject to external observation and scrutiny. Peasant families occupied shared living spaces in small homes—a peasant child growing up in a cottage where five or six people might live in just two rooms must have been well aware of all of the physicalities of life, from childbirth, to sex, to death, by the time they reached adolescence. Even the aristocracy did not expect the kind of privacy that is common for ordinary people today: with servants constantly in attendance, helping them to dress and undress, preparing their beds for them at night, and always waiting close to hand, an aristocrat was accustomed to sharing their most intimate personal space. Even internal thoughts were subject to scrutiny by the Church through the sacrament of Confession, and heretical beliefs were severely punishable. All of these factors contributed to an environment where the scope for individualism was narrowly circumscribed by the established social framework.

Such at least was the theory. Yet material realities were changing drastically in Chaucer's lifetime, and social realities would sooner or later have to change as well. Landlords took legal action against villeins who tried to shirk the obligations of servitude, but in a rapidly changing market environment, landlord and tenant alike often found advantage in trading rigid service relationships for much more versatile cash-rent transactions. Even landlords who tried to continue traditional forms of villeinage met with increasing resistance from their tenants: servitude was losing its status as a cultural norm, and discontented peasants could easily find another landlord desperate for tenants to people his plague-ravaged estate. Personal status and social relationships were visibly moving in the direction of a free-market model.

People's spiritual worlds were also more complex than official church orthodoxy would have liked. In spite of the universal system for religious education, religious belief had probably never been very uniform. The quality of religious instruction was not always very good, especially in remote parts of the country in parishes served by poorly trained priests. Even those individuals who received the proper education were not merely passive vessels filled with church doctrine. Peasants from the southern French village of Montaillou in the early fourteenth century are known to have reshaped and even rejected church teachings in formulating their own personal systems of belief, and the same could easily have been true of England, even though no English village is as well documented as Montaillou.

Official doctrine also competed with strains of folklore and other currents of belief. Superstition remained a vibrant part of popular culture. Places and events outside of human habitation, understanding, or control perennially become the domains of the supernatural, and such places and events were all around Chaucer and his contemporaries. Forests, moors, mountains, and marshes in the physical landscape; the domains of sickness and health, birth and death; even day-to-day chemical processes like making butter or smelting iron: all of these areas were fertile grounds for the superstitious imagination.

Scholarly culture also offered frameworks for magical understanding of the universe outside the core doctrines of Christian belief. When Chaucer wrote a treatise on the astrolabe for his son Lewis, it was to teach skills necessary for astrology, which formed a part of any well-educated person's intellectual toolkit. Chaucer's *Canon's Yeoman's Tale* satirizes the unscrupulous dealings of a self-styled alchemist who preys on people's dreams of turning lead into gold, but educated people in Chaucer's day genuinely believed that alchemy was a real science, even if it was abused by false practitioners like the Canon.

**A MORALIST DISCUSSES MEDICINE
AND MAGIC, c. 1405–1410**

To heal men's wounds and keep them fresh and clean, black wool and oil are good medicines without any charm, as experience shows well. But if men think that it is worth nothing without a charm and set their faith principally in the charm, then it is a witchcraft to those who use it this way. But if a man in doing it say his Pater Noster or some holy prayer, calling on the grace of God in his doing, it is no witchcraft, but it is well done.

Translated by J. L. Forgeng from the Middle English in *Dives and Pauper*, ed. Priscilla Heath Barnum (London: Oxford University Press, 1976, 1980), 168–69.

These longstanding limits on doctrinal uniformity were supplemented in the 1300s by a rise in lay education and in an increasingly vibrant lay culture. In the early part of the Middle Ages, secular authorities had been obliged to rely heavily on the clergy to support their secular administration, thanks to the clergy's virtual monopoly on literacy. By Chaucer's day, this was no longer the case. Government, law, and literate culture were supported by a substantial class of educated laypeople—individuals like Chaucer himself, who were born into sophisticated urban households, and were raised to take part in the growing literate culture of the laity.

Such people inevitably became producers as well as consumers of doctrine. *The Canterbury Tales* concludes with a sermon by the Parson: the words are put into the mouth of a clergyman, but they are composed by a layman. Even though the sentiments are entirely orthodox, the very idea of a layman writing sermons marks a shift toward a culture in which lay people were increasingly assertive in religious affairs.

Increasing lay engagement with religion inevitably contributed to anticlerical sentiment and a willingness to look critically at shortcomings in the Church. Chaucer's unflattering portraits of the Pardoner, Monk, and Friar are at one level aimed at individuals who abuse their position in the Church, but such sentiments ultimately shaded over into criticism of the Church's authority, and contributed to Lollard beliefs and reformist sympathies throughout the literate classes.

Ultimately, it is not excessive to see in Chaucer's day the first stirrings of humanist individualism. Officially, Chaucer's society was a rigid class hierarchy in which individuals were expected to play out the scripts that were determined for them at birth. In reality, we can see emerging in Chaucer's culture—and manifested in Chaucer's own work—an emerging marketplace of ideas, in which diverse individuals from all walks of life each have a story to tell—some pleasant, some unpleasant, but all worth the hearing, and integral to the story of the human pilgrimage. It is perhaps because of this emerging modernity that Chaucer is the earliest poet in English to whom a modern reader can truly relate.

NOTES

1. Martin M. Crow and Clair C. Olson, *Chaucer Life-Records* (Austin: University of Texas Press, 1966), 477–78.

2. Edith Rickert, *Chaucer's World* (New York: Columbia University Press, 1948), 258–59.

3. M. C. Seymour, ed. *The Bodley Version of Mandeville's Travels* (London, New York, Toronto: Early English Text Society, 1963), 3.

4. Seymour, *Mandeville*, 5, 67–69.

5. Seymour, *Mandeville*, 139.

6. P. Hamelius, ed., *Mandeville's Travels* (London: Early English Texts Society, 1919), 1.119–20.

GLOSSARY

acolyte—A cleric in minor orders who assisted a priest or deacon in his duties.

alderman—A member of a city council.

ale—A form of beer made without hops.

apprentice—A young person learning a craft or trade.

archdeacon—A church officer assigned to assist the bishop in administering his bishopric, having especial authority for church courts.

aristocracy—The second estate of medieval political theory, the warrior class. The term is a modern one: medieval English had no clear-cut word for this class as a whole, although the adjective "gentle" was applied to people of this class.

astrolabe—An astronomical instrument.

Ave Maria—A formulaic prayer to the Virgin Mary, deriving from the words spoken by the Archangel Gabriel to Mary announcing the conception of Christ.

baldric—A belt or sash worn across the shoulder to the opposite hip.

banneret—See **knight banneret.**

basinet—A form of close-fitting helmet.

bondman—A villein or serf.

boonwork—An extra labor service owed by a villein to the manor lord.

brazier—A vessel for holding coals to provide heat.

breech—A man's undergarment, vaguely comparable to modern boxer shorts.

canon law—The body of law administered by the Church, pertaining to such topics as morality, religious observation, and marriage.

carding—The process of brushing wool so that the fibers are free of tangles and run in a single direction.

champion settlement—A system of agricultural organization in which each holding consists of strips of land scattered about a village, as contrasted with **woodland settlement.**

citizen—An inhabitant of a town having the full rights and privileges of the town.

coat-armor—A military cloth overgarment, typically padded and quilted and sometimes bearing heraldic symbols.

coathardie—A close-fitting civilian coat.

cob-iron—An iron supporter for a spit.

coif—A small, close-fitting head covering made of fabric or leather, sometimes padded for military use; also, a "mail-coif," a comparable head covering made of mail, covering the head, neck, and upper shoulders.

commons—The third estate of medieval political theory, those obliged to work for a living.

communion—The religious ceremony in which the communicants receive wine and/or bread as the blood and body of Christ.

confession—The religious observation in which a person confesses his or her sins to a priest or friar.

confirmation—The religious ceremony by which a young person is fully admitted as a member of the church.

cottar—The smallest sort of landholding commoner, holding insufficient land to support a family without doing additional labor.

couter—A piece of armor protecting the elbow.

Credo—The formulaic statement of Christian belief, also called the Creed.

cuirbouilli—Leather made pliable by soaking or boiling, molded into shape, and hardened by exposure to low heat. It was commonly used as material for armor.

cuisse—A piece of armor protecting the thighs.

dagging—A notched or zig-zag edge on fabric or armor.

dean—A church administrator subordinate to an archdeacon, or in charge of the chapter of clergymen at a cathedral.

demi-greave—A small piece of armor protecting the upper shin.

distaff—A staff used by spinners to hold the fibers ready to be fed onto the spindle.

doublet—A fabric undergarment, sometimes padded and quilted, designed to provide extra warmth and support for the hose; also, a similar military undergarment providing extra protection as well as support for the arm and leg armor.

ember days—The Wednesday, Friday, and Saturday after the first Sunday in Lent (six weeks before Easter), after Whitsunday (six weeks after Easter), after Holy Cross Day (September 14), and after St. Lucy's Day (December 13). These days were observed with fasting and penance.

estate—One of the three divisions of society according to medieval theory (clergy, aristocracy, commons).

ewer—A water-jug.

extreme unction—The religious ceremony preparing a person for death.

fallow field—A field left idle for a season to allow it to recover for future planting.

fleece—The raw wool as shorn off the sheep.

franklin—The most prosperous form of landholding free commoner.

friar—A member of a mendicant order of regular clergy. Like monks, friars were subject to the rule of their order; unlike monks, they were not allowed to own personal property.

fulling—A washing process that served to thicken woolen cloth and give it a smooth surface resistant to water and wind.

furze—A low-growing, spiny shrub.

Galen—The ancient Greek physiologist who formulated the theory of the Four Humors.

gelding—A castrated livestock animal.

gentle—See **aristocracy.**

gesso—A solution of gypsum and glue used to seal a surface for painting.

greave—A piece of armor protecting the shin.

groom—A male common servant ranking below a yeoman and above a page.

guild—The modern term for medieval organizations which regulated the practice of a craft or trade in a particular town; in medieval England they were known as misteries.

gusset—A small piece of fabric inserted into a garment for additional room, or a piece of mail inserted to cover a vulnerable point in a harness of armor.

habergeon—A mail shirt.

hainselin—A kind of short jacket.

harness—A suit of armor or its components.

holding—See **landholding**

hose—Cloth leggings, reaching to the groin on men and to the knee on women.

husbandman—A small but self-sufficient landholding commoner; also, a general term for a farmer.

journeyman—A craftsman or tradesman who has completed apprenticeship but does not possess a business of his own, working instead for others.

jupon—Garment that can be worn over armor, or beneath a breastplate, but over other harnesses.

knight bachelor—An ordinary knight.

knight banneret—A class of knight ranking above an ordinary knight bachelor.

lame—An articulated band of armor, comparable to the individual shell pieces on a lobster's tail.

landholding—A parcel or quantity of land rented to a holder in accordance with the custom associated with that landholding.

latten—A copper alloy, of variable composition, but sometimes containing zinc, tin, and lead.

laver—A special water jug designed for washing.

lay peerage—The secular aristocracy of the House of Lords in Parliament, as opposed to the Bishops and Abbots who also sat in the House of Lords.

leech—An informally trained medical practitioner.

lime—Calcium oxide, a chemical available from limestone and other sources, that can be used to make a hard-drying coating for buildings.

livery—Heraldic clothing or emblems associated with a noblemen and given to his followers as a sign of their allegiance.

lower house—The House of Commons in Parliament.

lye—An alkaline solution obtained by percolating water through wood ashes.

mail—A form of armor consisting of small interlocked rings of iron or steel.

man-at-arms—A fully armored soldier, typically equipped with a horse.

Martinmas—The feast of St. Martin, November 11.

master—A fully qualified craftsman or tradesman having his own shop.

master of arts—A graduate of a university.

mercer—A merchant who retails various goods, particularly cloth.

messuage—The plot of land on which a house stands.

minor orders—A status of clergyman not fully a priest; clerks in minor orders did not take a vow of celibacy.

order—An organization of regular clergy (such as monks, friars, or nuns) belonging to a single structure and following a common rule of religious life.

ordination—The religious ceremony by which a person is admitted into the priesthood.

page—The lowest rank of servant, usually a young boy.

parson—The priest of a parish church.

Pater Noster—The Lord's Prayer, especially in its Latin form.

pauldron—The piece of armor covering the shoulder.

poleine—The piece of armor covering the knee.

poll tax—A "head tax" on every person in England, first levied in 1377.

pommel—The knob on the end of a sword-grip.

pottage—Stew.

prior—A monastic official ranking just below an abbot, either assisting the abbot in running the monastery or administering a priory, a less substantial version of the monastery.

quillons—The lateral projections on a sword, designed to protect the hand.

reader—A cleric in minor orders who read the biblical lessons for church services.

rector—The person or institution receiving the income associated with a parish church.

regular clergy—Clergy subject to a specific rule of religious life, such as monks, friars and nuns, in contrast with **secular clergy.**

rerebrace—The piece of armor covering the upper arm.

rule—A particular system of life and organization for an order of regular clergy.

sabaton—The piece of armor covering the foot.

secular clergy—Clergymen such a priests, whose primary function is to serve the religious needs of the public.

simony—The sale of church offices.

slop—A kind of loose outer garment, which might be "cutted," reaching only to the hips.

splint—A style of armor consisting of long strips of metal riveted to cloth or leather.

squire—A man of aristocratic estate ranking below a knight; also, an aristocratic assistant to a knight.

surcoat—A civilian or military overgarment, which might be loose or tailored.

tabard—A loose, poncho-shaped overgarment, typically with flaring sleeves and skirt.

tablet weaving—A style of weaving in which the "warp" or lengthwise threads are manipulated with small pierced cards.

tonlet—A horizontal piece of armor skirting attached to a breastplate to protect the abdomen.

tonsure—The distinctive hair style of the clergy, involving the shaving of the crown of the head and cropping the rest of the hair.

trivet—A three-legged gridiron for cooking over a fire.

usury—Moneylending at excessive rates of interest.

vambrace—The piece of armor covering the forearm.

vicar—A priest who administers a parish church for an absentee rector.

villein—An unfree common landholder, subject to more feudal taxes, services, and restrictions than a free landholder.

weft—In weaving, the thread that is passed back and forth horizontally through the longitudinal, or warp, threads.

whey—The thin liquid remaining after the curds are removed from curdled milk.

woodland settlement—A system of agricultural organization in which each holding is a discrete parcel of land, as contrasted with **champion settlement.**

yeoman—The highest rank of male common servants; in the fourteenth-century the name was coming to be applied to the upper rank of landholding free commoners as well, replacing the older term **franklin.**

APPENDIX: THE MEDIEVAL EVENT

As well as being a general introduction to daily life in the fourteenth century, this book is intended to facilitate medieval living history. We have included enough information to allow a group to organize a living history event, or to allow an individual to participate in such an event. The suggestions in this appendix are geared towards a living history event, but elements will apply equally to medieval fairs or feasts, school pageants, and other sorts of activities in which there is some attempt to recreate a historical milieu.

If you think you might be interested in trying medieval living history, the easiest route is to find an already existing organization. These groups have become relatively easy to find thanks to the Internet; a few examples are listed in the Guide to Resources.

TAKING PART

For the individual preparing to take part in a living history event, the first step will be to choose what sort of person you will be representing and to assemble an appropriate kit of personal equipment. For the beginner, we strongly suggest someone toward the lower end of the social scale, as this makes the equipment easier and less expensive. The higher your social status, the richer and more elaborate your personal property would be, the more servants you would have, and the more sophisticated your entertainments. Some of the basic requirements are listed in boldface.

1. The chapter on clothing is designed to provide all necessary information to assemble a basic outfit. For a man, an outwardly plausible outfit would require at least **headgear** (probably a hood), a **kirtle, hose,** and **shoes.** For a woman, it would require **headgear,** a **kirtle,** and **shoes.** Both men and women might also want a **belt** and **purse.** Depending on the circumstances of the event, you may also need to provide basic eating equipment, all of which is described and/or illustrated in the text. This would mean a **bowl, knife, spoon,** and **drinking vessel.** Suppliers of reproduction wares are not hard to find through the Internet; a few ideas are offered in the Guide to Resources.

2. If you are taking on the role of a particular medieval person, what do you own? If you are portraying an individual with a particular position in society, you have clothing and other possessions. Is your best clothing wool or silk? Are your buttons of silver or pewter?

3. You will probably also get more out of the re-enactment if you devote some time to the person inside the clothes. What's in your head? What would you have known or believed? What was your place in society? This book should help in addressing some of these questions. Do you think the current order of things is just and proper, or do you have reservations? Is England's clergy about what England needs, or would significant pruning be desirable? Nobles and gentlemen claim many rights from those beneath them. Are they right to do so? Can you read? Write? How much do you know about the Bible and the past? Other countries? Do you know other languages? For a more intimate view of how medieval people saw themselves, you might take a look at some of the books they wrote. The Chaucerian Bookshelf in the Bibliography offers some useful suggestions.

4. What's your place in society? Where do you live? What sort of family do you have? How do you make a living, and what's your family income?

5. You will probably have more fun at the event if you look at the section on entertainments and, if possible, practice some of them beforehand. Many can be learned on the spot, but the more you know ahead of time the more comfortable you are likely to feel. Practicing medieval skills can also enhance your recreation of the Middle Ages: writing, fingerloop braiding, cooking, and so on.

6. You can also have a more rewarding experience if you are prepared to hold a conversation in character and on medieval subjects.

If you are doing a first-person recreation of a medieval person, you should try to avoid obvious modernisms. It will improve the experience of those around you, and you may enjoy it more yourself. A truly accurate recreation of premodern speech isn't necessarily an achievable or even desirable goal. If you actually speak in fourteenth-century English, hardly anyone will be able to understand a thing you say!

Focus instead on content. Avoid modern subjects. Here are some alternatives:

Fifty men-at-arms defeat a hundred. Which would you rather be, the worst of the 50 or the best of the hundred?

At a tournament "Which is to be more highly prized: the one who loses two horses or three in one day while attacking or defending quite openly, or the one who keeps his horse very close the whole day and endures and bears well the pulls and blows and everything that comes his way?"

Knights say they perform deeds of arms for the honor of their ladies. Is that so, or do they really do it for their own honor?

A man's wife is under an enchantment: she will be hideous during the day (when others can see her) but beautiful at night (when he sleeps with her). Or the reverse can be true, but the man must choose one or the other, forever. Which should he choose?

When Adam delved and Eve span, who was then a gentleman? That is, since we are all equally descended from that pair, how can nobles claim that they are worthier than commoners?

There are many styles of music, vocal and instrumental. Which is best?

What is the greatest adornment of the mind, nobility of arms or letters?

Is it better for a man to be brave or wise?

Who was the wickedest woman in the Bible?

These sorts of questions were actually popular conversation topics during the Middle Ages. More examples can be found in Castiglione's sixteenth-century work, *The Book of the Courtier,* from which many of the preceding are cribbed.

Avoid modern slang and contractions. Avoid false archaicism. Medieval speech didn't sound archaic to medieval people, it sounded contemporary, because it was. Use thee and thou correctly or not at all. The second choice is much easier.

Some people have the talent of picking up the patterns of speech of another period by osmosis. If they read enough Chaucer or Froissart in translation, they are able to convey some sense of the flavor and construction of speech from that time. If you're one of them, great. If not, don't worry about it. It doesn't hurt to give the technique a try. If you're interested in an era, read some good books written during the period. At worst, you'll have read some good books and gained a better understanding of your of your period of interest.

ORGANIZING

If you are actually organizing a medieval living history event, you will need to attend to the following:

1. *Define and Disseminate the Goals:* The first step in organizing an actual event is to define its purposes. The following discussion addresses the issue from scratch; but if you are operating within an existing living history organization, your choices will naturally be shaped by the traditions of your group.

You may want to hold a fourteenth-century aristocratic tournament with twenty knights on a side, perfectly equipped in every detail, but unless you are incredibly wealthy or immensely fortunate in your choice of friends, something is going to have to give. You can be forgiving in the degree of authenticity you require in the knights' equipment, or perhaps a small deed of arms with three men-at-arms on a side will suffice. These are less ambitious goals, but you will still only be able to achieve them in a reasonable time if some of your participants are experienced re-enactors who already have some of the necessary equipment.

Even if you don't have a stable of armored knights at your disposal, there are plenty of viable alternatives. You might decide to hold a medieval picnic, with less expensive amusements, or a village festival, or a gathering of pilgrims at an inn. Your choice of setting should reflect your goals and resources.

So should the standards of authenticity you decide to set. The more accuracy you require, the more authentic your experience will be, but the smaller the number of people able or willing to take part. This is an important factor, since a larger number of participants will generally tend to add to the energy of the event.

You may choose to have somewhat easier standards for beginners or for your entire group while it is getting started. Some groups have several levels of acceptability in permitted items. Some things may be perfectly acceptable. Others are tolerated, but the owner is expected to replace them as soon as possible. Yet others would be allowed on a one-time basis, but permission would have to be renewed for each use.

You must make your own decisions about what level of authenticity to require, but here are some suggestions. Clothing of the wrong color, the wrong shape, or the wrong cut is more likely to spoil an effect than anything else. One basic test is to ask "Does it look right from ten feet away?" Some parts of the outfit require a disproportionate amount of time or expense to bring up to the standard of the rest. Shoes are one example. You might want to be a little more flexible there. Not all inaccuracies are equally grievous; one that is unobtrusive, or dictated by overwhelming necessity, may be less a matter of concern.

If you expect people to meet a certain standard of authenticity, that standard needs to be clearly articulated. We recommend compiling a list of "authoritative sources," people or texts one can turn to as a guide for how to prepare for the event. A source need not be perfect to be considered authoritative: it need only represent a degree of authenticity that you consider adequate for the purposes of your re-enactment. This book is in part written to provide an authoritative source of this sort.

Another question you will want to bear in mind is that of "playing character" or "playing persona." Not everyone is good at this kind of theatrics, and few people can keep it up for extended periods of time. It will help if you enunciate clear and realistic ideas as to what you expect in this direction.

Above all, we strongly recommend honesty: be absolutely clear about what you are doing. There is nothing inherently wrong with inauthenticity except when it gives people a misleading impression. For this reason, you should hold yourself to a higher standard if you are doing some sort of re-enactment for the public. Making compromises when you are amusing yourself is one thing, but the general public is less likely to recognize the difference between historical accuracy and practical compromises.

Always remember that complete accuracy is never really possible. Historical authenticity is best understood as a process, not a state. We could never actually *be* medieval people; at best, we can only strive to approach that goal without ever attaining it. At any given living history event, we are representing the Middle Ages only to the best of our current knowledge. If this is done well, we may actually achieve an atmosphere that does reflect historical reality, but we should never delude ourselves into believing that an experience of a living history event is tantamount to an experience of the past.

Whatever you decide, make sure that everyone knows what is expected of them. Writing up some sort of description of the event and circulating it among prospective participants is always a good idea.

2. *Provide for Creature Comforts:* No event can hope to work without certain essentials, notably food, drink, utensils, seating, and shelter. Food in particular can absorb a lot of effort. If your organizing group is small, we recommend keeping it as simple as possible, choosing dishes that will provide the greatest satisfaction for the least preparation unless some member has a desire to explore medieval cooking. You may want to rely on foods that can be prepared several days ahead of time. For a truer recreation, those planning the meal should consider:

   - What is in season this month, or available in a form that will keep? Is it a fast day, and if so how do you design a menu with permitted foods?
   - What portions do the different social levels get? Who sits with who?

3. *Define the Space:* As medieval buildings are few and far between, some effort is required to make the setting feel right. In the absence of a medieval hall, an outdoor event is one possibility, especially if you can provide some sort of medieval pavilion. If your event is held outdoors, don't overlook the importance of shade—and have an alternate plan in case of rain.

If the event is held indoors in a less-than-medieval setting, it will help if you can furnish the site with medieval household accoutrements of some sort. Wall hangings, tablecloths, banners, and candlelight can help to disguise the intrusions of the modern world (decorated wall hangings can be made with relative ease by tracing medieval designs onto a transparency and projecting them onto fabric with an overhead projector).

In any case, but particularly if you will be meeting outside, give some thought to climate and weather. In most parts of North America, seasonal differences are much more extreme than anywhere in northern Europe. If you want to be comfortable dressed like a medieval Englishman, you might want to schedule an outdoor event as early in spring or as late in fall as weather will permit. Another possibility is to set the event in southern France, parts of which were in English hands throughout the fourteenth century.

You will have a hard time making everything authentic, so it pays to concentrate your efforts. It is better to have half the site all medieval than the whole site half medieval. Clear boundaries can help keep the modern world from spilling into the re-creation. It helps to define which particular portions of the event space are to be "authentic." It is also useful to demark the beginning and end of the re-creation by some pre-arranged signal. Someone might welcome the guests at the official beginning and thank them at the end, or a special banner might be raised during the "authentic" portion of the event. If the event will be a long one, it may help to have "authentic" periods set off from "informal" ones. An entire day is a long time to stay in character as a medieval person, or to manage without eyeglasses, but many people can manage it for an hour or two at a time.

> 4. *Arrange Entertainments:* If the event is not fun, it will not succeed. In this book we have attempted to assemble a good selection of easily re-created entertainments. They will not only provide enjoyment and diversion but will make it easier to experience the event as a medieval person. Talking or consciously acting like a person from the fourteenth century requires a positive effort of will, but taking part in a medieval amusement makes it easier to forget your modern self. The most convivial entertainments are those that several people can take part in at once. You will need to ensure that any necessary equipment is available, and it will help if the participants have some practice beforehand.

Another kind of entertainment is scripting. If one can have some sort of plot or plots happening at the event—comparable perhaps to the "host a murder mystery" format that has become an established type of party game—this may contribute to the interest of the occasion.

> 5. *Prepare the Participants:* It is not always easy to re-create the past, and it will help if the group takes an active part in preparing people for the event. Try to ensure that beginners have guidance available to them in assembling their outfits—sewing get-togethers are a good way of doing this. You might even set up a buddy system, teaming beginners with experienced people responsible for making sure they have everything they need.

The event will work best if there is a core of participants who know what they are doing. For this reason, it is worth having a series of workshops prior to the event at which people can practice games, dances, songs, social interaction, and the like. In addition, the day of the event is a good time to hold workshops for the benefit of out-of-town visitors. You should also be prepared to take an active hand in arranging the social relationships between the participants' characters. If everybody wants to be a noble lord or lady, and nobody wants to portray the rest of society, the recreation will have some big holes in it, and some major distortions. Some living history groups require participants who want to take an upper class role to support it with the clothing, jewelry and other possessions that such an individual would actually have owned. This is a powerful brake on the natural desire for everyone to end up in the upper crust. Encourage participants to come with pre-arranged social relationships among them. Recreating a medieval household is one option. A wealthy knight or minor noble would have staff, servants, and a military retinue, ranging from knights, squires, and gentlemen to pages and laborers. A servant is a comparatively easy and cheap character to re-create, and it can be a great deal of fun.

Chaucer's Canterbury pilgrims are another useful starting point. The number of female roles among the pilgrims themselves is limited, but it could be increased by adding some of the wives, sisters, daughters and female servants of the characters in the prologue. Mrs. Chaucer doesn't appear in the tale, but she was an interesting person in her own right. Chaucer's pilgrims are a good slice of society to emulate: nobody higher than a simple knight, nobody lower than an honest plowman, and most falling well between the two extremes. They are not a full cross-section of English society, but a good sample of what you might find on the Canterbury road in the 1380s—and they're a fun bunch of people (after all, they've been entertaining audiences for 600 years). Again, you may find it worthwhile organizing sessions to help arrange social relationships, before and/or on the day of the event.

For a class project, the teacher could create the necessary number of roles, and assign them at random, letting the students trade roles by mutual consent.

6. *Do It Again:* If the event was enjoyable, it will be even more so next time. You will already have assembled your basic equipment and core of participants, and you can build on it. Think of the things you can improve for your next event. Keep at it long enough, and you will be amazed what you can accomplish.

A GUIDE TO DIGITALLY ACCESSIBLE RESOURCES

When the first edition of this book was published, the Internet was only just beginning to become widely accessible. A bit over a decade later, it has transformed the landscape for people who are interested in studying the Middle Ages: museum collections from around the globe can be searched online; manuscripts are available in digital facsimile; makers of reproduction artifacts can easily be found through the web; people with similar interests are in constant contact through a variety of digital media.

It is impossible to map fully the ever-changing terrain of digital resources. The following survey is intended to suggest the range of resources that are out there and how to use them.

Among the many research resources now available, printed books remain essential. The classified bibliographies at the end of this book, and the smaller specialized reading lists in the footnotes, are intended to identify especially useful print resources.

REFERENCE RESOURCES

A general Web search engine such as Google or a partially filtered engine like Google Scholar can yield plenty of hits for any given topic. The information from Web sites needs to be viewed with skepticism, but playing around with a few search terms can be a good way to do some preliminary investigation and find your bearings on a topic. It is also important to remember that not everything that is available on the Web is accessible through these search engines: many specialized databases can only be searched by going to the database itself.

An essential tool for any kind of meaningful research is a union database of books and articles, such as WorldCat, which runs unified searches on the databases of libraries across North America and (to a lesser degree) around the world. Such resources are usually accessible through university and public libraries. An increasing number of digital books are accessible on the Web, either in full (generally only if they are out of copyright) or in limited previews. Tools like Google Book Search can help you locate some of these.

An outstanding resource is *British History Online* (www.british-history.ac.uk), a massive site with extensive online versions of primary and secondary source material relating to British history, searchable by period, region, topic, and other filters.

Among the most valuable specialized resources not accessible through a general search engine is the online version of the *Middle English Dictionary (MED)* (quod.lib.umich.edu/m/med). If you can identify a few relevant keywords for your topic, the *MED* can quickly put you in touch with pertinent primary source material: each entry includes not only definitions, but primary source quotes in which the word appears, with information on where the quotes came from.

If you want to find out something about medieval laundering, looking up the word *laundry* may get you in touch with sources that discuss it. However, running the searches can be a challenge due to the irregular spelling of Middle English (which does not actually include the form *laundry*). The surest way to track down a word is to look up its modern form in the *Oxford English Dictionary (OED)* (dictionary.oed.com; requires a subscription, which many public and research libraries will have). The *OED* will include medieval forms of the word, presuming it existed in Middle English: looking up *laundry* in the *OED* will eventually get you to Middle English forms like *lavendrie,* which will turn up in an *MED* search. Replacing vowels with wildcard symbols can also be helpful in running an *MED* search.

INTERNET PORTALS

A variety of specialized internet sites offer research leads for medieval studies. Among the best known examples are Labyrinth (labyrinth.george town.edu), Netserf (www.netserf.org), and the On-line Reference Book for Medieval Studies, or ORB (www.the-orb.net). These sites provide categorized lists of useful links including primary sources, modern scholarship, databases, discussion groups, and organizations.

There are also specialized portals. The Chaucer MetaPage (www.unc. edu/depts/chaucer/index.html) is not extensive, but can be a starting point for further investigation.

A site especially pertinent to the subject matter of this book is kept by one of the authors: www.willscommonplacebook.blogspot.com. It includes links to living history groups, suppliers, research resources, as well as short articles on a variety of topics.

PRIMARY SOURCE TEXTS ONLINE

Large quantities of primary source material are now freely available online. Two good places to start are the *Internet Medieval Sourcebook* (www.fordham.edu/halsall/sbook.html) and the *Corpus of Middle English Prose and Verse* (quod.lib.umich.edu/c/cme). There are multiple versions of Chaucer's works available online; one site with both Middle English and modernized versions is *Chaucer's Canterbury Tales* (www.canterburytales.org). See also *British History Online* under Reference Resources.

MANUSCRIPTS

Bit by bit, medieval manuscripts are being digitized in whole or in part and made available on the web. Many of these will not show up on search engines: typically one has to go to the hosting database. One of the most developed is the one for early manuscripts at Oxford University (image.ox.ac.uk). The Bibliothèque Nationale in Paris has an online collection of images from select fourteenth- and fifteenth-century manuscripts in its collection (www.bnf.fr/enluminures/aaccueil.htm). The British Library (www.bl.uk) is working to put some of its holdings online, although the major Chaucerian-period holdings remain to be fully digitized. European libraries, including the British Library, can be searched at www.theeuropeanlibrary.org.

Especially relevant to this book is the Ellesmere *Canterbury Tales*, a manuscript of Chaucer's most famous work produced not long after his death. Selected images are accessible online: www.liu.edu/cwis/cwp/library/sc/chaucer/chaucer.htm.

VISUAL RESOURCES

Using a general images search engine (such as Google Images) can be a quick way to locate visual sources about the Middle Ages, but not every image available on the web will be picked up by such a search. Visiting online databases of medieval manuscripts such as those mentioned above can turn up valuable materials that the general search engines will miss. One excellent example is Oxford Bodleian MS. 264, a copy of *The Romance of Alexander* made about 1338–1344, with additions made in England around 1400, and a major source of images relating to daily life. The manuscript is reproduced online in the Oxford University site: image.ox.ac.uk/show?collection=bodleian&manuscript=msbodl264.

Some manuscripts are reproduced only in part. Paris Bibliothèque Nationale MS Fr. 2813 is a late fourteenth-century copy of the *Grandes Chroniques de France,* telling the story of France from antiquity to the 1300s. Selected images can be seen at: www.bnf.fr/enluminures/manuscrits/aman5.htm.

INSTITUTIONS

An increasing number of museums are putting parts of their collections online; the list below is only a sampling.

Higgins Armory Museum (www.higgins.org). North America's only specialized museum of armor, and also the center for a program of study of early European martial arts treatises. The entire collection is accessible online.

Museum of London (www.museumoflondon.org.uk). Probably the world's premiere museum collection in the domain covered by this book, with extensive holdings of artifacts from the daily life of Londoners across the centuries. Parts of the collection are searchable online.

Weald and Downland Museum (www.wealddown.co.uk). Includes an outstanding collection of surviving medieval buildings, accessible through a virtual tour.

REPRODUCTIONS

One benefit of the internet is the ease with which a person can now find highly specialized wares. Reproductions of medieval artifacts are a case in point. There is a very large number of firms trading in such things; below are a few examples.

Arms and Armour (www.armor.com). Produces museum-quality reproductions of medieval weaponry.

Billy and Charlie's Pewter Goods (www.billyandcharlie.com). High-quality cast spoons, badges, buttons, buckles, and fittings in lead-free pewter.

Historic Enterprises (www.historicenterprises.com). A general purveyor of medieval reproductions, including clothing, accessories, and arms and armor.

Buying goods through the Web can be tricky; a good strategy is to consult beforehand with someone who has experience with the sellers. Living history groups can be a great resource in this respect, and they are typically very generous with their time and knowledge. The Company of the Wolfe Argent has a useful page of selected suppliers with whom they have worked (www.wolfeargent.com/merchants.htm).

ONLINE FORA

There are quite a few online discussion groups specializing in various topics relating to the Middle Ages. Lists of such groups can be had through the medieval internet portals as listed above. One group especially pertinent to this book is Chaucernet (pages.towson.edu/duncan/descchau. html), an academic discussion group focusing mostly on Chaucerian literary studies, and to a lesser degree on other literature of fourteenth-century England.

AUDIO-VISUAL SOURCES

Chaucer's works have been recorded in multiple versions over the years. Some are available online through the Chaucer Metasite (academics. vmi.edu/english/audio/audio_index.html). One source of commercially available recordings source is the Chaucer Studio (creativeworks.byu. edu/chaucer).

Various educational films relating to the subject matter of this book have been produced over the years. An example is *A Prologue to Chaucer* (Films Media Group, 1986). This and other A-V media sources are available through Films for the Humanities (ffh.films.com). Another source for various educational videos is the Medieval Video Collection from the University of Toronto www.utoronto.ca/ic/mediadistribution/videocol lection/mediev.html.

An impressive video interpretation of a single fourteenth-century manuscript is the Luttrell Psalter film (www.luttrellpsalter.org.uk).

The multimedia CD-ROM has also been applied to Chaucer studies: an example is *The Canterbury Tales*, also available from Films for the Humanities as listed above; another is *Chaucer: Life and Times* (Woodbridge, CT: Primary Source Media Limited, 1995).

Quite a few recordings of medieval music have been produced over the years, a few of them specifically weighted toward Chaucer's period. Two of the most pertinent are *Songs from the Taverne: Ballads and Songs from the Time of Chaucer* (The Gift of Music/Classical Communications, 2003); and Carol Wood, *The Chaucer Songbook* (Eroica Classical Recordings, 2000).

Finally, there are a number of feature films that offer interpretations of Chaucer's world. *The Canterbury Tales* and *Gawain and the Green Knight* have been adapted for film multiple times, but one of the less expected films in this area is *The Return of Martin Guerre* (Fox Lorber, 1982). This film is set around the year 1500, but it is perhaps the best existing cinematic view of medieval village life.

Even the best movies set in the fourteenth century don't get the period entirely right. Sometimes the production designer doesn't have the resources or expertise to do the costuming or other details properly, as in the low budget *The Seventh Seal* and *The Navigator: A Medieval Odyssey*. Sometimes the film is less about the period than something else. *The Seventh Seal* was set in the fourteenth century, but Bergman was primarily using the setting to show the sort of existential doubt and crisis of faith a Lutheran pastor's son might feel in the second half of the twentieth century. Our sense of what is natural, stylish, or flattering is different from theirs, and this often shows up in the recreation of hairstyles and costume details, either unconsciously or because the production designer was afraid the audience wouldn't accept or understand an accurate recreation. In an extreme case like *A Knight's Tale,* the production designer deliberately modernizes the clothing and even soundtrack to make it more accessible to a modern audience even while retaining some properly medieval story elements. The movies can still be worth watching, but you need to be aware of their limitations as a recreation of the historical past.

RESEARCH ORGANIZATIONS

There are a variety of specialist organizations involved in researching areas covered by this book. Below are just a few examples:

> *Armour Research Society* (www.armourresearchsociety.org). Fosters study of arms and armor, particularly of the Middle Ages and Renaissance, through publications, conferences, and workshops.

> *Higgins Armory Sword Guild* (www.higginssword.org). Studies, teaches, and demonstrates historical combat techniques at the Higgins Armory Museum.

> *The New Chaucer Society* (artsci.wustl.edu/~chaucer). An academic organization specializing in Chaucer studies, and sponsoring conferences, a journal, and an online bibliography.

JOURNALS AND BOOK SERIES

Current research in any field can take a while to find its way into books. To get a handle on the most recent scholarship, it is often best to have a look at journal articles. Databases of article abstracts are included in reference resources like the *MLA International Bibliography* or *Historical Abstracts.* A few examples of specialist journals relevant to this book include *The Chaucer Review; Medieval Clothing and Textiles; The Journal of the Armour and Arms Society.*

LIVING HISTORY GROUPS

There are a variety of groups around the world involved in recreating aspects of medieval life. A few specialize in the fourteenth century, although even those that do not can sometimes be a pertinent resource for someone interested specifically in Chaucer's period.

> *La Belle Compagnie* (www.labelle.org). This group reenacts the household of a late fourteenth-century English knight.

The Society for Creative Anachronism (www.sca.org). Holds tournaments, feasts, and other activities inspired by the Middle Ages. The focus is not on recreating actual history, but the organization and Web site provide a forum for people with an interest in aspects of medieval life, especially in the domain of material culture.

The Wolfe Argent (www.wolfeargent.com). This group specializes in the fifteenth-century, but their Web site provides a forum for medieval living history in general, as well as a valuable list of suppliers of reproduction goods.

CLASSIFIED BIBLIOGRAPHIES

ABBREVIATIONS

AC	Alexander, Jonathan, and Paul Binski, eds., Age of Chivalry. Art in Plantagenet England 1200–1400
BL	British Library
CT	Geoffrey Chaucer, *The Canterbury Tales*
DMA	*The Dictionary of the Middle Ages*
HMSO	Her/His Majesty's Stationery Office
LP	*Luttrell Psalter.* British Library MS Add. 42130.
MED	*Middle English Dictionary*
RA	*Roman d'Alexandre.* Oxford Bodleian MS 264.
TS	*Tacuinum Sanitatis.* Cited by manuscript location (Casanatense, Paris, Vienna).
TBH	*Tres Belles Heures.* Paris, Bibliothèque Nationale nouv. acq. lat. 3093.

SUGGESTED READING

There are quite a few books available on life in medieval England, although they do not necessarily focus on the fourteenth century. An excellent recent introduction is Rosemary Horrox and W. Mark Ormrod, eds., *A Social History of England, 1200–1500* (Cambridge: Cambridge University Press, 2006). Older, but still an excellent reference resource, is Austin Lane Poole, ed. *Medieval England* (Oxford: Clarendon Press, 1958).

For an accessible, scholarly study of English society in Chaucer's day, Scott L. Waugh, *England in the Reign of Edward III* (Cambridge: Cambridge University Press, 1991) is a useful source. May McKisack's *The Fourteenth Century 1307–1399* (Oxford: Clarendon Press, 1959) remains one of the best introductions to political history and social structure in the period.

Among books aimed at a popular audience, Elizabeth Johnson, et al., *1381: The Peel Affinity: An English Knight's Household in the Fourteenth Century* (Harrisburg; Shumacher Publishing, 2007) is a living history group's photographic and narrative recreation of a year in the life of an English knight and his household, retinue, and tenants. Judith M. Bennett, *A Medieval Life: Cecilia Penifader of Brigstock, c. 1295–1344* (Boston: McGraw-Hill College, 1999) is an accessible introduction to peasant life in a period slightly before Chaucer, written by a leading scholar in the field. Another readable work in this area is the illustrated compendium by Frances and Joseph Gies: *Daily Life in Medieval Times* (New York: Black Dog and Leventhal Publishers, 1999).

A readable narrative account of the fourteenth century (although it may offer an excessively bleak picture of the period) is Barbara Tuchman, *A Distant Mirror: The Calamitous Fourteenth Century* (New York: Knopf, 1978). Good visual histories of the period are *Chronicles of the Age of Chivalry* (London: Weidenfeld and Nicholson, 1987) and *The Chronicles of the Wars of the Roses* (London: Viking, 1988). For general reference, *The Dictionary of the Middle Ages* (New York: Scribner, 1982) and Ronald H. Fritze and William B. Robison, *Historical Dictionary of Late Medieval England 1272–1485* (Westport, CT: Greenwood Press, 2002) are a good starting point.

For younger readers, Sheila Sancha's *The Luttrell Village* (New York: Crowell, 1982) and *Walter Dragun's Town* (New York: HarperCollins, 1987) are vivid introductions to medieval life in the country and town in a period slightly earlier than the scope of this book; they rely heavily on rich illustrations of reconstructed daily life, but both are well researched.

Additional readings on individual topics are suggested in the chapter notes.

CHAUCER

Brewer, Derek. *Chaucer and His World.* New York: Dodd, Mead and Co., 1978.

Chaucer, Geoffrey. *The Riverside Chaucer.* Boston: Houghton Mifflin, 1987.

Coulton, G. G. *Chaucer and His England.* New York: Putnam's, 1900.

Crow, Martin M., and Clair C. Olson. *Chaucer Life-Records.* Austin: University of Texas Press, 1966.

Furnivall, F. J. *The Cambridge MS. Dd.4.22. of Chaucer's Canterbury Tales.* London: Kegan, Paul, Trench, and Trübner, 1902.

Halliday, F. E. *Chaucer and His World.* New York: Viking, 1968.

Howard, Donald R. *Chaucer: His Life, His Works, His World.* New York: Fawcett, 1987.

Hussey, Maurice. *Chaucer's World: A Pictorial Companion.* Cambridge: Cambridge University Press, 1967.

Serraillier, Ian. *Chaucer and His World.* London: Butterworth, 1967.

A CHAUCERIAN BOOKSHELF

The following works were written by authors who were adults when Chaucer was alive.

Boccaccio, Giovanni. *Decameron.* Harmondsworth: Penguin, 1972. Shares Chaucer's diversity; indeed, Chaucer retells many of Boccaccio's tales.

Bonet, Honoré. *The Tree of Battles of Honoré Bonet,* transl. G. W. Coopland. Liverpool: University Press of Liverpool 1949. A learned clerk writes about law, justice, morality, and violence, legitimate and otherwise.

Charny, Geoffroi de. *The Book of Chivalry,* transl. Richard W. Kaeuper and Elspeth Kennedy. University Park: Pennsylvania State University Press, 1996. A knight writes about the ideals and obligations of knighthood.

Froissart, Jean. *Chronicles,* transl. Geoffrey Brereton. New York: Penguin 1978. A vivid and detailed contemporary chronicle; Froissart writes like an eyewitness even when he wasn't, providing details that may not always be accurate but are always true to the author's chivalric culture.

Kempe, Margery. *The Book of Margery Kempe,* transl. Barry Windeatt. New York: Penguin 1988. Written after Chaucer's lifetime by a woman who grew up during the late 1300s—this account of the author's lifetime of spiritual exploration is one of few substantial medieval works to come from us from an English laywoman.

Langland, William. *Piers the Plowman,* transl. J. F. Goodridge. New York: Penguin 1987. An allegorical exploration of contemporary society and morals, this was one of the most popular works in English during Chaucer's lifetime.

Mandeville, John. *Travels,* transl. C.W.R.D. Moseley. New York: Penguin 1983. Purporting to be the account of a fourteenth-century Englishman's journeys, this book was also very popular in Chaucer's day; it incorporates both fact and fantasy, and reflects popular ideas about the nature of the world.

Pisan, Christine de. *The Book of Deeds of Arms and of Chivalry,* ed. and transl. Sumner and Charity Cannon Willard. University Park: Pennsylvania State University Press 1999. Christine updates the late Roman military manual of Vegetius and Bonet's *Tree of Battles* with a great deal of practical contemporary advice such as the number of bowstrings and wheelbarrows to bring to a siege.

Power, Eileen, transl. *The Goodman of Paris.* Woodbridge: Boydell Press, 1928. A wealthy and aged Parisian writes moral and practical advice to his young wife regarding the management of her household.

Tolkien, J.R.R., transl. *Sir Gawain and the Green Knight, Pearl, and Sir Orfeo.* New York: Ballantine Books, 1975. Dating to the late fourteenth century, *Sir Gawain* is one of the finest examples of Middle English romance; it offers both chivalric adventure and sophisticated humor.

Wright, Thomas, transl. *The Book of the Knight of La Tour-Landry.* New York: Greenwood Press, 1969. A late fourteenth-century knight dispenses moral advice to his daughters illustrated by many anecdotes, some learned and classical, some lively and contemporary.

GENERAL AND REFERENCE SOURCES

Dictionary of the Middle Ages. New York: Scribner, 1982.

Dyer, Christopher. *Making a Living in the Middle Ages: The People of Britain 850–1520.* New Haven: Yale University Press, 2002.

Dyer, Christopher. *An Age of Transition? Economy and Society in England in the Later Middle Ages.* Oxford and New York: Oxford University Press, 2005.

Fritze, Ronald H. and William B. Robison. *Historical Dictionary of Late Medieval England 1272–1485.* Westport, CT: Greenwood Press, 2002.

Given-Wilson, Chris, ed. *An Illustrated History of Late Medieval England.* Manchester and New York: Manchester University Press, 1996.

Hart, Roger. *English Life in Chaucer's Day.* London: Wayland Publishers; New York: G. P. Putnam's Sons, 1973.

Hartley, Dorothy. *Lost Country Life.* New York: Pantheon, 1979.

Horrox, Rosemary, and W. Mark Ormrod. *A Social History of England, 1200–1500.* Cambridge: Cambridge University Press, 2006.

Loomis, Roger. *A Mirror of Chaucer's World.* Princeton: Princeton University Press, 1965.

McKisack, May. *The Fourteenth Century 1307–1399.* Oxford: Clarendon Press, 1959.

Middle English Dictionary. Ann Arbor: University of Michigan Press, 1952–2007.

Owst, G. R. *Preaching in Medieval England.* Cambridge: Cambridge University Press, 1926.

Poole, Austin Lane, ed. *Medieval England.* 2 vols. Oxford: Clarendon Press, 1958.

Rickert, Edith. *Chaucer's World.* New York: Columbia University Press, 1948.

Trevisa, John. *On the Properties of Things: John Trevisa's translation of Bartholomeus Anglicus' De Proprietatibus Rerum,* gen. ed. M. C. Seymour. Oxford: Clarendon Press, 1975.

Wood, Eric S. *Historical Britain: A Comprehensive Account of the Development of Rural and Urban Life and Landscape from Prehistory to the Present Day.* London: Harvill Press, 1995.

Woods, William. *England in the Age of Chaucer.* New York: Stein and Day, 1976.

Woolgar, C. M. *The Great Household in Late Medieval England.* New Haven: Yale University Press, 1999.

PRIMARY-SOURCE ANTHOLOGIES

Dobson, R. B. *The Peasants' Revolt of 1381.* London: Macmillan; New York: St. Martin's Press, 1970.

Goldberg, P.J.P. *Women in England, c. 1275–1525: Documentary Sources.* Manchester and New York: Manchester University Press, 1995.

Goldie, Matthew Boyd. Middle English Literature: A Historical Sourcebook Malden, MA: Blackwell, 2003.

Myers, A. R. *English Historical Documents, 1327–1485.* London: Routledge, 1996.

Rickert, Edith. *Chaucer's World.* New York: Columbia University Press, 1948.

POLITICAL HISTORY

Brie, Friedrich, ed. *The Brut or the Chronicles of Englande.* Early English Texts Society 131, 136. London: Kegan Paul, Trench and Trübner, 1906, 1908.

Froissart, Jean. *Chronicles.* Transl. John Jolliffe. New York: Modern Library, 1968.

Galbraith, V. H., ed. *The Anonimalle Chronicle, 1333–1381.* Manchester: Manchester University Press, 1970.

Grey, Sir Thomas, ed. *The Scalachronica: The Reigns of Edward I, Edward II, and Edward III.* Felinfach: Llanerch, 2000.

Hector, L. C., and Barbara F. Harvey, eds. *The Westminster Chronicle 1381–1394.* `Oxford: Clarendon Press, 1982.
Henry of Knighton, *Knighton's Chronicle 1337–1396.* Transl. G. H. Martin. Oxford: Oxford University Press, 1996.
John of Reading, *Chronica Johannis de Reading et Anonymi Cantuarensis.* Ed. James Tait. Manchester: Manchester Universtiy Press, 1914.
McKisack, May. *The Fourteenth Century 1307–1399.* Oxford: Clarendon Press, 1959.
Robbins, R. H. *Historical Poems of the XIVth and XVth Centuries.* Oxford: Clarendon Press, 1959.
Thomas of Malmesbury, *Eulogium Historiarum.* Ed. Frank Scott Heydon. Rolls Series 9. London: Longman, 1858–63.
Usk, Adam. *The Chronicle of Adam Usk, 1377–1421.* Ed. Chris Given-Wilson. Oxford: Clarendon Press, 1997.

SOCIETY

Astill, Grenville, and Annie, Grant, eds. *The Countryside of Medieval England.* Oxford: Blackwell, 1988.
Bailey, Mark. *The English Manor, c. 1200–1500.* Manchester: Manchester University Press, 2002.
Bellamy, John. *Crime and Public Order in England in the Later Middle Ages,* London: Routledge and Kegan Paul; Toronto: University of Toronto Press, 1973.
Brown, A.L. *The Governance of Late Medieval England, 1272–1461.* Stanford: Stanford University Press, 1989.
Coss, Peter. "An age of deference." In *A Social History of England, 1200–1500,* ed. Rosemary Horrox and W. Mark Ormrod. Cambridge: Cambridge University Press, 2006. 31–73.
Dyer, Christopher. *Standards of Living in the Later Middle Ages.* Cambridge: Cambridge University Press, 1989.
Dyer, Christopher. *Making a Living in the Middle Ages: The People of Britain 850–1520.* New Haven: Yale University Press, 2002.
Dyer, Christopher. *An Age of Transition? Economy and Society in England in the Later Middle Ages.* Oxford and New York: Oxford University Press, 2005.
Fryde, E. B. *Peasants and Landlords in Later Medieval England.* Stroud: Sutton, 1996.
Maddern, Philippa C. "Social mobility." In *A Social History of England, 1200–1500,* ed. Rosemary Horrox and W. Mark Ormrod. Cambridge: Cambridge University Press, 2006. 113–33.
McKisack, May. *The Fourteenth Century 1307–1399.* Oxford: Clarendon Press, 1959.
Miller, Edward, ed. *The Agrarian History of England and Wales. Volume III 1348–1500.* Cambridge: Cambridge University Press, 1991.
Radulescu, Raluca, and Alison Truelove. *Gentry Culture in Late Medieval England.* Manchester: Manchester University Press, 2005.
Rickert, Edith. *Chaucer's World.* New York: Columbia University Press, 1948.
Russell, Josiah Cox. *British Medieval Population.* Albuquerque: University of New Mexico Press, 1948.
Schofield, Phillipp R. *Peasant and Community in Medieval England, 1200–1500.* New York: Palgrave-Macmillan, 2003.
Swabey, Ffiona. *Medieval Gentlewoman: Life in a Gentry Household in the Later Middle Ages.* New York: Routledge, 1999.

Swanson, R. N. *Church and Society in Late Medieval England.* Oxford: Blackwell, 1989.

Waugh, Scott L. *England in the Reign of Edward III.* Cambridge: Cambridge University Press, 1991.

HOUSEHOLDS AND THE LIFE CYCLE

Bennett, Judith M. *A Medieval Life: Cecilia Penifader of Brigstock,* c. 1295–1344. Boston: McGraw-Hill College, 1999.

Bullough, Vern L. and James A. Brundage. *Handbook of Medieval Sexuality.* New York: Garland, 1996.

Cobban, Alan B. *English University Life in the Middle Ages.* Columbus: Ohio State University Press, 1999.

Dyer, Christopher. *Standards of Living in the Later Middle Ages.* Cambridge: Cambridge University Press, 1989.

Dyer, Christopher. *An Age of Transition? Economy and Society in England in the Later Middle Ages.* Oxford and New York: Oxford University Press, 2005.

Fleming, Peter. *Family and Household in Medieval England.* Houndmills, Hampshire and New York: Palgrave, 2001.

Goldberg, P.J.P. "Life and death: the ages of man." In *A Social History of England, 1200–1500,* ed. Rosemary Horrox and W. Mark Ormrod. Cambridge: Cambridge University Press, 2006. 413–34.

Hanawalt, Barbara. *Growing Up in Medieval London: The Experience of Childhood in History.* New York and Oxford: Oxford University Press, 1993.

Hanawalt, Barbara. *The Ties That Bound. Peasant Families in Medieval England.* New York and Oxford: Oxford University Press, 1986.

McSheffrey, Shannon. *Marriage, Sex and Civic Culture in Late Medieval London.* Philadelphia: University of Pennsylvania Press, 2006.

Orme, Nicholas. *From Childhood to Chivalry: The Education of the English Kings and Aristocracy, 1066–1530.* London and New York: Methuen, 1984.

Orme, Nicholas. *Education and Society in Medieval and Renaissance England.* London: Hambledon, 1989.

Orme, Nicholas. *Medieval Children.* New Haven: Yale University Press, 2001.

Piponnier, Françoise and Perrine Mane. *Dress in the Middle Ages.* New Haven: Yale University Press, 1997.

Radulescu, Raluca, and Alison Truelove. *Gentry Culture in Late Medieval England.* Manchester: Manchester University Press, 2005.

Rickert, Edith. *Chaucer's World.* New York: Columbia University Press, 1948.

Russell, John. *The Boke of Nurture.* In *The Babees Book,* ed. F. J. Furnivall. London: Trübner, 1868. 61–114.

Schofield, Phillipp R. *Peasant and Community in Medieval England, 1200–1500.* New York: Palgrave-Macmillan, 2003.

Shahar, Shulamith. *Childhood in the Middle Ages.* London and New York: Routledge, 1990.

Woolgar, C. M. *The Great Household in Late Medieval England.* New Haven: Yale University Press, 1999.

WOMEN

Amt, Emilie. *Women's Lives in Medieval Europe: A Sourcebook.* New York: Routledge, 1993.

Bennett, Judith M. *A Medieval Life: Cecilia Penifader of Brigstock,* c. 1295–1344. Boston: McGraw-Hill College, 1999.

Goldberg, P.J.P. *Women in England, c. 1275–1525: Documentary Sources.* Manchester and New York: Manchester University Press, 1995.

Labarge, Margaret Wade. *A Small Sound of the Trumpet: Women in Medieval Life.* Boston: Beacon Press, 1986.

Leyser, Henrietta. *Medieval Women: A Social History of Women in England, 450–1500.* New York: St. Martin's Press, 1995.

McIntosh, Marjorie Keniston. *Working women in English society, 1300–1620.* Cambridge: Cambridge University Press, 2005.

Phillips, Kim M. *Medieval Maidens: Young Women and Gender in England, 1270–1540.* Manchester; New York: Manchester University Press, 2003.

Shahar, Shulamith. *The Fourth Estate: A History of Women in the Middle Ages.* London and New York: Routledge, 2003.

CYCLES OF TIME

Bond, John J. *Handy Book of Rules and Tables for Verifying Dates within the Christian Era.* New York: Russell and Russell, 1966.

Cheney, C. R. *Handbook of Dates for Students of English History.* London: Offices of the Royal Historical Society, 1970.

Hanawalt, Barbara. *Growing Up in Medieval London. The Experience of Childhood in History.* New York and Oxford: Oxford University Press, 1993.

Homans, George Caspar. *English Villagers of the Thirteenth Century.* Cambridge, MA: Harvard University Press, 1942.

Maskell, William. *Monumenta Ritualia Ecclesiae Anglicanae.* Oxford: Clarendon Press, 1882.

Nicholas of Lynn. *Kalendarium,* ed. Sigmund Eisner. Athens: University of Georgia Press, 1980.

Orme, Nicholas. *Medieval Children.* New Haven: Yale University Press, 2001.

Pendrill, C. *London Life in the 14th Century.* London: Allen and Unwin, 1925.

Pythian-Adams, Charles. "Ritual constructions of society." In *A Social History of England, 1200–1500,* ed. Rosemary Horrox and W. Mark Ormrod. Cambridge: Cambridge University Press, 2006. 369–82.

Walter of Henley's Husbandry, ed. E. Lamond. London: Longman's, Green and Co., 1890.

Woolgar, C. M. *The Great Household in Late Medieval England.* New Haven: Yale University Press, 1999.

MATERIAL CULTURE

Alexander, Jonathan, and Paul Binski, eds. *Age of Chivalry. Art in Plantagenet England 1200–1400.* London: Royal Academy of Arts, 1987.

Astill, Grenville, and Annie, Grant, eds. *The Countryside of Medieval England.* Oxford: Blackwell, 1988.

Beresford, Maurice and John Hurst. *Wharram Percy: Deserted Medieval Village.* London: Batsford/English Heritage, 1990.

Blair, John, and Nigel Ramsay, eds. *English Medieval Industries.* London: Hambledon Press, 1991.

Campbell, B.M.S. *English Seigniorial Agriculture, 1250–1450.* Cambridge and New York: Cambridge University Press, 2000.

Charleston, R. J. *English Glass and the Glass Used in England* circa *400–1940*. London: Unwin, 1984.

Drogin, Marc. *Medieval Calligraphy: Its History and Technique*. Montclair: Allanheld and Schram, 1980.

Dyer, Christopher. *Standards of Living in the Later Middle Ages*. Cambridge: Cambridge University Press, 1989.

Dyer, Christopher. *Making a Living in the Middle Ages: The People of Britain 850–1520*. New Haven: Yale University Press, 2002.

Eames, Penelope. *Furniture in England, France and the Netherlands from the Twelfth to the Fifteenth Century*. London: Furniture History Society, 1977.

Egan, Geoff, and J. Bayley. *The Medieval Household: Daily Living c. 1150–c. 1450*. London: HMSO for the Museum of London, 1998.

Fryde, E. B. *Peasants and Landlords in Later Medieval England*. Stroud: Sutton, 1996.

Gies, Frances and Joseph. *Daily Life in Medieval Times*. New York: Black Dog and Leventhal Publishers, 1999.

Gottfried, Robert S. *Doctors and Medicine in Medieval England 1340–1530*. Princeton: Princeton University Press, 1986.

Grenville, Jane. *Medieval Housing*. Leicester: Leicester University Press, 1997.

Hornsby, Peter, Rosemary Weinstein, and Ronald Homer. *Pewter: A Celebration of the Craft 1200–1700*. London: Museum of London, 1990.

Kowaleski, Maryanne. "A consumer economy." In *A Social History of England, 1200–1500*, ed. Rosemary Horrox and W. Mark Ormrod. Cambridge: Cambridge University Press, 2006. 238–59.

Langdon, John. *Mills in the medieval economy: England, 1300–1540*. Oxford and New York: Oxford University Press, 2004.

London Museum. *Medieval Catalogue*. London: HMSO, 1967.

Lydgate, John. "Stans Puer ad Mensam." In *The Minor Poems of John Lydgate*, ed. H. N. MacCracken. Early English Texts Society 192. London: Trübner, 1934. 2.739–44.

MacGregor, Arthur. *Bone, Antler, Ivory, and Horn: The Technology of Skeletal Materials Since the Roman Period*. London and Sydney: Croom Helm, 1985.

McCarthy, Michael R. and Catherine M. Brooks. *Medieval Pottery in Britain A.D. 900–1600*. Leicester: Leicester University Press, 1988.

Mercer, Eric. *Furniture 700–1700*. New York: Meredith Press, 1969.

Metropolitan Museum of Art. *The Secular Spirit: Life and Art at the End of the Middle Ages*. New York: Dutton, 1975.

Miller, Edward, ed. *The Agrarian History of England and Wales. Volume III 1348–1500*. Cambridge: Cambridge University Press, 1991.

Myers, A. R. *London in the Age of Chaucer*. Norman: University of Oklahoma Press, 1974.

Rawcliffe, C. *Medicine and Society in Later Medieval England*. Stroud: Sutton, 1995.

Rickert, Edith. *Chaucer's World*. New York: Columbia University Press, 1948.

Robertson, D. W. *Chaucer's London*. New York: John Wiley and Sons, 1968.

Rogers, James E. Thorold. *A History of Agriculture and Prices in England*. Oxford: Clarendon Press, 1882.

Russell, John. *The Boke of Nurture*. In *The Babees Book*, ed. F. J. Furnivall. London: Trübner, 1868. 61–114.

Salzman, L. F. *Building in England Down to 1540*. Oxford: Clarendon Press, 1952.

Schofield, J. *Medieval London Houses.* New Haven and London: Yale University Press, 1994.

Wood, Eric S. *Historical Britain: A Comprehensive Account of the Development of Rural and Urban Life and Landscape from Prehistory to the Present Day.* London: Harvill Press, 1995.

Wood, Margaret. *The English Mediaeval House.* London: Phoenix House, 1965.

Woolgar, C. M. *The Great Household in Late Medieval England.* New Haven: Yale University Press, 1999.

Wrathmell, Stuart. *Wharram. A Study of Settlement on the Yorkshire Wolds VI. Domestic Settlement 2: Medieval Peasant Farmsteads,* York University Archeological Publications 8. York: York University, 1989.

CLOTHING AND ACCESSORIES

Blanc, Odile. "From Battlefield to Court: The Invention of Fashion in the Fourteenth Century." In *Encountering Medieval Textiles and Dress: Objects, Texts, Images,* ed. Désirée G. Koslin and Janet E. Snyder. New York: Palgrave Macmillan, 2002. 157–72.

Boucher, François, *2000 Years of Fashion.* New York: Abrams, 1957.

Christie, A.G.I. *English Medieval Embroidery A Brief Survey of English Embroidery Dating from the Beginning of the Tenth Century until the End of the Fourteenth.* Oxford: Clarendon Press, 1938.

Cowgill, J., M. de Neergard, and N. Griffiths, eds. *Medieval Finds from Excavations in London. 1: Knives and Scabbards.* London: HMSO, 1987.

Crowfoot, E., F. Pritchard, and K. Staniland, eds., *Medieval Finds from Excavations in London. Vol. 4: Textiles and Clothing.* London: HMSO, 1992.

Cunnington, Q. W. and P., *Handbook of English Medieval Costume.* London: Faber and Faber, 1952.

Cunnington, Q. W. and P., *The History of Underclothes.* London: Faber and Faber, 1981.

Davenport, Millia, *The Book of Costume.* New York: Crown Publishers, 1948.

Dyer, Christopher. *Standards of Living in the Later Middle Ages.* Cambridge: Cambridge University Press, 1989.

Egan, G., and F. Pritchard, eds., *Medieval Finds from Excavations in London. Vol. 3: Dress Accessories.* London: HMSO, 1991.

Goubitz, Olaf, Carol van Driel-Murray, and Willy Groenman-Van Waateringe. *Stepping through Time: Archaeological Footwear from Prehistoric Times until 1800.* Zwolle: Stichting Promotie Archeologie, 2007.

Grew F., and M. de Neergard, eds. *Medieval Finds from Excavations in London. 2: Shoes and Pattens.* London: HMSO, 1988.

Hartley, Dorothy, *Medieval Costume and Life.* London: Batsford, 1931.

Houston, Mary G., *Medieval Costume in England and France.* London: Black, 1939.

Kelly, Francis M., *A Short History of Costume and Armour.* London: Batsford, 1931.

Köhler, Carl, *A History of Costume.* London: Harrap, 1928.

Lester, Katherine Morris, and Bess Viola Oerke, *Accessories of Dress.* Peoria, IL: Manual Arts Press, 1954.

Netherton, Robin. "The Tippet: Accessory after the Fact?" In *Medieval Clothing and Textiles,* ed. Robin Netherton and Gale R. Owen-Crocker. Woodbridge, Suffolk, and Rochester, NY: Boydell Press, 2005. 115–32.

Newton, Stella Mary, *Fashion in the Age of the Black Prince.* Woodbridge, Suffolk: Boydell Press, 1980.

Nockert, Margareta, et al., eds., *Bokstensmannen Och Hans Drakt.* Falkenberg: Falkenberg Tryckeri, 1985.

Norlund, Poul, "Buried Norsemen at Herjolfsnes," *Meddelelser om Groenland* 67 (1924): 87–192.

Østergård, Else. *Woven into the Earth: Textiles from Norse Greenland.* Aarhus and Oxford: Aarhus University Press, 2004.

Piponnier, Françoise and Perrine Mane. *Dress in the Middle Ages.* New Haven: Yale University Press, 1997.

Rickert, Edith. *Chaucer's World.* New York: Columbia University Press, 1948.

Rutt, Richard. *A History of Hand Knitting.* Loveland, CO: Interweave Press, 1987.

Scott, Margaret, *A Visual History of Costume. The Fourteenth and Fifteenth Centuries.* London: Batsford, 1986.

Semenzato, Camillo, *Le Pitture del Santo di Padova.* Vicenza: Pozza, 1984.

Woolgar, C. M. *The Great Household in Late Medieval England.* New Haven: Yale University Press, 1999.

ARMS AND ARMOR

Anglo, Sydney. *The Martial Arts of Renaissance Europe.* New Haven: Yale University Press, 2000.

Arthur, Harold, Viscount Dillon. "On a MS. Collection of Ordinances of Chivalry of the fifteenth century." *Archaeologia* 57 (1840): 29–71.

Ayton, Andrew. *The Battle of Crécy, 1346.* Woodbridge, Suffolk: Boydell and Brewer, 2005.

Bartlett, Clive and Gerry Embleton. *English Longbowman 1330–1515.* 2nd ed. London: Osprey, 1997.

Blair, Claude. *European and American Arms, c. 1100–1850.* London: B. T. Batsford, 1962.

Blair, Claude. *European Armour circa 1066 to circa 1700.* New York: Macmillan, 1959.

Bradbury, Jim. *The Routledge Companion to Medieval Warfare.* London and New York: Routledge, 2004.

Contamine, Philippe. *War in the Middle Ages,* transl. Michael Jones. Oxford: Blackwell, 1984.

Cripps-Day, F. H. "The Armour at Chartres," *Connoisseur* 110:486 (1942): 91–95, 158.

De Vries, Kelly. *Infantry Warfare in the Fourteenth Century.* Woodbridge, Suffolk: Boydell, 1996.

DeVries, Kelly. *Medieval Military Technology.* Peterborough, Ontario: Broadview Press, 1992.

DeVries, Kelly, and Robert D. Smith. *Medieval Weapons: An Illustrated History of Their Impact.* Santa Barbara: ABC-CLIO, 2007.

Dufty, Arthur Richard. *European Armour in the Tower of London.* London: HMSO, 1968.

Edge, David, and John Miles Paddock. *Arms and Armour of the Medieval Knight.* New York: Defoe, 1988.

ffoulkes, C. *The Armourer and His Craft.* New York: B. Blom, 1967.

Forgeng, Jeffrey L. *The Medieval Art of Swordsmanship: A Facsimile and Translation of Europe's Oldest Personal Combat Treatise, Royal Armouries MS I.33.* Leeds; Union City, CA: Royal Armouries; Chivalry Bookshelf, 2003.

Forgeng, Jeffrey L., and Alexander Kiermayer. "'The Chivalric Art': German Martial Arts Treatises of the Middle Ages and Renaissance." In *The Cutting Edge: Studies in Ancient and Medieval Combat,* ed. E. B. Molloy. Stroud, Glocs.: Tempus, 2007. 153–67.

Froissart, Jean. *Chronicles,* transl. John Jolliffe. New York: Modern Library, 1968.

Gravett, Christopher. *English Medieval Knight 1300–1400.* London: Osprey 2002.

Macklin, H. W. *Monumental Brasses.* London: Sonnenschein, 1891.

Mann, J. G. *Wallace Collection. European Arms and Armour.* 2 vols. London: printed for the Trustees by W. Clowes, 1962.

Mellini, G. L. *Altichiero e Jacopo Avanzi.* Milan: Edizioni di Comunita, 1965.

Metropolitan Museum of Art. *The Bashford Dean Collection of Arms and Armor in the Metropolitan Museum of Art.* Portland, ME: Southworth Press for the Armor and Arms Club of New York, 1933.

Middle English Dictionary. Ann Arbor: University of Michigan Press, 1952–2007.

Norman, A. Vesey. *Arms and Armour.* New York: Putnam's, 1964.

North, Anthony. "Barbarians and Christians." In *Swords and Hilt Weapons.* New York: Weidenfeld and Nicolson, 1989. 30–43.

Oakeshott, R. Ewart. *The Archaeology of Weapons.* London: Lutterworth Press, 1960.

Oakeshott, R. Ewart. *Records of the Medieval Sword.* Woodbridge: The Boydell Press 1991.

Oakeshott, R. Ewart. *The Sword in the Age of Chivalry.* Woodbridge: The Boydell Press, 1991.

Porter, Pamela J. *Medieval Warfare in Manuscripts.* Toronto: University of Toronto Press, 2000.

Prestwich, Michael. *Armies and Warfare in the Middle Ages: The English Experience.* New Haven and London: Yale University Press, 1996.

Reed, Robert W., Jr. "Armour Purchases and Lists in the Howard Household Accounts: Part II." *The Journal of the Armour Research Society* 1 (2005): 65–105.

Rickert, Edith. *Chaucer's World.* New York: Columbia University Press, 1948.

Rothero, Christopher. *The Armies of Crécy and Poitiers,* Osprey Men-at-Arms Series 111. London: Osprey, 1981.

Soar, D. H. Hugh, with Joseph Gibbs, Christopher Jury, Mark Stretton. *Secrets of the English War Bow.* Yardley: Westholme, 2006.

Strickland, Matthew, and Robert Hardy. *The Great Warbow.* Stroud, Glocs.: Sutton, 2005.

Thordeman, B. *Armour from the Battle of Wisby 1361.* Stockholm: Kungl. vitterhets historie och antikvitets akademien, 1939.

Trapp, O. *The Armoury of the Castle of Churburg,* transl. J. G. Mann. London: Methuen, 1929.

Waldman, John, *Hafted Weapons in Medieval and Renaissance Europe.* Leiden and Boston: Brill, 2005.

Williams, Alan R. *The Knight and the Blast Furnace: A History of the Metallurgy of Armour in the Middle Ages and Early Modern Period.* Leiden: Brill, 2003.

FOOD AND DRINK

Bayard, Tania. *The Medieval Home Companion.* New York: HarperCollins, 1991.

Bennett, Judith M. *Ale, Beer and Brewsters in England: Women's Work in a Changing World, 1300–1600.* New York: Oxford University Press, 1996.

Cosman, Madeleine Pelner. *Fabulous Feasts.* New York: Braziller, 1976.

Dyer, Christopher. "English Diet in the Later Middle Ages." In *Social Relations and Ideas,* ed. T. H. Aston, P. R. Coss, et al. Cambridge: Cambridge University Press, 1983. 191–216.

Dyer, Christopher. *Standards of Living in the Later Middle Ages.* Cambridge: Cambridge University Press, 1989.

Egan, Geoff, and J. Bayley. *The Medieval Household: Daily Living c. 1150–c. 1450.* London: HMSO for the Museum of London, 1998.

Freeman, Margaret. *Herbs for the Mediaeval Household.* New York: Metropolitan Museum of Art, 1943.

Friedman, David, et al. *A Collection of Medieval and Renaissance Cookbooks,* 6th ed. Vol. I. private printing, 1991.

Friedman, David, ed. *A Collection of Medieval and Renaissance Cookbooks,* 4th ed. Vol. II. private printing, 1991.

Henisch, Bridget Ann. *Fast and Feast: Food in Medieval Society.* University Park: University of Pennsylvania Press, 1976.

Hieatt, Constance B., and Sharon Butler. *Curye on Inglisch,* Early English Texts Society special series 8. London: Oxford University Press, 1985.

Hieatt, Constance B., and Sharon Butler. *Pleyn Delit.* Toronto: University of Toronto Press, 1979.

Hieatt, Constance B., and Robin F. Jones. "Two Anglo-Norman Culinary Collections." *Speculum* 61:4 (1986): 859–82.

Le Ménagier de Paris. Paris: Crapelet, 1846. For translations, see Bayard, *Medieval Home Companion;* Power, *Goodman of Paris;* Friedman, *Collection,* vol. II.

Monckton, H. A. *A History of English Ale and Beer.* London: Bodley Head, 1966.

Power, Eileen. *The Goodman of Paris.* London: Routledge, 1929.

Scully, Terence, ed. and trans. *Chiquart's "On Cookery."* New York: P. Lang, 1986.

Taillevent. *The Viandier of Taillevent,* ed. and trans. Terence Scully. Ottawa: University of Ottawa Press, 1988.

Willan, Anne. *Great Cooks and Their Recipes from Taillevent to Escoffier.* Boston, Toronto, and London: Bulfinch, 1992.

Wilson, C. Anne. *Food and Drink in Britain from the Stone Age to Recent Times.* London: Constable, 1973.

Woolgar, C. M. *The Great Household in Late Medieval England.* New Haven: Yale University Press, 1999.

ENTERTAINMENTS: GENERAL

Brand, John, and Sir Henry Ellis. *Observations on Popular Antiquities.* London: Chatto and Wyndus, 1913.

Forsyth, Hazel and Geoff Egan. *Toys, Trifles, and Trinkets: Base-Metal Miniatures from London 1200 to 1800.* London: Museum of London/Unicorn, 2004.

McLean, Theresa. *The English at Play in the Middle Ages.* Windsor Forest, Berks.: Kensal Press, 1983.

Reeves, Compton. *Pleasures and Pastimes in Medieval England.* Oxford: Oxford University Press, 1998.

Rickert, Edith. *Chaucer's World.* New York: Columbia University Press, 1948.

Robbins, R. H. *Historical Poems of the XIVth and XVth Centuries.* Oxford: Clarendon Press, 1959.

Strutt, Joseph. *Sports and Pastimes of the English People.* London: Methuen, 1903.

ENTERTAINMENTS: GAMES

Alfonso X. *Das spanische Schachzabelbuch des Königs Alfons des Weisen vom Jahre 1283.* Leipzig: Hiersemann, 1913.

Cotton, Charles. *The Compleat Gamester [1674], in Games and Gamesters of the Restoration.* London: Routledge, 1930.

Dummett, David. *The Game of Tarot.* London: Duckworth, 1980.

Murray, H.J.R. *A History of Chess.* Oxford: Clarendon Press, 1913.

Parlett, David. *The Oxford Guide to Card Games.* Oxford: Oxford University Press, 1990.

Willughby, Francis. *Francis Willughby's Book of Games: A Seventeenth-Century Treatise on Sports, Games and Pastimes,* ed. David Cram, Dorothy Johnston, and Jeffrey L. Forgeng. Aldershot: Ashgate, 2003.

ENTERTAINMENTS: MUSIC AND DANCE

Arbeau, Thoinot. *Orchesography.* New York: Dover, 1967.

Castelli, Patrizia, Maurizio Mingardi, and Maurizio Padovan, eds. *Mesvra et Arte del Danzare.* Pesaro: Gualtieri, 1987.

Chappell, W. *Popular Music of the Olden Time.* London: Chappell, 1859.

Dixon, Peggy. *Nonsuch Early Dance vol. 1: Middle Ages to 15th-Century French.* London: privately published, 1986. Ordering information available at www.nonsuch-history-and-dance.org.uk.

Dobson, E. J. and F. Ll. Harrison. *Medieval English Songs.* New York: Cambridge University Press, 1979.

Gleason, Harold. *Examples of Music Before 1400.* Rochester, NY: Eastman School of Music, 1942.

Greene, R. L. *The Early English Carols.* Oxford: Clarendon Press, 1935.

McGee, Timothy. *Medieval Instrumental Dances.* Bloomington: Indiana University Press, 1989.

Rastall, Richard. *Two Fifteenth-Century Song Books.* Aberystwyth: Boethius Press, 1990.

Robbins, R. H. *Secular Lyrics of the XIVth and XVth Centuries.* Oxford: Clarendon Press, 1952.

Stainer, J.F.R. and C. *Early Bodleian Music.* London: Novello, 1901.

Wilkins, Nigel. *Music in the Time of Chaucer.* Chaucer Studies 1. Cambridge: D. S. Brewer, 1979.

Wood, Melusine. *Historical Dances.* London: Imperial Society of Teachers of Dancing, 1952.

CHAUCER'S WORLD

Childs, Wendy R. "Moving around." In *A Social History of England, 1200–1500*, ed. Rosemary Horrox and W. Mark Ormrod. Cambridge: Cambridge University Press, 2006. 260–75.

Clark, J., ed. *The Medieval Horse and Its Equipment, c. 1150–c. 1450*. Medieval Finds from Excavations in London 5. London: HMSO, 1995.

Duffy, Eamon. "Religious belief." In *A Social History of England, 1200–1500*, ed. Rosemary Horrox and W. Mark Ormrod. Cambridge: Cambridge University Press, 2006. 340–55.

Flint, Valerie I. J. "A magic universe." In *A Social History of England, 1200–1500*, ed. Rosemary Horrox and W. Mark Ormrod. Cambridge: Cambridge University Press, 2006. 293–339.

Frame, Robin. "The wider world." In *A Social History of England, 1200–1500*, ed. Rosemary Horrox and W. Mark Ormrod. Cambridge: Cambridge University Press, 2006. 435–53.

Friel, Ian. *The Good Ship: Ships, Shipbuilding, and Technology in England 1200–1520*. London: British Museum Press, 1995.

Gardiner, Robert, ed. *Cogs, Caravels, and Galleons. The Sailing Ship 1000–1650*. Conway's History of the Ship. London: Conway, 1994.

Hutchinson, Gillian. *Medieval Ships and Shipping*. London: Leicester University Press, 1994.

Lewis, C. S. *The Discarded Image*. Cambridge: Cambridge University Press, 1964.

Mannyng, Robert. *Handlyng Synne*, ed. F. J. Furnivall. Early English Texts Society 119, 123. London: Kegan Paul, Trench and Trübner, 1901, 1903.

Marsden, Peter. *Ships of the Port of London. Twelfth to Seventeenth Centuries A.D.* London: English Heritage, 1996.

Mirk, John. *Instructions for Parish Priests*, ed. E. Peacock. Early English Texts Society 31. London: Kegan Paul, Trench and Trübner, 1868.

North, J. D. *Chaucer's Universe*. Oxford: Clarendon Press, 1988.

Ohler, Norbert. *The Medieval Traveller*. Woodbridge, Suffolk: Boydell, 1989.

Rubin, Miri. "Identities." In *A Social History of England, 1200–1500*, ed. Rosemary Horrox and W. Mark Ormrod. Cambridge: Cambridge University Press, 2006. 383–412.

Swanson, R.N. *Church and Society in Late Medieval England*. Oxford: Blackwell, 1989.

Wood, Eric S. *Historical Britain: A Comprehensive Account of the Development of Rural and Urban Life and Landscape from Prehistory to the Present Day*. London: Harvill Press, 1995.

Woolgar, C. M. *The Great Household in Late Medieval England*. New Haven: Yale University Press, 1999.

NOVELS

Doyle, Sir Arthur Conan. *Sir Nigel*. London: G. Bell, 1906.
———. *The White Company*. London: Smith Elder, 1891.
Druon, Maurice. *The Iron King*. New York: Scribner, 1956.
———. *The Strangled Queen*. New York: Scribner, 1957.
———. *The Poisoned Crown*. New York: Scribner, 1957.

——. *The Royal Succession*. New York: Scribner, 1958.

——. *The She-Wolf of France*. New York: Scribner, 1961.

——. *The Lily and the Lion*. London: R. Hart-Davis, 1961.

Eco, Umberto. *The Name of the Rose*. San Diego: Harcourt, Brace, Jovanovich, 1983.

Hanse, Hella S. *In a Dark Wood Wandering*. Chicago: Academy Chicago, 1989.

Unsworth, Barry. *Morality Play*. New York; Doubleday, 1995.

Willis, Connie. *Doomsday Book*. New York: Bantam Books, 1992.

VISUAL SOURCES

Arano, Luisa Cogliati, ed. *The Medieval Health Handbook. Tacuinum Sanitatis*. New York: Braziller, 1976.

Avril, François. *Manuscript Painting at the Court of France*. New York: Braziller, 1978.

Backhouse, Janet. *The Luttrell Psalter*. London: British Library, 1989.

Basing, Patricia. *Trades and Crafts in Medieval Manuscripts*. London: British Library, 1990.

Dupont, Jacques and Cesare Gnudi. *Gothic Painting*. New York: Rizzoli, 1979.

Erlande-Brandenburg, Alain. *Gothic Art*. New York: Abrams, 1989.

The Four Seasons of the House of Cerruti. New York: Facts on File, 1984.

Hartley, Dorothy, and Margaret M. Elliot. *Life and Work of the People of England. A pictorial record from contemporary sources. The Fourteenth Century*. London: Putnam's, 1929.

James, M. R. *The Romance of Alexander: A Collotype Facsimile of MS Bodley 264*. Oxford: Oxford University Press, 1933.

Loomis, Roger. *A Mirror of Chaucer's World*. Princeton: Princeton University Press, 1965.

Ring, G. *A Century of French Painting 1400–1500*. London: Phaidon Press, 1949.

Thomas, Marcel. *The Golden Age of English Manuscript Painting*. New York: Braziller, 1979.

Trivick, Henry. *The Picture Book of Brasses in Gilt*. London: John Baker, 1971.

Warner, George F. *Universal Classic Manuscripts*. Washington and London, M. W. Dunne, 1901.

Warner, George F. *Queen Mary's Psalter: Miniatures and Drawings by an English Artist of the 14th Century Reproduced from Royal MS*. 2 B. VII in the British Museum. London: British Museum, 1912.

ILLUSTRATION SOURCES

Ashdown, Emily Jessie. *British Costume*. London: T. C. and E. C. Jack, 1910.

Bateson, Mary. *Mediæval England. English feudal society from the Norman conquest to the middle of the fourteenth century*. New York: G. P. Putnam's sons; London: T. F. Unwin, 1904.

Clinch, George. *English Costume*. Chicago and London: Methuen and co., 1910.

Fiske, W. *Chess in Iceland*. Florence: Florentine Typographical Society, 1905.

Furnivall, F. J. *The Harleian Manuscript of Chaucer's Canterbury Tales*. London: Kegan Paul, Trench, Trübner, and co., 1885.

Gay, Victor. *Glossaire Archéologique*. Paris: Librairie de la Société Bibliographique, 1887.

Griffiths, Nick, in J. Cowgill, M. de Neergard, and N. Griffiths, eds. *Medieval Finds from Excavations in London. 1: Knives and Scabbards.* London: Her Majesty's Stationery Office, 1987.

Hewitt, J. *Ancient Armour and Weapons in Europe.* Oxford and London: John Henry and James Parker, 1860.

Lundwall, E., in Nockert, Margareta, et al., eds. *Bokstensmannen Och Hans Drak.t* Falkenberg: Falkenberg Tryckeri, 1985.

Mitford, Susan, in F. Grew and M. de Neergard, eds. *Medieval Finds from Excavations in London. 2: Shoes and Pattens.* London: Her Majesty's Stationery Office, 1988.

Norlund, Poul, "Buried Norsemen at Herjolfsnes." *Meddelelser om Groenland* 67 (1924): 87–192.

Parker, John Henry. *Some account of domestic architecture in England from Edward I to Richard II.* Oxford and London: J. H. Parker and Co., 1882.

Ruding, Rogers. *Annals of the Coinage of Great Britain.* London: J. Hearne, 1840.

Santarem, Manuel visconde de. *Atlas composé de mappemondes, de portulans et de cartes hydrographiques et historiques.* Paris: E. Thunot, 1849.

Strutt, Joseph. *Sports and Pastimes of the English People.* London: Methuen, 1903.

Unwin, Christina, in E. Crowfoot, F. Pritchard, and K. Staniland, eds., *Medieval Finds from Excavations in London. Vol. 4: Textiles and Clothing.* London: Her Majesty's Stationery Office, 1992.

Woods, William. *England in the Age of Chaucer.* New York: Stein and Day, 1976.

Wright, Thomas. *History of Domestic Manners and Sentiments in England during the Middle Ages.* London: Chapman and Hall, 1862.

Zylstra-Zweens, H. M. *Of his array telle I no lenger tale.* Amsterdam: Rodophi, 1988.

INDEX

Page numbers in *italics* indicate illustrations.

About the Authors

JEFFREY L. FORGENG is Paul S. Morgan Curator at the Higgins Armory Museum in Worcester, Massachusetts, and Adjunct Associate Professor of Humanities at Worcester Polytechnic Institute. He has published extensively on topics including daily life in the Middle Ages and Renaissance, the Robin Hood legend, and the history of games, as well as medieval and Renaissance martial arts. Forgeng received his doctorate in Medieval Studies at the University of Toronto specializing in medieval and Renaissance languages and cultural history, and was for many years an editor for the Middle English Dictionary.

WILL McLEAN is an author, illustrator and independent scholar who has been active in medieval recreation and living history since 1975. He runs and takes part in recreations of medieval tournaments and other deeds of arms. He has published works on medieval deeds of arms, combat, physical culture, and society